Eden's Other Residents

Eden's Other Residents

The Bible and Animals

MICHAEL J. GILMOUR

Foreword by
Laura Hobgood-Oster

CASCADE *Books* • Eugene, Oregon

EDEN'S OTHER RESIDENTS
The Bible and Animals

Copyright © 2014 Michael J. Glmour. All rights reserved. Except for brief quotations in critical publications or reviews, no part of this book may be reproduced in any manner without prior written permission from the publisher. Write: Permissions, Wipf and Stock Publishers, 199 W. 8th Ave., Suite 3, Eugene, OR 97401.

Cascade Books
An Imprint of Wipf and Stock Publishers
199 W. 8th Ave., Suite 3
Eugene, OR 97401

www.wipfandstock.com

ISBN 13: 978-1-61097-332-8

Cataloging-in-Publication data:

Gilmour, Michael J.

    Eden's other residents : the Bible and animals / Michael J. Gilmour ; Foreword by Laura Hobgood-Oster.

    xviii + 170 p.; 21.5cm. Includes bibliographical references and indexes.

    ISBN 13: 978-1-61097-332-8

    1. Animals in the Bible. 2. Animals—Religious aspects—Christianity. 3. Ecology—Religious aspects. I. Hobgood-Oster, Laura. II. Title.

BT746 G60 2014

Manufactured in the U.S.A.

The previously unpublished hymn "Across a Sea of Chaos" by Rev. H. P. C. Broadbent appears with the author's permission, as do the photographs by Jake Fehr and Tim Henderson.

    New Revised Standard Version Bible: Catholic Edition, Copypright © 1989, 1993, Division of Christian Education of the National Council of the Churches of Christ in the United States of America. Used by permission. All rights reserved.

To Ned, Wilma, Guiness, Chloe, Fruit Loops, Tiny Tiger,
Mr. Laughter Cobblepots, and Waylon Smithers.
Friends and inspirations all.

"Across a Sea of Chaos"

Across a sea of chaos, dark and brooding,
The Spirit stirs; our Maker brings to birth
His plan for life ablaze with love and beauty,
And countless creatures on a fruitful earth.
Our fath'ring God within his heart rejoices
As he beholds their wonder and their worth.
Beneath a sea of violence and injustice
This precious life is drowning day by day.
Creation smeared by cruel exploitation;
The selfish path we tread with feet of clay,
We reach the end, our dignity distorted,
And see the Maker's image fade away.
Upon the sea a fragile ark is drifting,
A sign of hope that rises with the flood.
For Man becomes a servant of redemption
To bird and beast, as now he seeks their good.
The rainbow-God shows in a dove his mercy—
His love for all more clearly understood.
The chaos gone! Our God one day will conquer.
His love will bring a harmony complete,
As grief and pain, the sorrow all around us,
Are swallowed up in victory so sweet.
The Lamb of God will reign on high for ever,
As living creatures worship at his feet!

—REV. H. P. C. BROADBENT
COMMITTEE MEMBER WITH THE ANGLICAN SOCIETY
FOR THE WELFARE OF ANIMALS
(FOR THE TUNE "FINLANDIA")

Contents

Foreword by Laura Hobgood-Oster | ix
Preface | xi
Acknowledgments | xv
Abbreviations | xvi

1. Realizing Animals Matter | 1
2. Reading Animals in the Christian Bible | 26
3. Recognizing the Grace of God in Animal Creation | 56
4. Revisiting Animals in Religious Ritual | 92
5. Responding to the Groaning Creation | 113
6. Returning to the Garden: The Writings of William Bartram | 140

Bibliography | 155
Subject Index | 167

Foreword

GREYHOUNDS SPARK LIFE-CHANGING MOMENTS of conversion, compassion, and wisdom. Just ask the residents of the area of southern France around Lyon and many will tell the tale of Saint Guinefort, the holy greyhound and healer of children. As I tromped this terrain and witnessed the twenty-first-century rebirth of a beloved medieval animal saint, albeit one deemed a heretic in the thirteenth century, intriguing questions and possibilities entered my mind. Are humans finally on the verge of loosening our insistent grip on ourselves—the grip that places us at the center of all that is? Will we finally see that we are not the only species that matters? Will we, theologically, yield that position of centrality back to the divine and, ethically, include other animals in our circles of compassion? Hopes and possibilities, along with pitfalls and tragedies, mark the roads of those who pose these difficult, confrontational, and increasingly urgent questions.

For years, "animals and religion"—my answer to the question, "What is your area of teaching and research?"—was met with raised eyebrows and looks of bewilderment. What do animals and religion have to do with each other? And, more specifically in this case, what does Christianity have to do with animals? The resounding response, as Michael Gilmour articulates clearly and courageously, is—"everything."

A carefully crafted and thoughtful study of biblical texts and other important pieces of literature, *Eden's Other Residents* is, as Edward Said would say, a prophetic suggestion. Postcolonial readings of Jane Austen and postanthropocentric readings of the Apostle Paul play with each other in this much-needed challenge to traditional readings of texts. Expanding

Foreword

the cries for justice beyond the human, without denying the debate that expansion evokes, is the central message of the book. And these eloquent, knowledgable cries must be heard, especially now in the midst of an unprecedented age of human-caused extinction of countless species.

Gilmour's deep understanding of the historical contexts and exegetical possibilities of texts offers the reader new ways of thinking and of acting. He artfully examines animal–human–divine triads (or, in his words, triptychs), gracefully reads between the lines of well-known stories (such as Zacchaeus and Ruth), boldly examines difficult issues (including animal sacrifice), and cleverly relates theology with popular culture (Woody Guthrie makes a fascinating appearance).

As one reads through Gilmour's study, it becomes obvious that he is writing not just from a place of intellectual passion, but from an ethical commitment to new ways of thinking about justice and kindness in the Christian tradition. Gilmour's own greyhound conversion experience, his own Saint Guinefort moment, provided the catalyst for this urgent new direction in his scholarship. Learning the histories of the rescued, racing greyhounds who entered his home and realizing that their lives had been ones of pain and sorrow caused deliberately by humans, evoked from him the wisdom of the Torah: "When you see the donkey of one who hates you lying under its burden and you would hold back from setting it free, you must help to set it free" (Exod 23:4–5). Gilmour's words as he considers the other residents of Eden are a defense of, arguably, the most defenseless—a cry for freedom, justice, compassion, and consideration of animals.

Laura Hobgood-Oster
Professor of Religion and Environmental Studies
Southwestern University

Preface

THE THIRD-CENTURY *ACTS OF Thomas* includes a touching story about a donkey meeting the apostle during his evangelistic activities in India. While Thomas addresses a crowd on the side of a road, the animal approaches the servant of God and speaks, explaining he is of the "race" that assisted not only the prophet Balaam but also Jesus. "And now am I sent to give thee rest," the creature adds. Though reluctant to accept the animal's generous offer of service, the apostle eventually allows the donkey to carry him to the city gates. Once Thomas dismounts and blesses the creature, it immediately falls dead at his feet. The amazed crowd asks the man of God to raise it back to life but he chooses not to perform this miracle, reasoning that "he who gave it speech that it might speak was able also to make it not die." The incident ends with Thomas asking those present to show the animal the dignity of burial (*Acts Thom.* 39–41).[1]

This unusual tale encapsulates much that I consider in the present book. The storyteller behind it imagines nonhumans in communion with God and actively doing their Maker's bidding in the world ("I am sent [by God]" the donkey tells Thomas). We see too a mutually beneficial animal-human relationship, with the colt carrying the weary Thomas, who in turn gives the creature a blessing. Note also the subtle concern for animal well-being within the context of the religious life. The same crowd that listens to the apostle preaching the gospel reacts strongly when the donkey dies: they are "sorrowful," they ask Thomas to raise it from the dead, and they honor it with burial. All of this surprises the contemporary reader who is generally

---

1. Hennecke et al., eds., *New Testament Apocrypha*, 355–57.

Preface

not accustomed to Christian proclamation, storytelling, theological reflection, and moral teaching integrating animals to any great extent.

What interests me most about this tale is the assumption of continuity between the biblical world and postbiblical experience. A donkey speaks to the prophet Balaam in the Hebrew Scriptures so it is fitting one speaks to another prophet in a later age. In the Gospels a donkey carries Jesus to a city so naturally it happens as an apostle goes about the Lord's business. Animals are everywhere in the Bible and theologically proximate to humans, all alike created by and dependent on God, and existing for God's purposes. Our anonymous third-century Christian author is quite aware of this and finds it perfectly congruous for an apostle and a donkey, literally and figuratively, to walk the same road in their service to God.

The Bible includes not only stories with animal characters but also instructions concerning behaviors that impact other living things directly and indirectly. A story about a donkey assisting Thomas and the crowd's showing respectful concern for its welfare is not merely a sentimental fiction but instead a reflection of the high regard for animal life rooted in the Scriptures. The *Acts of Thomas* is commentary on what eventually becomes the Christian Old and New Testaments and reveals the writer's belief that what applies to prophets and apostles in bygone days applies also to those reading their histories, psalms, prophetic pronouncements, gospels, letters, and apocalypses centuries later. For this anonymous Christian there is continuity between sacred text and lived experience, and the God of the Bible is still active in the lives of those reading its sacred pages. To the extent we allow that the Bible has anything to teach contemporary readers, there is much to consider as we contemplate Eden's other residents.

Disclosure of authorial perspective and bias is *de rigueur* in religious studies. In this case, my interest in finding a basis to include animals within the moral purview of Christian theological reflection, in reaction to a long history of the erasure of nonhuman life in its ethical discourse, motivates all that follows. I confessed as much on Twitter while writing this book. On March 13, 2013, in the hours before the College of Cardinals selected the Jesuit Archbishop of Buenos Aires Jorge Mario Bergoglio to be pope, news outlets from all over the world trained their cameras on the chimney of the Sistine Chapel, waiting for signs of smoke that would announce to the world when the papal conclave reached its decision. To the amusement of many watching, a seagull perched there for a time. Half-jokingly, I tweeted the following at 12:11 CST: "Loving pictures of the seagull on the Sistine

Preface

Chapel chimney. Hoping it's a sign the next Pontiff will be a voice for non-human animals too!" At 2:20, after the announcement, I added another tweet: "Since the new pope goes by the name Francis, as in Francis of Assisi, I'm thinking that [the] seagull on the chimney had a hunch about the voting." A delightful coincidence, yes, but one bringing into focus the supposition considered here, namely, that animal life, the people of God, and the God of both belong together in Christian thought and praxis, and that theological reflection is stronger when it concerns more than just humanity's story in a God-made world.

July 3, 2013
Feast Day of St. Thomas (post-Vatican II)

Acknowledgments

It makes me smile to see greyhounds looking out from these pages, so I extend hearty thanks to Tim Henderson and Jake Fehr for permission to use their photos of Fruit Loops, Tiny Tiger, and Mr. Laughter Cobblepots. I am also grateful to Reverend Hugh Broadbent for permission to include his lovely hymn "Across a Sea of Chaos" as an epigraph. This image of non-humans and humans together aboard "a fragile ark" is a fitting preamble for musings on the interconnectedness of all living things. I am honored that Professor Laura Hobgood-Oster contributed the Foreword. Her important studies of animals in the Christian tradition both inspire and motivate, and I am so pleased that she is a part of this otherwise modest contribution to that conversation. And as always, I extend my deepest appreciation and love to Kyla, who makes our life together a peaceful Eden.

Abbreviations

1QS	*Rule of the Community*
AB	Anchor Bible
ACCS	Ancient Christian Commentary on Scripture
Acts Thom.	*Acts of Thomas*
Ag. Ap.	Josephus, *Against Apion*
Ant.	Josephus, *Jewish Antiquities*
Did.	*Didache*
JBL	*Journal of Biblical Literature*
JSOT	*Journal for the Study of the Old Testament*
Jub.	*Jubilees*
KJV	King James Version
LXX	Septuagint (the Greek OT)
m. 'Abot	Mishnah, *Avot*
m. Kelim	Mishnah, *Kelim*
m. Pesaḥ	Mishnah, *Pesahim*
m. Tamid	Mishnah, *Tamid*
m. Ter.	Mishnah, *Terumot*
NICNT	New International Commentary on the New Testament
NICOT	New International Commentary on the Old Testament
NRSV	New Revised Standard Version
NTL	New Testament Library

Abbreviations

OTL	Old Testament Library
RSV	Revised Standard Version
SP	Sacra Pagina
Spec. Laws	*On the Special Laws*
WBC	Word Biblical Commentary

1   Realizing Animals Matter

Generosity follows gratitude. We see this all the time in the Bible. Israel cares for strangers in the land knowing they too were once strangers, displaced and separated from the protections and comforts of home (Deut 24:17–18, 22). Zacchaeus gives away half his possessions to the poor and offers to restore fourfold anyone he defrauded. This in response to Jesus's kindness (Luke 19:8) even though it was not required of him, as it was of others (cf. Luke 18:22). Zacchaeus thus enacts that liberality of spirit Jesus encourages elsewhere. "[F]reely ye have received, freely give," as the KJV puts it.[1] Even when it is perfectly within one's rights to claim certain comforts and privileges, we often find instead self-sacrifice and an almost excessive liberality. The author of Ruth celebrates the heroine's *hesed*, kindness, evident in her willingness to leave her own people for Naomi's sake (1:16–18; 2:11–12, 18, 23). Boaz praises this *hesed* as well. Far from self-serving, Ruth has her mother-in-law's best interests in mind when claiming this man as redeemer rather than seeking someone younger to marry (3:10). And notice how often such stories of faith-motivated largesse spill across "boundaries." Israel's God-given bounty is not theirs to hoard but rather to share with sojourners in the land, indicating non-Israelites. Wealthy Zacchaeus reaches across the socioeconomic divide to the poor.[2] A kind Samaritan ignores racial and

---

1. I cite the NRSV throughout, unless indicated otherwise.

2. This is not condescension because Zacchaeus is himself a marginalized figure. Parsons argues Luke's portrayal of the man is insulting in a number of ways and yet this unlikely individual defies expectations by showing cheerful hospitality (*Body and*

religious differences when lending a helping hand to a Jew (Luke 10:25–37). When Ruth puts the wellbeing of another ahead herself, leaving behind her own family, people, and gods to do so, she even resists Naomi's pleas to do otherwise (Ruth 1:11–15). Freely ye have received, freely give, and in the process defy conventions, and avoid giving to those in a position to return the kindness (Luke 14:12–14). Where is the reward in that?

This book explores the limits of our individual and collective responses to the grace of God. It considers recurring injunctions reminding us to give when we receive, to give joyfully and not reluctantly, and to realize it is not up to us to determine "who is my neighbor." It asks whether we ought to reach so far across boundaries in showing *hesed* as to include all creation, not just our own kind (*Homo sapiens*).

Zacchaeus, Restitution, and Gratitude Unbidden

As noted, Zacchaeus gives away much of his fortune and publically announces his willingness to right wrongs with an almost reckless munificence. In doing so, he offers a compelling model for our purposes here (see the full story, Luke 19:1–9). The Bible does not speak of animals[3] and

---

Character, 97–108). He not only worked for unwelcome foreigners (the Romans) but also carried the stigma of his profession. Even if he did not exploit the taxation system for personal gain, neighbors likely harbored suspicions he did. Furthermore, within the context of Luke the accumulation of wealth is routinely criticized (6:24; 12:16–21; 16:19–31; 18:18–25). He is a needy individual in many respects, reaching out to others also in need. See too Resseguie, *Spiritual Landscape*, 108–9.

3. Using the term *animal* to indicate all nonhuman species, as I do throughout, is potentially misleading if taken to mean there is no kinship (biologically or theologically) with other living things. Various writers dealing with animal-human relationships grapple with terminology. Lisa Kemmerer, for one, explores the major religions of India (Hinduism, Buddhism, Jainism), China (Daoism, Confucianism), and the Middle East (Judaism, Christianity, Islam), as well as the world's indigenous traditions, mining their sacred texts and mythologies for ancient wisdoms concerning human responsibilities toward other-than-human creatures, and her preferred term is "anymals." This neologism—a contraction of "any" and "animal"—appears throughout her book, replacing other available labels like nonhuman animals, other animals, animals other than humans, and the like. She finds these cumbersome and fraught with a hierarchical dualism that elevates humans over all else and obscures the fact that they too are animals interconnected with other species. As she defines the term, "*Anymal* is . . . a shortened version of 'any animal that does not happen to be the species that I am'" and since the author of the book is a human being, "*anymal* refers to any animal who is not a human being" (*Animals and World Religions*, 17, italics original; full introduction to this linguistic choice, 14–18). Though I do not adopt this particular convention, I am fully sympathetic to these concerns. By my

ethical responsibilities owed to them by the people of God in any uniform, systematic sense. There are ambiguities, compounded by millennia of culture-bound interpretations that complicate efforts to articulate a biblically informed animal ethic. But try we must.

What Zacchaeus models is an act of generosity partially rooted in specific biblical teaching and partially derived from broader injunctions to kindness and care for the poor. He does what the Bible tells him explicitly to do *and more*, and it is in this convergence of the two, this largesse and willingness to go two miles instead of the one demanded, that perhaps we find "space" to include animals in the community of those deserving hospitality and the protection of God's people. Torah requires returning fourfold what one steals as restitution (Exod 22:1; cf. 2 Sam 12:5–6; both passages, incidentally, refer to theft of animals). Zacchaeus appears to take legislation protecting animal property (fourfold restitution) and extend it to theft in any form, which given his profession presumably includes taking more taxes from people than what is owed.[4] The other part of Zacchaeus's restitution—giving half his possessions to the poor—is not grounded in any specific law and, again, is not something Jesus asked of him. It stems from gratitude. It goes beyond the minimum required by law.[5] It involves the disciple freely choosing how best to honor the teacher who shows favor. It gives tangible expression to his newfound joy and shows awareness that what he has, he does not deserve.

Owing to the paucity of explicit instruction about other-than-human animals, and the ambivalences and ambiguities of biblical texts and subsequent Christian tradition concerning them, I offer Zacchaeus's response to grace as a way forward in thinking about Christian animal ethics.[6] Aware of requirements in Torah (Exod 22:1), Zacchaeus adapts its instructions as

---

use of *animal* and equivalents I do not mean to distinguish humans from other species as though there is no connection. Quite to the contrary, in the arguments that follow I insist on the interconnectedness of all life.

4. For brief introductions to the Roman system of taxation presupposed in the story, see Jeffers, *Greco-Roman World*, 142–46; and Schmidt, "Taxes."

5. Blomberg observes that rabbinic law discourages people from ever giving away more than 20 percent of their resources, so Zacchaeus goes well beyond expectations here (*Jesus and the Gospels*, 361). On another occasion, Jesus asks a man to give everything away to the poor (Matt 19:21; Mark 10:21; Luke 18:22), a demand illustrating how the call to discipleship often places unique obligations on individuals.

6. The very idea of Christian animal ethics likely sounds strange to some. An excellent place to start for some perspective is Jay McDaniel's helpful and accessible article "Practicing the Presence of God."

appropriate for his particular circumstances, thus capturing the spirit of restitution found in this legislation. It may be he never stole actual oxen or sheep but he found here a fitting way to make amends. Zacchaeus also exceeds this injunction, perhaps acknowledging that greed, or lack of trust in God, or lack of respect for his neighbors is at the root of his (at least hypothetical) fraudulent actions. Approaching the subject of the Bible and animals requires a similar consideration of *what the text says explicitly and what it implies.* We must read the words on the page but also what is between the lines and at the margins, as it were. To push this further yet, we must acknowledge the enormous gap between the worlds of the ancient poets and sages and our own. We cannot reconstruct fully or replicate attitudes toward/relationships with animals in ancient societies, and it would not necessarily address all our concerns or answer all our questions about this topic if we could. Instead, like Zacchaeus, we need to be creative in our approach to biblical teachings if they are to contribute meaningfully to our particular circumstances.

Since the God of the Bible values animals—this much is obvious—what are the implications for people of faith? I argue in the following pages that a believer's response to God's grace must be gratitude embodied in a self-sacrificing, exuberant generosity to others, and like behaviors displayed in the stories of Ruth and the Good Samaritan and a hundred others, this generosity ought to transgress boundaries. If reconciliation encompasses "all things" in heaven and earth (see, e.g., Rom 8:18–30; Eph 1:7–10; Col 1:15–20), then it befits the people of God to widen the ambit of care and concern to include "all things." Jesus does not tell Zacchaeus to give away half his property but the tax collector does. Naomi tells Ruth not to follow but she does anyway. Similarly, the Scriptures are not always clear what extending hospitality and kindness means for the community of God's people. Like Zacchaeus and Ruth we need to sort out the appropriate response to grace for ourselves, at times moving from general understanding of the tenor of God's word (in Zacchaeus's case, showing kindness to the poor) to specific actions (distributing his wealth to them even if not told to do so). Sometimes these choices appear strange (as in Ruth's case, from Naomi's perspective). In the following pages, I focus mostly on why we must incorporate animals within our ethical purview though I leave to readers to sort out for themselves what specific behaviors ought to follow.

A Religious Awakening

Animals as a consideration for the religious life? I came to the conviction that Christian compassion must be all-inclusive only gradually. It was a kind of religious awakening. Before this Damascus Road moment, there was no particular sense of moral obligation to animals, nothing beyond a typical revulsion at stories of cruelty occasionally flashing across the evening news. And I certainly did not allow animals into my theological thinking in any meaningful sense. It was almost as though the language of the Bible and Christian discourse was too familiar and my reading habits too entrenched to permit anything so jarringly different from the status quo, to allow that its ancient teachings have something pertinent to say about actual animals and my connections to them. It was a little like rereading a novel so many times there is little surprise left when Elizabeth Bennet finally marries Fitzwilliam Darcy, or Jane Eyre returns to be with Edward Rochester. The Bible is concerned solely with the children of Adam and Eve and their God, or so I assumed, and it was hard to imagine its story involving anything more.

This is not all that remarkable. Some passages seem to minimize the value of nonhuman creatures, thus reinforcing this attitude of indifference. One prayer recalling the Priestly creation narrative (i.e., Gen 1:1—2:4a)[7] declares, "You have given [human beings] dominion over the works of your hands; you have put all things under their feet, all sheep and oxen, and also the beasts of the field, the birds of the air, and the fish of the sea, whatever passes along the paths of the seas" (Ps 8:6–8; cf. Sir 17:2–4; Wis 9:2–3). To be sure, the psalmist certainly asserts God's high view of people for those inclined to doubt such a wondrous truth ("what are human beings that you are mindful of them?" [8:4]) but this is not synonymous with denigrating the rest of creation. This last part, that celebration of humanity is not necessarily a diminishing of the rest, did not register for me early on and I was not inclined to pick up that thread and see where it might lead. I see now that whatever "dominion" and putting "all things under their feet" means, it is not license to deny the value of the rest of sentient life on the planet. The wellbeing of all creatures is a recurring theme in Scripture, though this notion is easily and often overlooked. Even one of God's own prophets struggles to appreciate this, failing to recognize that divine concern and compassion extend to both people (even Gentiles) and animals (Jonah

---

7. For a convenient and succinct description of the Priestly material in the Old Testament, see Soulen and Soulen, *Handbook of Biblical Criticism*, 127–28.

4:11). Like Jonah my Bible reading and theologizing remained stubbornly myopic and human-centered in their orientation.

Along with many others, a general awareness of environmental concerns seeped into my consciousness over the years though initially it was far from a theologically pressing matter.[8] Now-familiar neologisms like climate change, habitat destruction, and carbon footprint slowly entered the collective lexicon and there was a new realization of the fragility of our planet. A few modest lifestyle choices and attitudes became the norm. Most now give at least some passing thought to recycling, the fuel efficiency of vehicles, and the type of light bulbs used. For me there was also some vague awareness of stresses placed on certain species and morally objectionable behaviors toward other living things. Cutting off a shark's fins for soup, then releasing it still alive into the ocean to die a slow death is senselessly cruel by any measure. So too is force-feeding ducks and geese to make *foie gras*[9] and killing elephants to support a black market trade in ivory trinkets. But do such issues fall under the purview of a biblically rooted Christian ethic? Said differently, should Christians order soup or buy products that involve such waste, suffering, and disregard for nonhuman life?

Finding God on the Racetrack

Over time, a plodding awakening to questions of animal wellbeing began to take shape for me. An early step occurred with the realization that the negative consequences of human indifference to other-than-human

---

8. For a compelling introduction to environmental questions in religious perspective, see Deane-Drummond, *Eco-Theology*, which includes an excellent chapter on biblical literature. While she acknowledges the complexities of these writings, she finds much for those approaching environmental ethics to build on, noting, among other things, that "principles of intrinsic value, interconnectedness, custodianship, voice, resistance and purpose serve to promote eco-justice" and that such themes as Sabbath "are instructive in providing a way of shaping theological commitments to give space and time for creation and for liturgical celebration in building up an ethos that fosters ecological sensitivity" (97). On animals specifically, see too her chapter "Animal Ethics," in *Ethics of Nature*, 54–85.

9. This causes the liver to grow unnaturally, something considered a culinary delicacy but a practice involving excruciating pain for the bird. "The owner generally holds the neck of the goose between his legs, pouring the corn with one hand and rubbing it down the neck with the other. When this process ceases to be effective, the owner uses a wooden plunger to compact it still further" (Schwartz, *Judaism and Vegetarianism*, 33–34); "employees shove a metal tube down the bird's throats [*sic*], and into their stomachs; this process is repeated two or three times each day. The metal tubes cause painful bruising, lacerations, sores, and can even rupture organs" (Kemmerer, *Animals and World Religions*, 305).

life are not always so remote from every day experience as sharks and elephants. We all touch the animal world in one way or another, whether directly through such things as food, clothing, and entertainment choices, or indirectly through our collective contributions to pollution and climate change with their adverse impact on, say, the hunting needs of polar bears. This much I accepted. A modest step forward in my "conversion" but there was more to learn.

I refer often throughout the following pages to moments when animals, humans, and God meet in biblical narratives, what I refer to variously as triadic sites of revelation or triptych narratives in which interactions between these three realms result in a new discovery or insight.[10] We see this in the story of Jonah and his fish, to return to the prophet mentioned above, when God hears him and corrects his itinerary while deep inside that creature's belly. In effect, God "speaks" to his human prophet through the fish and the consequences are enormous. God spares Nineveh's many residents, animals among them, in consequence of this triadic encounter. We often refer to Jonah as a reluctant prophet but perhaps we ought to shift the emphasis and acknowledge the great fish as a willing and obedient one.

To return to my "conversion" story, the arrival of retired racing greyhounds into my home represented a further stage in my awakening. Learning their tragic stories as part of the heartless racing industry nudged my general awareness of human-caused animal suffering away from vague abstractions toward the very real situation of these suffering dogs. Greyhound racing is a cruel business in which the lives of these gentle giants are expendable when not profitable. Young dogs typically have six opportunities to place in the top four positions in their maiden runs, which means they must demonstrate profitability for their owners. If they fail to do so, the tracks usually euthanize them. Racing itself is extremely dangerous for the dogs given their speed (upward of 70 kilometers/45 miles an hour) and the limited space on crowded tracks. Broken bones, torn ligaments and tendons, dislocated toes, and "spikes" (when the claw of one dog cuts another) are common. Electrocution is possible "from falling into the cradle that holds the electric lure."[11]

---

10. There is similar vocabulary in Hobgood-Oster, *Holy Dogs and Asses*, in which she examines animals in (mostly) postbiblical Christian hagiographies, visual arts, and rituals, referring at times to "animal-human-divine relationships" (79 etc.). Cf. Bauckham's similar use of triangular and quadrilateral imagery (the latter allowing for inanimate creation as well) in *Bible and Ecology*, 146–47.

11. Branigan, *Adopting the Racing Greyhound*, 52. This book offers a wonderful

Eden's Other Residents

**My greyhound Fruit Loops running for fun, not competition.
Photograph by Jake Fehr (Winnipeg, Manitoba).**

Bringing dogs from this world into my home proved revelatory and highly motivating. I see them as synecdochic, not just a part of animal creation representing the whole of animal creation, but also a part of the abused animal world (track greyhounds) representing the whole of the abused animal world. But again, what if anything does religion have to do

---

introduction to the breed and various details about the race industry. See too Branigan, *Reign of the Greyhound*. I am aware that there are philosophical objections to keeping pets and that the preference for specific breeds not only proliferates puppy mills but also introduces health concerns over long periods of time. Though we ought to do all we can to reduce the number of domestic animals born, it remains that the already-born dogs, cats, and more fill shelters and rescues, and they need care. For disussion of various ethical questions raised by human-pet relationships, see Bok, "Keeping Pets"; Tuan, "Animal Pets"; and Serpell, "People in Disguise." For theological perspectives on companion animals, see Webb, *On God and Dogs*, and briefly, McDaniel, "Practicing the Presence of God," 134, 144.

with this?[12] Here followed the next step in my lumbering, somewhat reluctant progress toward the subject matter, which involved bringing my frustration about human caused animal suffering into dialogue with the Bible.

The wonderful Hebrew phrase *tsa'ar ba'alei chayim* indicates the tradition of showing kindness to animals, or causing no sorrow, pain, or harm to living creatures, a theme deeply rooted and widely represented in Jewish teaching.[13] This concept ultimately derives from Torah and its many mandates to protect animals from undo distress:

> When you see the donkey of one who hates you lying under its burden and you would hold back from setting it free, you must help to set it free (Exod 23:4–5; cf. Deut 22:4).

> For six years you shall sow your land and gather in its yield; but the seventh year you shall let it rest and lie fallow, so that the poor of your people may eat; and what they leave the wild animals may eat (Exod 23:10–11).

> Six days you shall do your work, but on the seventh day you shall rest, so that your ox and your donkey may have relief, and your home born slave (Exod 23:12; cf. Deut 5:13–14).

> When an ox or a sheep or a goat is born, it shall remain seven days with its mother . . . you shall not slaughter, from the herd or the flock, an animal with its young on the same day (Lev 22:27–28).

> If you come on a bird's nest, in any tree or on the ground, with fledglings or eggs, with the mother sitting on the fledglings or on the eggs, you shall not take the mother with the young. Let the mother go, taking only the young for yourself, in order that it may go well with you and you may live long (Deut 22:6–7).

> You shall not plow with an ox and a donkey yoked together (Deut 22:10).

---

12. In chapter 2, I explain how one of these dogs contributed to my theological contemplation.

13. Kalechofsky, "Hierarchy, Kinship, and Responsibility," 91; Kemmerer, *Animals and World Religions*, 174–77; Schwartz, *Judaism and Vegetarianism*, 15–39; Webb, *On God and Dogs*, 22; Tirosh-Samuelson, "Judaism and the Care for God's Creation," 297: "On the basis of Deuteronomy 22:6, which forbids the killing of a bird with her young because it is exceptionally cruel, the rabbis articulated the general principle of *tza'ar ba'aley hayyim* (literally 'distress of living things') that prohibits the affliction of needless suffering on animals." The rabbis considered this one of the seven laws given to Noah "and, therefore, binding on all humans, not just on Jews" (ibid.).

Though the cultural contexts behind such legislation seem remote, it is obvious that the religious thinking behind these instructions includes high regard for nonhuman life. These passages present animal wellbeing as a concern of the religious life, and acts of kindness toward them are requisite for those who worship God. Laboring domestic animals keep and benefit from the Sabbath along with the children of Israel. And clearly this incorporation of animals into legislation goes beyond the mere economic wisdom and production strategies of ancient farmers aware that a rested animal is a more productive animal. This is true but there is more to it because "wild animals" and birds one happens to come across during an afternoon stroll also deserve consideration. With respect to the latter, notice the promise that follows the injunction against taking both mother and fledglings at the same time: "in order that it may go well with you and you may live long" (Deut 22:7). On one level, these words indicate the wisdom of conservation (as also in 20:19–20, which rules against unnecessary destruction of trees) and suggest it is in the community's best interest to "let the mother go." But there is also divine favor attached to compliance, indicating that on another level, God looks kindly on the beneficiaries of this compassion. Human-animal relationships are a theological matter.

When I started to reread the Bible with this new set of concerns and questions in view, it was like discovering a completely new story (as if Elizabeth Bennet refused Mr. Darcy's proposal a second time!). A world of animals was indeed present in the pages of holy Scripture all along, and as it turns out, these other characters are more than scenery in a wholly human story. Animals are instead part of the great drama revealed in its pages.

Animals and the Bible?
A Rather Strange Choice of Subject, Isn't It?

It was a difficult decision to dedicate the lion's share of a precious and rare sabbatical to the study of animals and the Bible, for a few reasons. For many, the subject is on the fringe, a low priority for both biblical studies departments and the church. Also in the back of my mind was Andrew Linzey's story about a fellow student chastising him for his interest in animal theology: "I don't know why you're spending all your time on this. They're only animals—for heaven's sake!"[14] Similarly, the French poet, playwright, and art historian Jean-Christophe Bailly observes that "dec-

14. Linzey, *Creatures of the Same God*, ix.

larations of intense feelings on the subject of animals quite often not only fall flat but give rise to a sort of embarrassment, rather as though one had inadvertently crossed a line and gotten mixed up in something untoward, or even obscene." Bailly adds, "Nothing is more painful . . . than the choice one has to make: pull back discreetly or forge ahead obstinately and speak out."[15] Sometimes the decision to speak out for animals generates outright hostility. Philosopher Tom Regan is an employee at a university that kills thousands of animals every year in the name of scientific research and he reports that some of his faculty colleagues do not take kindly to his efforts as an advocate on behalf of those creatures.[16]

Strange as it sounds, geography is another factor making my decision to write on this subject difficult. I live and work in a Canadian prairie province heavily dependent on agriculture and livestock production. According to the Manitoba government, the province's pork industry, for instance, "grew out of humble beginnings before the turn of the century and expanded to approximately 2 million hogs by 1990 . . . In 2001, approximately 1668 hog operations across the province produced nearly 6.4 million hogs—over 20 percent of the Canadian total—19 percent of these hog operations produce weanlings only, 33.1 percent are farrow to finish, and 47.9 percent are feeder operations."[17] According to a study coming out of the University of Manitoba, "directly and indirectly, the pig/pork industry in Manitoba generates over $1 billion of economic benefit and roughly 12,000 jobs in the province. These levels were much higher in the early 2000s, but declined due to the industry's recent poor financial situation."[18]

This presents a challenge for me because as the government report makes clear, hog (and other animal) production has a long history in the region and is consequently part of its social and cultural fabric. The second report speaks to its economic importance as a major employer and revenue-generating export. Many of my students, friends, and neighbors are from farming families reaching back generations whose stories are included in these statistics, their livelihood deriving from the land. I worry that addressing the topic of animal ethics at all is potentially offensive or

---

15. Bailly, *Animal Side*, 4.

16. Regan, *Defending Animal Rights*, xi. In chapter 9 of the same book ("Work, Hypocrisy, and Integrity"), he reflects on the moral dilemma he faces working for an institution guilty of (as he sees it) unethical practices.

17. Manitoba Government, "Pork," n.p.

18. Oleson and Honey, "Agricultural Review," n.p.

insulting to them, especially since I am an urbanite with no real experience of farm life to speak of, a deficit that no doubt disqualifies me to comment on animals, in their view.

At the same time, large, mechanized farming operations inevitably subject animals to physical and emotional distresses, and it is morally questionable, to my mind, whether regional traditions, economics, and the market's demand for cheap meat justify the suffering of so many living things.[19] That much suffering occurs among animals raised, transported, and slaughtered as part of the food industry is not in doubt. While working on this book, a video surfaced illustrating horrific abuses at a hog farm only a few hours from where I live. According to a Canadian Broadcasting Corporation report, it includes images of "agitated pigs with open sores in tiny cages, adult animals being euthanized using bolt guns in the head and piglets being euthanized by slamming them against the floor."[20] Unfortunately, this is not an isolated incident, and reports of animals suffering in the food processing industries are not hard to come by. At minimum, citizens of Manitoba certainly have moral obligations to ensure that the treatment of farm animals is as humane as possible because we all derive economic benefits from the industry, even if we do not eat meat. Surely most do not dispute this.

Another challenging dynamic at play in choosing to explore this topic derives from the nature of the Bible itself. I comment further on my reading strategies below, but a few words on the subject are in order here. To try to encapsulate in a simple statement "what the Bible says about animals" or "a biblically based animal ethics" is impossible. There are endless complexities, not least of which is the enormous gulf between the times, places, cultures, and worldviews represented among the diverse writings

---

19. On the disturbing realities of industrial farming, see Mason and Finelli, "Brave New Farm," 158–70, and Kemmerer, *Animals and World Religions*, 291–315. Berkman's poignant account in "Are We Addicted to the Suffering of Animals?" highlights the plight of pigs on pp. 127–30. For philosophical perspectives on the practices of industrial husbandry and the ethical questions they pose, see Walters' chapter "Animals, Pain, and Factory Farms" in *Vegetarianism*, 9–29 (on pork production, 25–26); Rachels, "Vegetarianism"; and Gruen, "Empathy and Vegetarian Commitments." The term *factory farming* gained widespread currency with the 1975 publication of philosopher Peter Singer's *Animal Liberation*. According to the updated 2009 edition, "The use and abuse of animals raised for food far exceeds, in sheer number of animals affected, any other kind of mistreatment" (95). Walters puts the number of "domesticated food animals" slaughtered each year "between 20 and 25 billion" worldwide (*Vegetarianism*, 18).

20. CBC, "Animal Abuse Alleged," n.p.

of the Hebrew Bible and the Christian Scriptures, on the one hand, and contemporary readers, on the other. The Bible and the long history of its interpretation present us with a widely diverse range of opinions.

Commenting on the ancient world more generally, Stephen R. L. Clark reminds us that the evidence available "is often as confused and confusing as present-day human attitudes to the nonhuman. Thinking ourselves back into the mind-frame of Classical Antiquity is an exercise in imaginative sympathy. Different aspects of that time and place attract different scholars' attention, especially as they must, inevitably, bring their own preoccupations with them, however detached they strive to be."[21] Within postbiblical Christian tradition, we need only compare the different views of, say, Thomas Aquinas and Albert Schweitzer to illustrate the range of perspective. The former is representative of those whose theological concern rests almost exclusively on the human story and who maintain ethical consideration need not extend to nonhuman creation. As he puts it in his *Summa Theologica*, animals are "naturally enslaved and accommodated to the uses of others" and "charity does not extend to irrational [nonhuman] creatures" (1.64.1; 1.65.3).[22] The latter is representative of those who see God's compassion encompassing all life. Schweitzer organizes his views around the guiding principle of "reverence for life." The phrase suggested itself to him when watching hippopotamuses from a boat in Africa that "plodded along in our same direction."[23] The image is a fitting symbol, suggesting commonality and movement toward a common destination among "all things that have breath," as he puts it elsewhere in the context of a prayer.[24] This spectrum—from focus on humanity and indifference to all else, to reverence for all life—is a spectacular one for its breadth, and these dissimilar conclusions and many more between have defenders throughout the history of Christian thought.

---

21. Clark, "Animals in Classical and Late Antique Philosophy," 38.

22. For analysis of Aquinas's views, see Yamamoto, "Aquinas and Animals," and Deane-Drummond, *Ethics of Nature*, 67–74. On the Thomistic tradition and the natural world more broadly, see Wynn, "Thomas Aquinas"; and Scheid, "Saint Thomas Aquinas."

23. Schweitzer, *Reverence for Life*, 25.

24. "O heavenly Father, protect and bless all things that have breath; guard them from all evil, and let them sleep in peace" (Schweitzer, *Reverence for Life*, 44). The language recalls Gen 7:22. For discussion of Schweitzer's "reverence for life" principle in light of critiques by Karl Barth, see Linzey, *Animal Theology*, 3–12.

Eden's Other Residents

Animals and Biblically Aware Writers and Thinkers

> Imagination is one of the characteristic marks of the humane person, as also are empathy, compassion, love, sympathy, and the ability to see and respond to the needs of others despite superficial barriers of race, class, or . . . species. It is not clear that the kind of science that would condemn the use of imagination and story-telling in constructing its proofs can ever lead to the humane responses that are the hallmark of human moral understanding.
>
> —CATHERINE OSBORNE[25]

Theologians are not the only ones giving serious thought to these issues. Though most of the present book looks directly at biblical literature (chapters 2 through 5), I frame this central section with brief examples of the Bible's influence on more recent authors. The reason for doing so is to illustrate that the Bible does not exist as a mere abstraction, removed from the "real world" and its "real animals." The value of its teachings about creation in all its magnificent diversity is negligible if it remains only ink on paper. It is only when people embrace and embody its ideals that its transformative potential is realized. Creative writers who integrate the Bible into their work, considering what it adds to our understanding of human-animal relations, contributed much to my "conversion," and so it is I close this opening chapter in rather unlikely fashion, with reflections on a Victorian novelist and poet whose writings reveal a deep belief in the Christian's obligation to care for animals. Anne Brontë illustrates what it means to extend a sense of community to all living things, and she recognizes that the biblical call to protect the vulnerable is no less limited by species than by race, gender, or social standing. Though fiction is her medium, she is clear that morality in the "real world" is her actual concern. I end the book discussing another writer who believes the same. The eighteenth-century Quaker, explorer, artist, and naturalist William Bartram depicts a journey through parts of southeastern North America as a visit to paradise, and his 1791 travelogue is reminiscent of Genesis, complete with a generous understanding of humankind's "dominion." To my mind, both writers model a Christian compassion for animals grounded in the Bible that is worthy of emulation. They

---

25. Osborne, *Dumb Beasts*, 139. She makes these remarks when discussing Aelian's version of the well-known story of Androcles and the lion. The man helps the animal with an injured paw, and when the two meet later in the Roman arena, the grateful lion spares his life (see 135–39, 148–50).

Realizing Animals Matter

share the conviction that the world is God's and everything in it and assume this foundational truth demands we tread lightly on Eden's other residents.

The intervening chapters examine biblical literature. The intent is not an exhaustive or systematic overview of what the Bible says about other-than-human species but rather a deliberately provocative presentation aiming to disrupt more traditional/habitual perspectives on biblical texts. These readings are often experimental and playful rather than exegetically rigorous, by-products of curiosity and the conviction that selective and biased reading habits usually conspire, consciously or otherwise, to erase animals from much Christian discourse. They are meditations rather than commentaries that attempt to subvert this pattern, more concerned to raise awareness of possible ways the Bible speaks to moral questions in our day than to reconstruct meanings these texts had for their first audiences. This approach to the Bible is the focus of chapter 2, where we examine the challenges and opportunities presented to us when "reading animals" in the Christian Scriptures. From this consideration of hermeneutical questions we turn to three chapters that cohere thematically, if loosely, around the topics of creation (chapter 3), animal sacrifice (chapter 4), and visions of eschatological peace and restoration (chapter 5).

Running with a Coyote: Timothy Findley's *The Wars*

Robert went inside at one point to request of Captain Leather that he be allowed to take the horses and mules he had just brought forward and make a strategic retreat with them so they might be saved. But Captain Leather . . . was adamant in his refusal . . . Finally, when the shells began to land in the barnyard, Robert couldn't stand it any longer and he said to Devlin: "I'm going to break ranks and save these animals . . . It cannot be called disobedience to save these animals."[26]

If the greyhounds awakened something on an emotional level, animal aware and religiously sensitive poetry and novels stirred things on a more intellectual one. The realization that my early concerns about indifference and cruelty to animals is a moral concern the Bible addresses, however obliquely, came not directly from Scripture itself, strangely enough, but rather the Bible as mediated through creative writing. With Tom Regan and Andrew Linzey, I believe strongly that literature can "reconnect us with

---

26. Findley, *Wars*, 201, 202.

the world of animals,"²⁷ and I owe much to writers who serve to disrupt my Bible reading habits and stir up fresh questions. Tzachi Zamir puts it eloquently: "Situated between emotional appeals and defensible claims, between rhetoric and argument, the literary text is able to address us not as targets to be politically mobilized. Nor does it position us as judges of arguments that need to be appeased. Mirroring our actions and practices for us, alerting us to what we see, the subtle fingers of literature fleetingly touch and leave us. Unexpectedly, it is the soft touch which can mount a powerful punch."²⁸ Similarly, the philosopher Catherine Osborne observes there is much to learn from poetry and stories because "arid argument is not always (or perhaps ever) the way to grasp moral truths—such as coming to understand what it is to take a humane attitude, and not a sentimental attitude, towards the other inhabitants of the world we live in."²⁹

Wisdom emerges in the most unlikely places. Of writers who depict animals and their relations with humanity, acknowledging simultaneously the beauties and horrors those interactions involve, Canadian novelist Timothy Findley stands out for me. Animals feature prominently in his work, memorably in *The Wars* in which we read about the experiences of World War I officer Robert Ross. Two incidents in this story—one at the beginning of the novel, the other at the end—are worth noting in this regard.

The first occurs soon after young Ross arrives in Lethbridge, Alberta, for military training in 1915 and depicts the harmonious interaction of a man and an unexpected companion. Ross is running in a field when he sees a coyote and decides to follow it, the animal appearing initially not to notice. The peacefulness of the moment and even the animal's hospitality is unexpected. When the animal stops to drink, Ross, still watching from a distance, hears the lapping "and the sound seemed to satisfy his own thirst." After this, once the animal moves away from the water, "it looked directly at him—right at Robert, with its tail slightly lowered—and barked. Then the tail began to wag. The coyote had known he was there the whole time . . . Now it was telling Robert the valley was vacant: safe—and that Robert could proceed to the water's edge to drink."³⁰ This beautiful

27. Regan and Linzey, *Other Nations*, xviii.
28. Zamir, "Literary Works and Animal Ethics," 953.
29. Osborne, *Dumb Beasts*, viii. Poetry and art, she adds, "rather than science and argument, are the kinds of things that can change our sense of which features of the world demand our attention and our love" (11; cf. 5, 138).
30. Findley, *Wars*, 27, 28. For the full episode, see 25–28. For a biblical example of animal concern for a human's wellbeing, see my reading of Mark 5:1–20 and parallels

harmony between species and even mutual concern for the other's wellbeing has no counterpart in the relationships between people during wartime, as depicted later in the novel, and so this prairie image haunts all that follows as a paradise lost.

The second incident reveals how broken and troubled Ross becomes as the fighting rages across Europe's battlefields. Just as the coyote's gesture signals a cross-species concern for another, so too does Ross's attempts to save horses and mules threatened by enemy shells and trapped in burning barns.[31] Ross is contemptuous of those who are cruel to animals and indifferent to their distress, something evident in his panicked efforts to save these creatures amid the terrifying shelling of enemy combatants and his effortless execution of Captain Leather (a suggestive name illustrating that man's lack of concern for animals), who tries to prevent him from doing so: "Robert shot him between the eyes."[32]

Ross witnesses a complete disregard for the sanctity of life—human and animal—during the Great War and is desperate to recover something of his youthful idealism by protecting those innocent of the horrific crimes committed by soldiers on all sides of the conflict. With respect to animal-human relations, Findley suggests respect, compassion, dignity, hospitality, and generosity are not species specific and that humanity at its worse has much to learn from such unlikely teachers as coyotes and horses.

Findley's writing often demonstrates sensitivity to injustice and abuses of power, particularly the victimization of vulnerable characters at the margins of society, a category that includes animals.[33] In *The Wars*, the novelist juxtaposes violence with cross-species empathy. Part of the story's power derives from the constant paralleling of brutality and kindness that forces

---

in chapter 3.

31. Findley, *Wars*, 201–3, 210–13.

32. Ibid., 203. See too 66–69 regarding a very different situation involving distressed animals.

33. Animals are also prominent in Findley's 1984 novel *Not Wanted on the Voyage* and they often suffer as a result of "Noah's" cruelty and despotism. Findley finds the "dominion" language of Genesis harsh and potentially destructive. He explains that *Not Wanted on the Voyage* envisions an alternative version of the biblical story of Noah and the ark; it is "an allegory about a strong-willed man who lost touch with his God, and so decided to make up his own rules and say that God had given them to him. And that, in this book, is how we gained 'dominion over nature'—we gave it to ourselves, claiming that our right to it came from God" (Findley, *Stone Orchard*, 111; for further notes on *Not Wanted on the Voyage*, see too Findley's *Inside Memory*, 215–34). For analysis of Findley's ark novel, see Gilmour, "Postmodern Flood."

readers to acknowledge the dissonance between them. This technique also occurs in the work of the Victorian novelist and poet Anne Brontë.

Wisdom, Folly, and Animals in *Agnes Grey* and *The Tenant of Wildfell Hall*

> For at the window of my house I looked through my casement,
> And beheld among the simple ones, I discerned among the youths, a young man void of understanding,
> Passing through the street near her corner; and he went the way to her house,
> In the twilight, in the evening, in the black and dark night:
> And, behold, there met him a woman with the attire of an harlot, and subtil of heart.
> (She is loud and stubborn; her feet abide not in her house:
> Now is she without, now in the streets, and lieth in wait at every corner.)
> So she caught him, and kissed him, and with an impudent face said unto him,
> I have peace offerings with me; this day have I payed my vows.
> Therefore came I forth to meet thee, diligently to seek thy face, and I have found thee.
> I have decked my bed with coverings of tapestry, with carved works, with fine linen of Egypt.
> I have perfumed my bed with myrrh, aloes, and cinnamon.
> Come, let us take our fill of love until the morning: let us solace ourselves with loves.
> For the goodman is not at home, he is gone a long journey:
> He hath taken a bag of money with him, and will come home at the day appointed.
> With her much fair speech she caused him to yield, with the flattering of her lips she forced him.
> He goeth after her straightway, as an ox goeth to the slaughter, or as a fool to the correction of the stocks;
> Till a dart strike through his liver; as a bird hasteth to the snare, and knoweth not that it is for his life.
> Hearken unto me now therefore, O ye children, and attend to the words of my mouth.
> Let not thine heart decline to her ways, go not astray in her paths.
> For she hath cast down many wounded: yea, many strong men have been slain by her.
> Her house is the way to hell, going down to the chambers of death.
> (Prov 7:6–27, KJV)

The least known of the much-celebrated Brontë sisters is in many respects my "muse" for all that follows because in her two novels I discovered, for the first time, a biblically informed concern for animal wellbeing. Next to sisters Charlotte and Emily, whose novels are among the best known in the English language, Anne is somewhat obscure, yet in her work we find not only a striking illustration of the reception of biblical literature in creative writing but also a compassionate theology that allows room for other-than-human life. Consider her 1847 debut work *Agnes Grey*, in which the beleaguered titular governess recalls a conversation between herself and her pitiless young male charge:

> I observed, on the grass about his garden, certain apparatus of sticks and corn, and asked what they were.
> "Traps for birds."
> "Why do you catch them?"
> "Papa says they do harm."
> "And what do you do with them when you catch them?"
> "Different things. Sometimes I give them to the cat; sometimes I cut them in pieces with my penknife; but the next, I mean to roast alive."
> "And why do you mean to do such a horrible thing?"
> "For two reasons: first, to see how long it will live—and then, to see what it will taste like."
> "But don't you know it is extremely wicked to do such things? Remember, the birds can feel as well as you; and think, how would you like it yourself?"[34]

This dialogue between the sadistic Tom Bloomfield and Agnes Grey raises obvious concerns about cruelty. Anne Brontë's novel suggests that arguments for interspecies compassion had at least some currency in mid-nineteenth-century England. According to Ivan Kreilkamp, *Agnes Grey* appeared "at a moment when a nascent 'animal rights' movement—not yet called by that name—was taking its place as a powerful social force in England," more than twenty years after the founding of the Society for the Prevention of Cruelty to Animals.[35] Of particular interest for the present study is Agnes's idea of an affinity between humans and animals: "the birds can feel as well as you." This statement precedes Charles Darwin's *On the Origin of Species* by more than a decade, and yet there is openness to the idea that the distance separating humans from nonhumans is not so great.

34. Brontë, *Agnes Grey*, 18.

35. Kreilcamp, "Petted Things," 88. For remarks on Brontë's *Agnes Grey*, see esp. 87–89.

Indeed, notions of kinship between sentient beings were common in pre-Darwinian British writing. The assumption of a gap between the species "may not have been so definite, or even so preexisting" as is often supposed, and even "in the Victorian or pre-Victorian context, the shift from the human to the nonhuman animal frequently required no very great leap."[36] Commenting on Victorian literature more widely, Harriet Ritvo adds that others share Agnes Grey's views: "On both the physical and the rhetorical levels the relationships between people and animals had long seemed indeterminate and fluid . . . there was no consensus about the content of the dichotomy that distinguished people from the rest of animate creation."[37]

For the pious Anne Brontë, her vision of the proximity between animals and humans does not derive so much from philosophical and scientific discourse as from the Bible. Informing this perspective in part is the book of Proverbs with its assertion that wisdom and righteousness manifest themselves in the proper treatment of animals. The reverse is also true. Foolishness and unrighteousness are synonymous with ill treatment of animals: "A righteous man regardeth the life of his beast: but the tender mercies of the wicked are cruel" (Prov 12:10 KJV).[38] Brontë does not express these ideas in anything like a systematic commentary on Proverbs but rather dramatizes its wisdom, giving life to its values in the characters of her 1848 novel *The Tenant of Wildfell Hall*.

Soon after her marriage to Arthur Huntingdon, the story's protagonist, Helen, writes in her diary about a quarrel with her new husband: "Arthur had told me, at different intervals, the whole story of his intrigue with Lady F—, which I would not believe before. It was some consolation, however, to find that, in this instance, the lady had been more to blame than he; for he was very young at the time, and she had decidedly made the first advances, if what he said was true. I hated her for it, for it seemed as if she had chiefly contributed to his corruption."[39]

36. Ritvo, "Our Animal Cousins," 48.

37. Ibid. The Victorian period saw dramatic cultural shifts regarding human-animal relations, including the opening of zoos, more widespread pet ownership, and increased use of animals in laboratory experimentation. It is likely Brontë found the last disturbing, to the extent she was aware of it. For discussion of scientific research involving animals in the nineteenth century, see White, "Experimental Animal in Victorian Britain"; Li, "Mobilizing Christianity in the Antivivisection Movement"; Mayer, "Laboratory Animals"; and Preece, "Darwinism, Christianity, and the Great Vivisection Debate."

38. I cite the Authorized Version (KJV) in this section because it is the version Anne Brontë uses.

39. Brontë, *Tenant of Wildfell Hall*, 194.

This is an intriguing lack of precision, replacing the woman's full name with a capitalized letter and dash. Brontë uses this device regularly in *Agnes Grey* but not often in *The Tenant of Wildfell Hall*, which makes it all the more conspicuous on this occasion. Withholding the full name suggests broad applicability, perhaps a universal meaning that resists reduction to a particular person or incident. Indeed, Brontë is explicit that she intends *The Tenant of Wildfell Hall* to educate her readers and warn them against certain behaviors.[40] It follows that this nameless woman, Lady F—, serves as a model of infamy, a paradigm of villainy whose particular location in time and space is of secondary importance. She is a classic *femme fatale*.

Despite Brontë's lack of precision in naming this woman, I suggest we can identify her further. Notice what Helen writes about her new husband's affair: he was a young and unmarried man at the time it happened; the woman was the first to make sexual advances; and she was married at the time she seduces Arthur Huntingdon. This is also, of course, what we learn about the "young man void of understanding" described in Prov 7:6–27 (v. 7; cited above). A married woman draws a simple youth away from the path of wisdom, ultimately leading him to the "chambers of death" (as the KJV so eloquently puts it; v. 27). The nameless Lady F— in *The Tenant of Wildfell Hall* is, I propose, Lady Folly, a frequent designation for the temptress in Proverbs 1–9 who is the counterpart to Lady Wisdom.

We find citations and allusions to Scripture throughout this novel but Proverbs in particular informs and motivates Helen's actions and conversations. Almost everything she does concerns the moral formation of her child and her husband. Helen believes her God-given reason to exist is to "educate [her son] for heaven," keeping the boy from following his wicked father's example, what she calls his "contaminating influence."[41] Her language alludes to, and her actions live out, the Proverbs maxim "Train up a child in the way he should go: and when he is old he will not depart from it" (Prov 22:6). She defines motherhood as being the boy's "instructor, friend—to guide him along the perilous path of youth, and train him to be God's servant while on earth."[42] Similarly, she frequently speaks of her marriage as an opportunity to

---

40. "My object in writing [*The Tenant of Wildfell Hall*] was not simply to amuse the Reader, neither was it to gratify my own taste, nor yet to ingratiate myself with the Press and the Public: I wished to tell the truth, for truth always conveys its own moral to those who are able to receive it" (ibid., 39, from the preface to the second edition).

41. Ibid., 216, 280; cf. 217, 222, etc.

42. Ibid., 217; cf. Prov 3:6; 4:11; etc.

foster an ethical core in her husband, to "lead him back to the path of virtue," again using a metaphor familiar from Proverbs.[43]

Helen warns all those she meets to choose life rather than death. Said differently, she embodies Lady Wisdom of Proverbs 1–9 and calls out to her husband Arthur Huntingdon, "the young man void of understanding, Passing through the street near [the] corner" where Lady Folly dwells (Prov 7:7–8). Arthur Huntingdon is an allegory, embodying the consequences of one choosing to ignore Lady Wisdom: one who "committeth adultery with a woman lacketh understanding," and "he that doeth it destroyeth his own soul" (6:32).[44]

Arthur is, then, the Proverbs fool but not only because he listens to Lady Folly and ignores Lady Wisdom (Helen). He also abuses animals. For Anne Brontë, the mistreatment of animals is unambiguously a moral failure, and one she links to Christian theological and biblical teaching. This is true of young Tom, who tortures birds in *Agnes Grey*, and it is true of the fool Arthur Huntingdon in *The Tenant of Wildfell Hall*. When constructing her symbolic portrayal of wisdom and folly in her depictions of Helen and Arthur, Brontë includes a number of references to their respective attitudes toward animals as ways of depicting and assessing their morality. We see this in an episode involving their dog: "his favourite cocker, Dash, that had been lying at my feet, took the liberty of jumping upon him and beginning to lick his face. He struck it off with a smart blow; and the poor dog squeaked, and ran cowering back to me." The dog's movement here enacts the harmony envisioned by such wisdom texts as Prov 12:10. The wise (Helen) are at peace with nonhuman creation and attentive to its needs, and fools (Arthur) are not.

Arthur later calls the dog back "but Dash only looked sheepish and wagged the tip of his tail. He called again, more sharply, but Dash only

---

43. Brontë, *Tenant of Wildfell Hall*, 280. Owing to the extent of biblical references in the novel, it is possible Brontë has 1 Pet 3:1–2 in view as well. These verses refer to believing wives quietly influencing their unbelieving husbands, nudging them toward belief.

44. The incident where Helen introduces the shorthand "Lady F—" is brief, and only occasionally does she refer back to it. However, a much longer story appearing in her diary concerns another of Arthur Huntingdon's affairs, one occurring after his marriage to Helen. His friend Lord Lowborough marries and soon after, the new Lady Lowborough begins flirting with Arthur and she eventually seduces him (Brontë, *Tenant of Wildfell Hall*, 265 etc.). It is interesting to note that Lady Lowborough is the only other titled female character of significance in the novel apart from Lady F—, something suggesting a link between the two. Lady Lowborough is also an incarnation of Lady F—, Lady Folly of the book of Proverbs.

clung the closer to me [Helen], and licked my hand as if imploring protection. Enraged at this, his master snatched up a heavy book and hurled it at his head. The poor dog set up a piteous outcry and ran to the door."[45] This book actually hits Helen, which not only hints at domestic abuse (Helen asks if he intended to hit her) but is also an affront to wisdom, which she personifies. On other occasions, Arthur pulls Dash's ears, shoots "hapless partridges," engages in foxhunts for entertainment, and shows no compassion for a sick horse.[46] Arthur's behavior recalls that of another disagreeable Brontë character, the hypocritical Rector Mr. Hatfield in *Agnes Grey*, who, Nancy Brown reports, "kicked my poor cat right across th' floor."[47]

For Anne Brontë, cruelty to animals "was the sure mark of a villain," an observation Angeline Goreau supports with comments by a visitor to the Brontë home who reported, "The Brontës' love of dumb creatures made them very sensitive of the treatment bestowed upon them. For any one to offend in this respect with them was an infallible bad sign, and a blot on the disposition."[48] In a similar vein, Stevie Davies argues that in *Agnes Grey* "animals are fellow beings with an ethical claim on human protection. Tenderness towards animals is a major index of moral worth, elevating the curate [Edward Weston] above his 'superior' [the Rector Mr. Hatfield], Agnes above her employer."[49] Apart from her fiction, Anne's values are evident in her disapproval of riders whipping horses. For this reason she welcomed the development of rail travel.[50]

We also see Anne's high esteem for animals and emotional attachment to them in her long poem "Self-Communion," in which she records her grief over the death of a sparrow. Here her religious values align with this sympathy for other living things:

> How can it stand alone?
> That heart so prone to overflow
> E'en at the thought of other's woe,
> How will it bear its own?
> How, if a sparrow's death can wring

---

45. Ibid., 196.
46. Ibid., 207, 154, 198, 236.
47. Brontë, *Agnes Grey*, 148.
48. Goreau, editorial note in ibid., 260 n. 8. The visitor she cites is Ellen Nussey, who visited the Brontës at Haworth in 1833.
49. Davies, "'Three distinct and unconnected tales,'" 85–86.
50. Chitham, *Anne Brontë*, 160, 185.

> Such bitter tear-floods from the eye,
> Will it behold the suffering
> Of struggling, lost humanity?
> The torturing pain, the pining grief,
> The sin-degraded misery,
> The anguish that defies relief?[51]

These lines not only reveal the Bible's influence on Brontë's writing (cf. Jesus's words about sparrows in Matt 10:29) but as this is an autobiographical poem, they reveal her own sensitivity to other creatures. Biographer Edward Chitham refers to "the Brontës' great love of animals" in comments about this poem, adding, "it seems likely that Anne shared this family trait very early."[52]

Like the fool of Proverbs, Arthur Huntingdon's decisions destroy him. He falls prey to Lady F—, Lady Folly, and a symptom of this corruption is his callous disregard of animals and an abdication of duties toward them. He goes down to what Proverbs calls "the chambers of death," never able to embrace Lady Wisdom even though Helen invites him to do so right up until his last breath. Wisdom, Proverbs tells us, was present at creation, beside the Creator "like a master worker," "rejoicing in his inhabited world" (Prov 8:30–31). To hear Lady Wisdom's voice, Anne Brontë tells us, is to rejoice alongside Wisdom, sharing her delight in all God's creatures, eschewing cruelty to them in all its manifestations.

Anne Brontë's vision of human–animal relations derives from her fervent faith and theological reflection.[53] The ideal of compassionate sympathy for all creatures is more than sentimentalism; it is rather an obligation embedded in biblical teaching, as she understands it. As we move on to consider some of the biblical writings that possibly inform those conclusions, her short poem "Views of Life" offers a fitting segue:

> Because the road is rough and long,
> Shall we despise the skylark's song?

---

51. Brontë, "Self-Communion," in Benson, ed., *Brontë Poems*, 306; full poem, 303–15.

52. Chitham, *Anne Brontë*, 20.

53. Another plausible influence informing Anne Brontë's attitude toward animals is the eighteenth-century poet William Cowper, whose poem "Winter Walk at Noon" comments on the "worth of beasts." Linzey describes Cowper's poem as "an impressive essay on the theology of the Fall and restoration of the animal creation" ("Is Christianity Irredeemably Speciesist?," his editorial introduction to *Animals on the Agenda*, 254 n. 12; cf. xiii). Brontë refers to Cowper as the "celestial Bard" in her 1846 poem "To Cowper" (included in the Talley edition of *The Tenant of Wildfell Hall*, 410–11, citing here 410). The latter poem does not mention animals but demonstrates her familiarity with his work.

> No! while we journey on our way
> We'll notice every lovely thing
> And ever as they pass away
> To memory and hope we'll cling.[54]

May we also notice all lovely things that God places in our path, and in the pages of our Bibles.

---

54. Taken from Chitham, *Anne Brontë*, vii.

2   Reading Animals in the Christian Bible

As we set out to read animals in the Bible with attention to ethical concerns we face a number of hurdles. In this chapter I call attention to just five of them, each overlapping with the others in various ways, and offer suggestions on how we might hone our Bible reading habits so as to be inclusive of all Eden's residents. For the first of these, I take my cue from a journal entry from November 8, 1874, by the poet and Jesuit priest Gerard Manley Hopkins.

Looking at the Same Animals but Seeing Something Different: Unity and Diversity within the Community of Faith

Hopkins reports seeing "a vast multitude of starlings making an unspeakable jangle." Here as elsewhere in his writing we find the poet taking great delight in nature: "They would settle in a row of trees; then, one tree after another, rising at a signal they looked like a cloud of specks of black snuff or powder . . . then they would sweep round in whirlwinds—you could see the nearer and farther bow of the rings by the size and blackness; many would be in one phase at once, all narrow black flakes hurling round, then in another; then they would fall upon a field and so on."

For the poet, the scene evokes contemplation and curiosity: "I thought they must be full of enthusiasm and delight hearing their cries and stirring and cheering one another." But Hopkins's companion that day was not thinking about poetry or content simply to watch the starlings at play. William Splaine wanted a gun, declaring then "it would rain meat."[1]

I find in this incident a kind of parable. Like many of the parables in the New Testament Gospels, it challenges deeply entrenched patterns of thought and behavior, while resisting singular and simplistic explanations and commentaries. Parables force us to rethink the familiar and they disrupt expectations. They pose questions previously thought answered. This particular "parable" reminds us that there are different ways of looking at the world, and evaluating whether one is better than the other is not always straightforward. For one thing, it is interesting to note that the two men with such divergent reactions to the starlings' "unspeakable jangle" are both deeply religious. Gerard Manley Hopkins and William Splaine are priests, which is to say they take the religious life and the Christian Bible seriously. Their responses to the avian spectacle occur, we might say, within the context of a worldview informed by Christian tradition, theological reflection, the Bible, and a commitment to institutional religion. Presumably each responds to the birds' flight in a manner he thinks consistent with that faith-based frame of reference. For his part, Splaine might say the wonders of creation are gifts for human pleasure, there to be used in whatever way we see fit, which for him means sport hunting and "meat." On some level, Hopkins seems to disagree with Splaine's position. He was no vegetarian so not necessarily opposed to hunting for food, but there is no mistaking that his stirring description of the starlings contrasts sharply with Splaine's violent outburst, indicating that in his view the birds offer something far more important than a meal or a sharpshooter's delight.

Also noteworthy is the exuberance displayed by each man. Splaine's outburst is hyperbolic ("it would rain meat"). Even if joking, the bravado promises the shooter's performance would rival nature's impressive display (i.e., it would be more spectacular than the birds sweeping round in whirlwinds). For Hopkins, however, the scene evokes more than a smile. It inspires poetry. He is less interested in the entertainment potential of the birds than their contributions to the inner life of the imagination, and even his spirituality. The natural world often contributes to his meditations on God. Put side by side, we see here two different ways of viewing nonhuman species among those similarly grounded within a single religious tradition—one characterized by conquest, violence, and consumption (Splaine), the other by reverence and awe for natural wonders (Hopkins).

---

1. Hopkins, *Major Works*, 221–22.

Finally, I note that Hopkins does not explicitly condemn or condone Splaine's comment, even in the privacy of his journal. We can easily imagine the poet wincing at Splaine's outburst, given the way the poet celebrates the birds' breathtaking beauty, but he resists overt commentary on his friend's words. We do not know as much about William Splaine as we do Gerard Manley Hopkins but there is no reason to doubt he was as pious and well meaning as his poet-friend. The two walked together in Wales despite their differences, a symbol perhaps of Christian fellowship amid diversity of opinion. I aim to emulate that spirit of unity here, recognizing that well-meaning, pious, competent thinkers disagree regarding the ethics of human interaction with the natural world and interpretations of the Bible. At the same time, animal issues represent a moral issue of extreme urgency and one demanding theological arguments in defense of the defenseless. Debate, even within the community of faith, is necessary and inevitable.

While Hopkins's gentleness is commendable, some dismiss such behavior as mere sentimentalism devoid of a theological basis. What is more, some early Christian writing seems to support Father Splaine more than Father Hopkins, appearing to minimize the value of animals as objects meriting ethical consideration. Perhaps the clearest example of this is a remark by St. Paul.

When the Bible Resists Animal-Friendly Bible Reading, or, What's Paul's Beef with Oxen?

In a few short words, the Apostle Paul appears to dispense with Mosaic legislation requiring proper care of animals (see examples cited in the previous chapter) and at the same time he seems to rule out a high estimate of their worth within a Christian worldview. According to Deut 25:4, "You shall not muzzle an ox while it is treading out the grain." According to St. Paul, these words are about people, not animals (1 Cor 9:9–10). For readers interested in making connections between the Christian Bible and animal compassion, this passing remark presents a considerable impediment. One theologian finds that "the severest blow dealt by the Bible to religiously grounded concern for animals [is this] almost flippant way that St. Paul disposes of the literal meaning of that Deuteronomic text."[2] From an animal compassion point of view, the anthropocentric nature of the passage is dan-

2. Gaffney, "Catholic Morality," 102.

gerous because it appears to offer license to ignore animal ethics outright. At the same time, this is the most explicit New Testament statement (along with its parallel in 1 Tim 5:17–18) touching on human responsibility to animals, owing to the citation of Deut 25:4. It is therefore both an obstacle and an opportunity for animal theology. Is there a way to read 1 Cor 9:9–10 that does justice to Paul while minimizing bias against nonhuman species among his readers?

Slavery and Animals, Jane Austen and Paul the Apostle: An Analogy

Before addressing this question, I offer a somewhat clumsy analogy. It is fascinating to follow the great postcolonial theorist Edward W. Said as he grapples with Jane Austen's 1814 novel *Mansfield Park*, a book he clearly cherishes as much as he does its author. His challenge lies in the fact that slavery and empire provide the backdrop for the comfortable upper-class setting of the story. In *Culture and Imperialism*, Said acknowledges he wrestles with "a paradox" when reading this Austen novel, one that, he says, "I have been impressed by but can in no way resolve. All the evidence says that even the most routine aspects of holding slaves on a West Indian sugar plantation were cruel stuff. And everything we know about Austen and her values is at odds with the cruelty of slavery."[3] Readers of Paul concerned with animal compassion face a similar dilemma. Everything we know of the apostle and his values appears to be at odds with cruelty and indifference. Though he is silent about obligations to animals and applies Deut 25:4 to people, this is not the same thing as muzzling hungry oxen or kicking puppies. He simply does not address animal compassion issues directly. This leaves us, like Edward Said, with "a paradox" not easy to resolve.

At one point in Jane Austen's *Mansfield Park*, the upright Fanny Price speaks to her uncle Sir Thomas Bertram who owns an estate in Antigua, questioning him "about the slave trade." Following the question, Austen writes, "there was such a dead silence!"[4] Said finds this moment suggestive because it indicates "that one world could not be connected with the other since there simply is no common language for both." In this particular setting and historical moment there was no vocabulary available to the

---

3. Said, *Culture and Imperialism*, 95–96.
4. Austen, *Mansfield Park*, 178. Austen's use of an exclamation mark heightens the ideological import of this momentary break in the conversation.

characters to confront directly and explicitly the ethical problems attached to slaveholding plantations. To read works like *Mansfield Park* accurately, Said adds, we need to read them "in the main as resisting or avoiding that other setting, which their formal inclusiveness, historical honesty, and prophetic suggestiveness cannot completely hide."[5] The "dead silence" Austen refers to hints at her discomfort with an economy relying on slave labor, a scourge lying beneath the surface of the wealthy English characters that populate her novels. Said's efforts to find resistance to slavery in Austen is loosely analogous to Christian animal compassion advocates wanting to find moral direction in St. Paul, even though the apostle does not address the topic explicitly. Consider Said's conclusion:

> It would be silly to expect Jane Austen to treat slavery with anything like the passion of an abolitionist or a newly liberated slave . . . Yes, Austen belonged to a slave-owning society, but do we therefore jettison her novels as so many trivial exercises in aesthetic frumpery? Not at all . . . if we take seriously our intellectual and interpretive vocation to make connections, to deal with as much of the evidence as possible, fully and actually, to read what is there or not there, above all, to see complementarity and interdependence instead of isolated, venerated, or formalized experience that excludes and forbids the hybridizing intrusions of human history.[6]

We cannot jettison Paul in matters of Christian animal ethics any more than postcolonial theorists can ignore one of the great novelists of the English language. Said's reading of Austen is elegant and forceful for its simplicity. All he does is highlight the potential of a pregnant pause in a conversation between two characters, that "dead silence," and there finds room to wrestle with the pressing moral questions that shape and inform his study of culture, history, literature, and politics. The discomfort of the characters regarding the slave trade hints at Austen's own discomfort and that of others in her society.

Edward Said offers further comments on reading great writers—like Austen and Joseph Conrad—whose ideas seem out of step with the standards of our time in *Freud and the Non-European*. "My approach tries to see them in their context as accurately as possible," he writes, "but then . . . I see them contrapuntally, that is, as figures whose writing travels across temporal, cultural and ideological boundaries in unforeseen ways to emerge

---

5. Said, *Culture and Imperialism*, 96.
6. Ibid.

as part of a new ensemble *along with* later history and subsequent art."[7] This is a promising strategy for those seeking to find value in the Bible for animal and environmental ethics, even though both of these concerns as we understand them are largely foreign to the biblical writers. We need to read the Bible *along with* and in light of the unique circumstances of our own times and places.

The Problem with 1 Corinthians 9:9–10

Back to Paul. What, then, is the problem with 1 Cor 9:9–10? Noah J. Cohen finds that "examination of the biblical, Talmudic, and medieval jurisprudence concerning the lower creatures reflects a coherent system of humane legislation whose purpose is to defend the [nonhuman] creation."[8] Unfortunately, laws rest on precedent and interpretation and so the protections they afford animals vary in different times and places among both Jews and Christians. Noting this, Roberta Kalechofsky then mentions Paul's reading of Deuteronomy in 1 Cor 9:9–10 as an example of exegetical retreat from the original sense of the passage. With the exception of Paul, she adds, such an elastic interpretation "is never applied to the law concerning the muzzling of the ox."[9] Many others also find Paul's reading of Deuteronomy at least unusual, if not problematic:

> The passage about the ox was as nonallegorical as everything else in the book of Deuteronomy . . . Like certain other passages in that same book, it is plainly intended to be read as a piece of divine legislation in behalf of animals, despite some inconvenience to human greed . . . It is indeed "for oxen that God is concerned," and to at least that extent he "does not speak entirely for our sake." The Mosaic law does envisage animal interest, does legislate animal rights, and to that extent does represent animals as moral objects.[10]

In a chapter surveying views about animals in the ancient world, philosopher Stephen R. L. Clark observes that the Hebrew Bible includes several rules about the proper treatment of animals (listing among examples

---

7. Said, *Freud and the Non-European*, 24 (italics original).

8. Cohen, *Tsa'ar Ba'alei Hayim*, 1; cited in Kalechofsky, "Hierarchy, Kinship, and Responsibility," 95.

9. Kalechofsky, "Hierarchy, Kinship, and Responsibility," 95, 96.

10. Gaffney, "Animal Experimentation," 151; as cited in Kalechofsky, "Hierarchy, Kinship, and Responsibility," 96.

Deut 14:21; 22:4 cf. Luke 14:5; Deut 22:6–7 cf. Lev 22:28; Deut 22:10; Lev 19:9–10; 23:22; 25:6–7; Wis 11:14). He notes Deut 25:4 as well but recognizes the ramifications of Paul's subsequent commentary: "Unfortunately, it was early decided by the mainstream Churches, following a remark of Paul, that the animal welfare laws were only allegorical, that we are linked by no 'community of law' [Augustine, *Morals of the Manichaeans*], and even that a concern for animals was a sign, as it had been for the more doctrinaire of pagan thinkers, of a poor moral sense."[11]

Clearly the *reception* of biblical literature, quite apart from anything we might describe as an original or authorial intent, has consequences in earliest Christian thinking about animals. The influence of Paul's citation and interpretation of the Deuteronomy regulation about oxen in 1 Corinthians, from 1 Tim 5:17–18 to the present, invites and even encourages a diminished sense of their importance as creatures deserving moral consideration. Some who are not specialists in Pauline literature recognize this,[12] as well as some who are. Among astute readers in the latter category, no less a scholar than Albert Schweitzer is blunt in his assessment of Paul's use of Torah in 1 Cor 9:9–10: "Of course Paul's exegesis is here at fault," he writes. "It is part of the greatness of the legislation of Deuteronomy, that in this and so many other ordinances it does imply that God concerns Himself about the animal creation."[13]

Occasionally those drawing on biblical and Christian theological tradition in support of animal compassion causes appear angered, frustrated, or even embarrassed by Paul's reference to oxen in 1 Cor 9:9–10. Others who happily mine Rom 8:18–23, Col 1:15–23, and other passages in support of a Pauline vocabulary of inclusion ignore these verses altogether, even though, again, they are among the most explicit words about animal care in the New Testament (i.e., meaning the citation itself, regardless of

---

11. Clark, "Animals in Classical and Late Antique Philosophy," 54.

12. Consider, for instance, the widely read 1975 publication *Animal Liberation*, in which philosopher Peter Singer argues that "if a being suffers there can be no moral justification for refusing to take that suffering into consideration" (8). He does not find much value in the Bible to support his position, however, finding that while the Old Testament shows only "flickers of concern for their sufferings," the New Testament "is completely lacking in any injunction against cruelty to animals, or any recommendation to consider their interests." He then mentions 1 Cor 9:9–10 with obvious disdain: "Saint Paul insisted on reinterpreting the old Mosaic law that forbade muzzling the ox that trod out the corn: 'Doth God care for oxen?' Paul asks scornfully. No, he answered, the law was intended 'altogether for our sakes'" (191).

13. Schweitzer, *Mysticism of Paul the Apostle*, 320.

Paul's commentary on it). Paul's remark about oxen is conspicuous by its absence in such cases, particularly because it is one of a very few places where he mentions animals at all. Those who do comment on 1 Cor 9:9–10 tend to keep their remarks short and/or dismissive. "In Paul's anthropocentric and allegorizing hermeneutics," Stephen H. Webb writes, "this humane law from Moses really applies to Christian missionaries who should be rewarded for their evangelism, not animals who should be fed when they work the fields. Paul does not even consider the alternative of a literal reading of the text."[14] In these verses Norm Phelps finds Paul "deciding that God has no concern for animals, and therefore we need have none," a position indicating the apostle "rejected both his Jewish background and the teachings of Jesus in favor of his Greek background," which is a largely Aristotelian view of the world.[15]

The Opportunity Presented by 1 Corinthians 9:9–10

But all is not lost. If 1 Cor 9:9–10 is a Gordian knot for Christian animal compassion advocates, the metaphor dares us to approach the impossible with creativity. This is what Edward Said does. He finds meaning in Jane Austen's "dead silence" and his recommendation to allow dialogue between old books and ideas, and the concerns and interests of later readers, is a productive one. Jane Austen was not an abolitionist, true, but *Mansfield Park*, subtly and simply—by means of an uncomfortable pause, "a dead silence"—offers Said an opportunity to add Austen's voice to literary resistance to empire. He does not misread Austen or deny her historical moment but deliberately and creatively shapes his engagement with her novel in the direction of opposition to colonialism and slavery. We have a loose equivalent to Jane Austen's "dead silence" in Paul's somewhat unexpected use of Deut 25:4.

What particularly intrigues me is the broader context of the law Paul cites, which is, as is often the case with Paul, an important clue to understanding his thought.[16] Animal compassion advocates bristle at the apostle's words in part because he had non-animal illustrations available to support

14. Webb, *On God and Dogs*, 25.
15. Phelps, *Dominion of Love*, 164; full discussion occurs on 155–64.
16. For discussion of Paul's use of subtle allusions and short citations to refer to larger sections of text and underlying narrative structures, see, e.g., Hays, *Echoes of Scripture*, throughout; and Wright, *Paul*, 7–8, 10.

his argument, even in the immediate context of Deut 25:4. At least since Chrysostom in the fourth century (ca. 349–407), readers have recognized Paul's appeal to a Torah regulation about oxen was an odd choice. To make the point that laborers deserve pay, Chrysostom observes the example of the priests who had access to various offerings was available to Paul (e.g., Lev 2:3, 10; 7:31–34; 10:12–13).[17] For his part, Calvin saw in Deut 24:14–15 an illustration well suited to Paul's purposes, with its warning against depriving poor and needy laborers of their daily wages. More recently, Joseph A. Fitzmyer agrees that Deut 24:14–15 "would have been a more apt OT text to suit Paul's argument."[18] Nevertheless, while Paul's choice of the oxen passage is unusual, it is simultaneously a compelling opportunity.

This Deuteronomy text sits in the midst of several references to the necessity of protecting the wellbeing and dignity of defenseless people, including divorced women (Deut 24:1–4), poor or needy laborers (24:14–15), aliens in the land, orphans, and widows (24:17–21; 25:5–10). As Richard B. Hays puts it, this context promotes "dignity and justice for human beings."[19] The single mention of animals in this long section about compassion for the defenseless is conspicuous, and Paul's short citation brings to the reader's mind *the whole extended community of those in need of generosity and hospitality*. God is not concerned with human life alone but rather with all life. Deuteronomy does not limit this expectation of care of the defenseless to humans alone. Animals, like widows, laborers, priests, orphans, and the poor, fit within a broader category of those worthy of special attentions and protections. To speak of caring for laboring animals is to speak of caring for vulnerable human beings. To speak of caring for vulnerable humans beings is to speak of caring for laboring animals. They are all alike to those in a position to serve, support, and defend. Paul appeals to this broader section of Deuteronomy and its concern for those in need, people and animals, and applies it to a very specific situation.

Other writings more or less contemporary with Paul also appeal to Deut 25:4 in contexts concerned with the care of needy people. Josephus writes of provisions for the poor and those travelling in the land, citing the injunction against muzzling oxen in support (*Ant.* 4.8.231–34). Agricultural regulations in the Mishnah also allude to the oxen verse in comments about poor

---

17. Chrysostom, *Homilies on the Epistles of Paul to the Corinthians*, 21.5. Taken from Bray, *1–2 Corinthians*, 82.

18. Fitzmyer, *First Corinthians*, 362.

19. Hays, *First Corinthians*, 151.

Israelites and poor priests who glean in the fields (*m. Ter.* 9:2–3). This is a beautiful image. This slippage between a Torah mandate concerning animals and the care of vulnerable people in Paul, Josephus, and Mishnah is analogous to Jane Austen's "dead silence" in that it is a subtle opening in the text permitting a perspective on a vexing moral concern. Paul slides comfortably from oxen to people, from one species to another. This precedent offers us a bridge, allowing us to draw on an old Pauline letter for direction in a present-day conversation about Christian obligations to animals. Dare we credit Paul with a "prophetic suggestiveness" in 1 Cor 9:9–10, as Said does for Jane Austen? Allowing this, Paul's great insight in these verses is that God is not concerned with oxen *only* in Deut 25:4, any more than other laws demanding generosity, hospitality, protection, and compassion are about human beings *only*. The ethical vision of Deuteronomy and Paul is an all-encompassing one, extending to every living thing in need of our care. It is not ours to choose where we direct our concern. It is not ours to choose who is our neighbor.[20]

Some argue that a central motif of Pauline ethics is "other-regard," a lovely catch-all indicating that the call to imitate Christ's self-giving on behalf of others extends beyond narrowly defined human communities to encompass all creation.[21] If we approach 1 Cor 9:9–10 this way, it opens this otherwise embarrassing passage to new possibilities.

To find a living word in biblical literature requires us to move constantly from the particular to the general, from specific instances of a principle to broader applicability. Torah tells us to feed oxen. Paul extrapolates from this law, finding in it justification to care for God's messengers. If Scripture requires we feed our flocks and herds, it also requires we feed those preaching the gospel (1 Cor 9:14). A law about animals is also a law about people. The reverse is also true. The Bible's numerous calls for justice and compassion toward people are not limited to the specific instances cited. They are calls to care for all God's creatures.

We cannot easily identify Paul as an animal advocate in our efforts to address contemporary ethical concerns about their plight any more than Edward Said can easily call Jane Austen an abolitionist, yet in both cases these writers have contributions to make to these respective discourses. The tendency to ignore or minimize 1 Cor 9:9–10 is to miss an opportunity to

---

20. Cf. Jesus's use of Sabbath regulations concerning proper treatment of animals (Matt 12:9–14; Luke 13:12–16; 14:4–5). Here too the required care of animals, even on the Sabbath, serves to justify Jesus's ministry of healing humans.

21. See Horrell et al., *Greening Paul*, 5; Horrell, *Bible and the Environment*, 86, 141.

read a brief, subtle word about animal compassion in the Bible. There are others too, if we look closely.

Selective Bible Reading and the Problem of a "Pick-and-Choose" Approach to Christian Ethics

Another challenge for considering animals in biblical perspective is our tendency to read selectively. Christian readers who maintain the religious authority of the Bible usually insist that all Scripture is inspired by God (cf. 2 Tim 3:16), though practically speaking, many of its pages do not make it into regular rotation as liturgy, sermon texts, or private reading material. It is not easy, hermeneutically speaking, to integrate Leviticus or Obadiah into daily Christian living in quite the same way as Psalm 23 or Philippians. Even within the New Testament, the genealogies of Matthew and Luke or the visions of John the Seer or the argumentation of Hebrews often perplex as much as illuminate.[22]

But first things first. Why animals? Are they really so important that their place in the Bible warrants our attention? The questioning response of some is sharper yet: Are there not more pressing matters plaguing our world that demand our attention and take precedence over concern for dolphins and ducks? Such scourges as poverty, human trafficking, preventable or treatable diseases, natural disasters, and many more all clamor for the Christian's attention and resources. Does it not make more sense to address these problems before tackling others?

The issue, however, is not the neglect of one in order to address another. They are all critically important. Furthermore, a "pick-and-choose" approach to ethics is problematic for various reasons. To start, there are always other issues demanding our attention, but the call to love neighbor as self does not come with permission to care for some while deferring care of others, as though love and grace—from God or God's people—are in short supply. To borrow the language of Torah, the poor, widows, orphans, and strangers in the land are all our responsibility (e.g., Deut 24:19–21) and extending a hand to only a select few misses the point. Kindness and justice

---

22. Selectivity is not unique to Christianity. In his study of animals in Islamic traditions and cultures, Richard C. Foltz observes that many are "only partially aware of what is taught" and "highly selective" about the teachings they choose to embrace and practice (*Animals in Islamic Tradition*, 4, as cited in Kemmerer, *Animals and World Religions*, 4). On animals in Islamic tradition, see too Kemmerer's chapter 7 and Foltz's article "'This She-Camel of God.'"

characterize the people of God in all their relationships and stem from an awareness of their own vulnerability and God's past intervention on their behalf: "Remember that you were a slave in the land of Egypt; therefore I am commanding you to do this [i.e., feed the poor, etc.]." And notice again that animals fall within the purview of the Deuteronomist's logic here because they are present in the immediate context. God showed mercy to you, you show mercy to them. You were a slave in Egypt and God showed you kindness, so do not muzzle your hardworking ox (Deut 24:22; 25:4).

Another problem with approaching ethics selectively and/or postponing some issues to another day is that rarely does "another day" ever come. We always have the poor with us (Mark 14:7), which indicates our inability to complete the task of distributing resources equitably, but this does not mitigate our duties to do all we can to meet the needs of others. Humanity seems bent on destroying itself, but our inability to overcome the Cain complex does not lessen our obligation to be peacemakers. For Paul, the ultimate end of creation's groaning is an eschatological hope (Rom 8:18–25),[23] but this does not excuse Christians from seeking to spread, embody, and serve as witnesses to the kingdom of God now and praying for its world-transforming presence, for conditions today to be the same on earth as they are in heaven (Matt 6:10).[24] Our situation is a little like that of Ezekiel, who, when told to speak, learned also that his audience would not listen (3:4, 7). Our job is to care for others and work for peace regardless of the prospects of success, and even if our efforts inevitably prove insufficient to meet all needs.

Alternatives to Selective Reading and Pick-and-Choose Ethics

What is needed is an approach to Bible reading cognizant of our tendency toward human centeredness. I recommend three general strategies for broadening our awareness of the scope of biblical literature with respect to nonhuman life as alternatives to our habitual erasure of animal presence in theological discourse.

23. For a very informative study of this passage, see Gaventa's chapter "The Birthing of Creation" in *Our Mother Saint Paul* (51–62). She argues against the prevailing view that "creation" in this section of Paul's argument refers to all things apart from humanity. Instead, she finds Paul's sense of creation here to include "*all of humanity* along with *the remainder of creation*" (54; italics original). For her reasons, see 53–55.

24. Crossan understands Paul to mean that as divine heirs, "we are responsible . . . never to increase but always alleviate the 'groaning of creation' (Rom. 8:17–22)" (Crossan, *Greatest Prayer*, 155).

Eden's Other Residents

"Prophetic Suggestiveness"

I take the first from Edward Said's strategy for reading Jane Austen noted above. As seen, he is not only mindful of her historical moment but also aware of her sensitivity to the horrors of slavery. He finds in her work an anticipation of justice, a "prophetic suggestiveness." Said makes a deliberate effort to read Austen with attention to a guiding concern (slavery) and his interpretive strategy permits a constructive, progressive, and creative engagement with *Mansfield Park*. Said does justice to Austen's novel while confronting its disturbing historical setting. Similarly, the Bible does not speak often or in a sustained manner about the proper treatment of animals, but that does not mean it has nothing to contribute to the issue.[25] We need to seek out biblical equivalencies to such poignant silences (Austen) and "prophetic suggestiveness" (Said).

Divine-Animal-Human Triads

Second, as noted in the opening chapter, I propose we pay close attention to those biblical stories where we find divine-animal-human triads. Triptychs are artworks divided into three parts. As a heuristic to facilitate reflection on animals in the diverse writings of the Bible, I adapt the term here to indicate poignant moments involving a convergence of divine, animal, and human characters. This recurring triadic pattern takes many forms but the hypothesis guiding my reflections is that attention to these moments of convergence helps us recognize the essential place of animals for Christian biblical theology. To cover, remove, ignore, or destroy any one panel in a triptych causes irreparable disruption to the message(s) conveyed by the piece as a whole. Analogously, inattention to animals in Bible reading distorts the picture, leading us to overlook an important theme within its pages.

This may appear a strange pattern to search out but such divine-animal-human triads are often striking and illuminating. Consider, to illustrate, the tale of Balaam, his donkey, and the sword-wielding angel (Num 22:22–35). Notice it is the donkey who sees the angel, not the prophet, as one might expect (Num 22:23), which serves to illustrate the spiritual capacity of animals. Balaam's donkey is a greater prophet than he is because

---

25. E.g., Kazez finds the Bible's message about animals to be "a mixed one, bordering on contradictory" (Kazez, *Animalkind*, 15). Cf. Hobgood-Oster, *Holy Dogs and Asses*, 43–46. When writing about the ecological implications of biblical texts, Horrell notes they are "ambivalent and ambiguous" (Horrell, *Bible and the Environment*, 117).

the animal is aware of the divine in a way he is not. This animal's actions also save Balaam from certain physical death. "If it had not turned away from me," the angel of the Lord says to Balaam with reference to the donkey, "I would have killed you and let it live" (Num 22:33). The donkey is not only a vehicle of material blessing by saving his life but also of spiritual revelation, providing an occasion for Balaam to hear the word of the Lord (22:35) and repent (22:34), which in turn proves valuable for Israel collectively because the prophet eventually blesses them (see 24:10). The story also provides the Bible's clearest reference to animal abuse. The angel condemns Balaam's behavior in beating the innocent donkey and threatening its life (22:27–32).

Animals are not always passive participants in these narrative triads but often the unlikely prophets whose innocence, actions, and distinctive "voices" combine to reveal theological insights to the human characters around them. Writers naturally foreground stories about people and nations, which explains why we easily lose sight of those animals that inhabit spaces—literally and literarily—on the margins. Within these triads, however, animals easily overlooked as extraneous detail often prove to be integral to moments of anagnorisis where people make critical discoveries. David (human) learns nothing without the ewe lamb (animal) in a parable told by Nathan (divine representative). In this triad, in which the prophet explicitly serves as the divine mouthpiece ("the LORD sent Nathan" [2 Sam 12:1]), the fictional animal is obviously central in eliciting the king's moral outrage, something evident in the required reparation for the heinous crime of taking a man's beloved pet ("restore the lamb fourfold" [2 Sam 12:6; cf. Exod 22:1]).

In the gospel story of the cock's crow, we find another triadic relationship illuminating a human failure. Here it is the Apostle Peter who displays weakness, nobly asserting his courage and loyalty to Jesus one moment (Matt 26:31–35; Mark 14:27–31; Luke 22:31–34; John 13:36–38), then falling short of that mark the next. The bird's cry is more than an indicator of time as the evangelists tell the story. Instead, the incident reinforces their assertions that Jesus is lord over creation because he uses part of that creation (the bird) to "speak" for him. The scene is poignant because Peter's final denial coincides with the bird's cry (Matt 26:24; Mark 14:71–72; Luke 22:60; John 18:27). The Synoptics signal that Peter remembers Jesus's words about the cock, thus highlighting the miraculous quality of the story (Matt 26:75; Mark 14:72; Luke 22:61). Jesus is a prophet in the writers' estimation, correctly assessing the human condition and anticipating Peter's response.

The bird "speaks" to Peter, who immediately understands the significance of the cock's cry ("he went out and wept bitterly" [Matt 26:75; Luke 22:62]). The bird "speaks" to Jesus, letting him know when the predicted denial occurs ("the cock crowed. The Lord turned and looked at Peter" [Luke 22:60–61]). The bird also "speaks" to those of us reading the story, confirming the evangelists' claims that Jesus is lord of creation and a prophet who understands the human condition.[26] In both stories, the writers use animals (a ewe lamb, a cock's crow) to demonstrate to human characters (David, Peter) their moral failings.[27]

All-Inclusive Language

Third, I urge we take seriously the Bible's many all-encompassing terms and phrases that logically include animals even when not mentioned explicitly. Nonhuman creatures are ubiquitous in biblical literature, perhaps more so than many realize. They are often a hidden presupposition, their presence assumed rather than explicit. This is clear from such common phrases as "all creation" or "all things" or "all flesh."[28] This is one reason why simple appeal to the number of times words like *fish*, *birds*, or *beasts* appear in a concordance is not a reliable measure of their textual presence in the Bible. They appear far more often than such terms alone indicate. An animal-sensitive reading of the Bible is a bit like a hike in the woods. As we walk through a forest, we may not always see them but we know there are all manner of creatures around us. We do not need to flip over that rock to know there are worms and insects underneath. Birdcalls carry on the wind from high above, while others are closer, perhaps from a songbird perched on nearby branches though still out of sight. There is a world of aquatic

---

26. The cock is rich in symbolism throughout the ancient Near East, the Greco-Roman world, and church history. For surveys, see the brief articles by Brumble ("Cock," 149–51) and Penner ("Cock," 93–94).

27. Human failings often mar the ideal harmony in these divine-animal-human triptychs. For instance, though Torah forbids worshiping idols in the likeness of earth's various creatures (Deut 4:15–19), it still occurs, a disruption of an ideal triadic harmony occasionally ridiculed (e.g., Rom 1:23). At the other end of the spectrum, God censures human indifference toward animals under their care (e.g., Exod 23:10–12; Prov 12:10).

28. On the significance of such all-inclusive language, see, e.g., Horrell et al., *Greening Paul*, 89–96 (here with reference to Col 1:15–20 but a recurring theme throughout), and Bauckham, *Bible and Ecology*, 142; for his lengthy list of New Testament passages using *ta panta* (all things), see 199 n. 1. For detailed analysis of the Christ hymn in Colossians, see too Lohse, *Colossians*, 41–61.

life below the surface of that nearby stream or lake, and we see tracks in the mud or snow more often than the bears, moose, wolves, or rabbits that made them. In an analogous way, animals are both present and hidden in the Bible. Sometimes they are hard to miss: Adam names them, Noah sails with them, priests sacrifice them, David and other warriors ride them into battle. But on other occasions, their presence in the text is less obvious, as though lurking in the shadows of our imagined forest.

In the midst of stories largely focused on people it is easy to overlook the implications of terms like "all things" or "the world," especially if reading is influenced by a world-denying eschatology that assumes the earth is temporary and doomed to destruction.[29] As we ponder the pressing ecological crises of the twenty-first century, it is essential we recognize the disastrous implications of a theological indifference to our world. We need to appreciate that while the Bible is concerned with spiritual matters, the material world is no less in view in the language of the prophets and apostles. Theological constructs that dismiss the value of the earth and its diverse nonhuman inhabitants are at odds with the situation envisioned by biblical writers who emphatically declare the world and everything in it "very good" (Gen 1:31) and envision a coming together of the divine and material (as in, e.g., Matt 6:10) and the renewal of all things (as in, e.g., Rev 21:1–5).

Attention to these three broad ideas—the Bible's all-encompassing language, human-animal-divine triads, and the less concrete "prophetic suggestiveness" of biblical writers—goes some way toward helping us find valuable theological resources to support what we might call Christian animal ethics.

Bestial Imagery and Rhetoric

The next obstacle to an animal-sensitive reading of the Bible concerns a commonplace literary and rhetorical device. We constantly find animal metaphors highlighting negative attributes of individuals or groups of people, and this stylistic pattern potentially prejudices our attitudes toward the nonhuman. Examples are legion. When Paul writes of fighting with "wild animals at Ephesus" (1 Cor 15:32), he does not envision a literal battle

---

29. About which, see e.g., Maier's fascinating "Green Millennialism"; Horrell, *Bible and the Environment*, 7–8, 16–17; Wright, *Surprised by Hope*, passim; Habel, *Rainbow*, 84–85.

with beasts like those occurring in the Roman Coliseum.[30] Paul's Roman citizenship protected him from such a fate. Instead, he indicates the human adversaries present in Ephesus (16:9), defining them in bestial terms that emphasize aggression and violence.[31] The author of 2 Peter also depicts opponents of the gospel in a way that denies their humanity. They are instead "irrational animals, mere creatures of instinct, born to be caught and killed" (2 Pet 2:12). Though the simile intends to highlight behaviors of human false teachers in the church (cf. 2:1), the choice of language subtly and indirectly minimizes animal worth because they lack forms of reason the author recognizes. This dehumanizing description of the false teachers and their followers continues a few verses later as the author introduces proverbial phrases about a dog returning to its vomit and a washed sow wallowing in mud (2:22).

To return to Paul, the idolatry he describes in Rom 1:18–23 presents us with another example of animal imagery carrying sinister connotations. He refers to the exchange of the glory of the immortal God "for images resembling . . . birds or four-footed animals or reptiles" (1:23). Such idolatry occurs famously under Aaron's leadership when the people worship a golden calf (Exod 32:4, 8). The concern here is inappropriate religious allegiance and not directly animals, yet it belittles real animals just the same by associating them with human misbehavior.[32] For this reason, it is important not to confuse an author's rhetorical strategies with theological values. Paul distinguishes worship of creation from worship of the Creator (Rom 1:25). The issue is obviously misdirected allegiance and not creation itself. Of course, this widespread use of animal imagery is not unique to the ancients.[33]

---

30. Regarding which, see e.g., Hobgood-Oster, *Holy Dogs and Asses*, 28–29. For the view that Paul refers to battling evil spirits in this verse, not literal animals or human opponents, see Williams, "Apocalyptic and Magical."

31. Fee, *First Epistle*, 770. In his view, the animals "must be understood metaphorically" (full discussion, 770–71). Bailey observes shared themes between 1 Corinthians and Amos, and since Amos refers to lions (1:2; 3:4, 5, 8; 5:19), a bear (5:19), and a snake (5:19), this might provide a clue about the specific "wild animals" Paul has in mind in 1 Cor 15:32 (*Paul through Mediterranean Eyes*, 503; full survey of 1 Corinthians-Amos parallels, 500–508).

32. On other occasions, writers describe and celebrate prized physical, emotional, or spiritual qualities through bestial similes and metaphors, as in, for example, use of the term *dove* in Song 5:2, 12; 6:9; etc.

33. Among modern novelists, Salman Rushdie employs bestial imagery and zoomorphism in a wide variety of ways, often in the service of commentary on politics and

Also challenging are Jesus's uses of lesser-to-the-greater (*qal wa-homer*) forms of argumentation involving flora and fauna:

> "Look at the birds of the air; they neither sow nor reap nor gather into barns, and yet your heavenly Father feeds them. Are you not of more value than they?" (Matt 6:26; cf. Luke 12:24).

> "Are not two sparrows sold for a penny? Yet not one of them will fall to the ground apart from your Father . . . So do not be afraid; you are of more value than many sparrows" (Matt 10:29, 31; cf. Luke 12:6, 7).[34]

> "Suppose one of you has only one sheep and it falls into a pit on the Sabbath; will you not lay hold of it and lift it out? How much more valuable is a human being than a sheep!" (Matt 12:11–12).

These comforting words are entirely consonant with numerous other passages referring to the sustaining of all creation by a generous, caring God. The psalmist reminds us that "all" look to God for their food in due season and that God causes grass to grow "for the cattle, and plants for people to use" (Ps 104:27, 14). The young lions roar, "seeking their food from God," and Jesus's followers do the same, in effect, each time they pray, "Give us this day our daily bread" (Matt 6:11; cf. Luke 11:3; *Did.* 8.2).

Jesus's formulation of this basic theological truth about God's provision for all creation is challenging because he seems to belittle nonhuman life.[35] If God cares for those insignificant, worthless birds, Jesus seems to say, then of course he cares for something as important as you. It is important to notice, however, that Jesus does not deny that sparrows have value, and God's attention to them suggests quite the opposite: "Are not two sparrows sold for a penny? Yet not one of them will fall to the ground apart from your Father" (Matt 10:29). The issue is not so much the relative value of birds and humans in God's eyes—God's love extends to all living things, as Psalm

---

society. For discussion of this technique as it occurs in his novels *Midnight's Children, Shame, The Satanic Verses,* and *Shalimar the Clown,* see Gilmour, "Goats and Gods, Demons and Dogs."

34. The fall of a sparrow likely refers to hunting, not natural death (cf. Amos 3:5). See Bauckham, "Jesus and Animals I," 42–43.

35. For illuminating discussions on this issue, see N. Alexis-Baker, "Humans Are More Important than Animals?," 43–46; and Bauckham, "Jesus and Animals I," 42–46, also in Bauckham, *Living with Other Creatures,* 91–96. Linzey finds in Jesus's remarks here "an *inclusive* understanding of divine generosity, one that is in contrast to past and present humanocentrism" (*Animal Theology,* 35, emphasis original).

104 demonstrates—but instead the value of these birds for those in Jesus's audience. The low monetary value attached to these birds (two for a penny in Matthew, five for two pennies in Luke) indicates these small creatures have little usefulness for humans as commodities in a market context, but that is very different than saying birds, or by extension all animals, are of little worth in God's eyes. Jesus simply demonstrates the extent of God's concern and care by showing its manifestation among the most unlikely of recipients *in the audience's estimation*. If it happened that Jesus addressed this lesson to the poor man in Nathan's parable, who loved and cared for his ewe lamb "like a daughter" (2 Sam 12:3), the assertion "How much more valuable is a human being than a sheep!" (Matt 12:12) would likely fall flat and require another comparison.

In effect, Jesus allows a premise that is somewhat incomplete in order to present his major thesis. A similar thing occurs in the Psalms with another animal-human contrast. Here we read that "young lions suffer want and hunger, but those who seek the Lord lack no good thing" (34:10). Does God disregard the needs of lions? Obviously not because, as just noted, God listens to the lions' roar/prayer (Ps 104:21, 27–28). Hierarchy is no more the point for the poet of Psalm 34 than for Jesus. The writer of Psalm 34 teaches that those who are faithful to God want for nothing (34:9). These "holy ones" are apparently vulnerable because the poet writes of "fears," being "saved from every trouble," judgment on "evildoers," and cries "for help" (34:9, 4, 6, 16, 17). The psalmist and those he addresses are weak and subject to abuse by the wicked. The situation is therefore the reverse of the one in Jesus's lessons. The insight found in the Gospels is that God cares even for useless and valueless birds (from a human perspective), so take comfort. The insight of the psalm is that whereas even the mighty, fearless lion may lack basic needs, you who fear the Lord, you who are insignificant and vulnerable to the violence of the wicked, and much weaker than the mighty lions, even you "lack no good thing" (34:10).

As these few passages illustrate, we must tread carefully around bestial imagery serving as commentary on (usually negative) human behaviors. The same holds for those employing human-animal comparisons to inspire confidence in God's trustworthiness. These stylistic techniques potentially distract us from other animal-affirming themes in the Hebrew Bible and Christian Scriptures.[36]

---

36. On the importance of recognizing real animals in Christian storytelling, not just animals as symbols, see Hobgood-Oster, *Holy Dogs and Asses*, 15. Not doing so, she argues, is "escapist" and reinforces human claims to superiority and domination,

Animal Cruelty in the Bible

This recurring tendency to depict human corruption in relation to animals helps us understand occasional scenes of brutality toward nonhumans in biblical narratives. One bizarre example of this occurs in Judges with one of Samson's attacks on the feared Philistines: "Samson went and caught three hundred foxes,[37] and took some torches; and he turned the foxes tail to tail, and put a torch between each pair of tails. When he had set fire to the torches, he let the foxes go into the standing grain of the Philistines, and burned up the shocks and the standing grain, as well as the vineyards and olive groves" (Judg 15:4–5).

There is no way to redeem Samson's treatment of these animals, which is nothing short of callous and a flagrant disregard for other living things, particularly given the obvious fact that he did not lack the courage, skill, and strength to kill his human enemies in other ways. There must be care, however, not to assume the mere presence of such a story is an endorsement of the act or evidence of the storyteller's indifference to animals. Many assume so, but the situation is just the opposite.

I agree with Kowalski that the act described is "patently cruel" but disagree with his assumption that this is evidence that the author "gives no hint of sympathy for the poor creatures," and that the book "that lauds [Samson's] exploits has scant concern for the four-legged members of the earth community."[38] Instead, the first thing we must ask is whether Samson is indeed a hero in the book of Judges, as Kowalski and others assume, and so whether the writer actually lauds his exploits. This is far from obvious. The Lord indeed blesses and stirs Samson (13:24–25), and his birth is both momentous and miraculous, announced in advance by an angel (13:2–23) after Israel falls prey yet again to the Philistines (13:1). But this does not mean

---

and involves the "erasure" of animals from history (19; see too *Friends We Keep*, 5). For helpful overviews of this widespread biblical imagery, see Fleming, "Animals, Symbolism of" and Fleming, "Birds, Symbolism of."

37. Or perhaps jackals, as some prefer to translate *shual* (e.g., Boling, *Judges*, 234, 235 n. 4). In support of this, Soggin notes that foxes are not only rare in Palestine but also "solitary animals and would be virtually impossible to tie together" (246). Jackals, on the other hand, are plentiful and travel in packs. Regardless of the specific species in view, Soggin further observes that the scene is difficult to visualize: "it seems more to be the product of a good idea than to draw on an effective knowledge of the animal world" (246). In the end, it makes no difference to the point made here whether the story is real or imagined, or what species the storyteller has in mind.

38. Kowalski, *Bible according to Noah*, 4.

Eden's Other Residents

Samson is heroic and an ideal Israelite in any sense. God alone is the hero of the book of Judges, often using flawed leaders despite their ineptness and moral shortcomings. After all, Samson resists his parents' better judgment (14:3; cf. Prov 1:8–9); eats from an unclean carcass, something forbidden by Torah (14:8–9; cf. Lev 11:24, 30); engages a prostitute (Judg 16:1); and, by revealing the secret of his hair (16:17; cf. 13:5), allows himself to be defeated and subjugated by the wiles of a woman, something shameful in its patriarchal setting. Samson is deeply flawed, and we must read the story of his cruel treatment of three hundred foxes in light of this larger presentation of his character. This is the same literary strategy employed by Anne Brontë in *The Tenant of Wildfell Hall*, discussed in the opening chapter. The story of the foxes reinforces this presentation, showing Samson to be yet another of Israel's weak leaders, which is consistent with a central theme of the book of Judges as a whole: "another generation grew up after [Joshua's generation], who did not know the LORD or the work that he had done for Israel" (2:10). A high view of animals is part of Israel's worldview and only wicked fools treat them cruelly (cf. Prov 12:10).[39] Samson is one such fool.

Similarly disturbing are references to Joshua and David hamstringing horses (Josh 11:6, 9; 2 Sam 8:4). This is also extremely cruel, an act acknowledged as such in Gen 49:6–7 with respect to oxen. One commentator observes that in "the ancient world this was, apparently, an accepted military practice . . . These wars must be judged in their own cultural setting in spite of such practices as unnecessary cruelty to animals, inhumane treatment of prisoners of war, and what appears to be a form of colonialism or empire building."[40] Note, however, that despite Joshua and David's military prowess and their employment of this particular tactic, it is God who gives the victory over their enemies (Josh 11:8a; 2 Sam 8:14b). The authors of Joshua and 2 Samuel do not single out this violence against horses for censure, but neither do they allow such brutality to stand alone as the source of victory. God gives the victory *despite* this indifference to animals.

Rather than resorting to a reading strategy that rejects certain passages, or recommends forms of revision to produce what Kowalski calls an "environmentally friendly edition" of the holy books,[41] a better way forward

---

39. Though Prov 12:10 has domestic animals specifically in view, it still suits the situation described in Judges in that the foxes are animals under Samson's control in this scene. For illuminating discussion of Prov 12:10, which highlights the sympathy humans ought to have for fellow-creatures, see Bauckham, *Bible and Ecology*, 138–40.

40. Anderson, *2 Samuel*, 132, 134.

41. Kowalski, *Bible according to Noah*, 6; cf. 115–16.

for those wanting to further environmental and animal welfare causes is a robust engagement with all of Scripture. The reality is that the Jewish and Christian Scriptures *in toto* function as the foundational writings for communities of faith, and if we hope to motivate religiously inclined people to take creation care and animal ethics seriously, a more productive way forward involves confronting those texts, not turning away from them.

Regarding this last claim, an important caveat is necessary. It would be wonderful if an animal equivalent to *The Green Bible* were possible. I would be the first to buy it. The most distinctive feature of this curious 2008 publication is that it highlights in green font "the rich and varied ways the books of the Bible speak directly to how we should think and act as we confront the environmental crisis facing our planet."[42] As much as I appreciate *The Green Bible*, it does give the impression that bringing the biblical writings into dialogue with recent environmental concerns is an uncomplicated process, a simple matter of gathering up the requisite passages as if that alone is sufficient to remove the ambiguities regarding creation care.[43]

Unfortunately, bridging the hermeneutical gap between ancient writings and modern queries is never straightforward. As noted already, the place of animals in the experience of biblical writers is nothing like the situation in our day. They knew nothing, for instance, of the use of animal models in biomedical research or genetic manipulation of feed animals to maximize profits. What is needed is an approach to Bible reading and theological discourse that looks for spaces in the text, "prophetic suggestiveness" (Said), creativity, and visions of inclusiveness that allows us to extrapolate from ancient literature a basis to articulate a Christian compassion for animals. This does not mean recovery of an animal-friendly meaning is possible in every instance, or that there is a satisfying answer for every question that arises. Obscurities persist.[44]

42. Maudlin et al., *Green Bible*, 1–15.

43. No doubt many dismiss the premise of this edition of the Bible outright based on certain eschatological assumptions. If 2 Pet 3:10 and like passages indicate that an inevitable, catastrophic conflagration is the earth's ultimate and inescapable fate, then little motivation remains to care about such matters as pollution, human-caused climate change, habitat and species loss, or the just treatment of animals. The alternative is that such poetic and apocalyptic texts dramatically depict a cosmic transformation and renewal of the world, not its annihilation.

44. I have in mind here the provocative approach to ecological questions and biblical literature outlined in Horrell, *Bible and the Environment*, and Horrell et al., *Greening Paul*. I return to their work below. For Horrell's review of *The Green Bible*, see his "Timely Idea Deeply Flawed."

Consider just one example of the limited nature of *The Green Bible* with respect to the ambiguities of Scripture. Not surprisingly, Deut 25:4 appears in green font as an animal-affirming instruction (do not muzzle an ox while it is treading grain), but New Testament citations of that passage in 1 Cor 9:9–10 and 1 Tim 5:17–18 are not green. Apparently the editors assume these early Christian readings of Deuteronomy sever completely any connection to animal life. As I argue above, however, if we read 1 Corinthians creatively, searching out opportunities in Paul's language permitting inclusivity, his commentary on the oxen legislation is potentially among the most important statements about animals in the New Testament (i.e., it indicates animals are part of the broader community of the vulnerable to which the people of God owe care and protection). If correct, the passage ought to appear in green font.

Paradigm Shifts Are Never Easy: Nurturing Animal-Sensitive Bible Reading

Though I examine the biblical literature addressing human interaction with animals, I acknowledge that articulating a systematic, unambiguous statement of Christian responsibility toward them remains difficult. At the same time, the biblical writers speak often enough about other-than-human life that avoidance of the subject is not an option. My conclusions are modest, with emphasis on two primary themes.

First, since there is clear concern for animal wellbeing in Scripture, the church cannot simply appeal to the "dominion" language of Genesis as license to ignore the issue, or as permission to treat other sentient beings in any way we wish. As discussed in chapter 3, the sense of this dominion mandate is subject to debate with opinions ranging from gardening/caretaking/stewardship,[45] on the one hand, to unrestrained conquest and consumption, on the other. Worth noting when considering the meaning and scope of "dominion," however, is that the Bible includes references to the natural world as independent of human presence, something that puts the issue in some perspective. God brings rain to lands where no one lives,

---

45. Phelps is one of many assuming this is the sense of the Genesis passage: "We can love God concretely only by loving God's creation . . . The 'dominion' or 'stewardship,' [sic] that the Bible tells us God has given us over the other living beings in the world is simply an opportunity to love God concretely by protecting and nurturing God's creation" (*Dominion of Love*, 36, italics original).

places devoid of human life (Job 38:26). Here creation exists for God alone; it is neither for humanity nor in any way dependent on humanity. As we contemplate what "dominion" means, we do well to recognize its limits because much of the natural world thrives quite apart from Adam's presence. This alone ought to temper our hubris, be it an exaggerated estimation of our ability to care for the world or an unbridled exploitation on the assumption it is ours to do with as we see fit.

Second, I recommend an approach to the question of animal ethics that is theologically proleptic in nature.[46] Biblical glimpses into ideal or eschatological fullness and wholeness—Isaiah's peaceful kingdom, a return to Eden (with its plant-based diet), Paul's promise of redemption for the groaning creation, John's vision of New Jerusalem coming to earth and the renewal of the world (Rev 21:1—22:5), and so on—inspire a reappraisal of our attitudes toward other sentient life. Our choices and behaviors in the present embody kingdom ideals just as Jesus's table fellowship in the Gospels anticipates the eschatological banquet. Animal compassion represents one way in which the church can enact "thy will be done on earth as it is in heaven." By living peaceably in the present with all creation, we serve as witnesses to an eschatological hope, the kingdom of God coming in all its fullness.

Paradigm Shifts

The now hackneyed term *paradigm change* or *paradigm shift* indicates occasions when people give up certain assumptions about a subject and adopt others. The term originates in the sciences, in the work of Thomas Kuhn, whose 1961 book *The Structure of Scientific Revolutions* claims the history of science comprises two tendencies. On the one hand is the community of thinkers who share certain assumptions about the world and about their work within it, and on the other, those radical, revolutionary thinkers who question the received wisdom and propose new ways of viewing their subjects. Before 1600, to illustrate, it was common to

---

46. Consider, e.g., Bauckham, *Bible and Ecology*, 166–68, and "Reading the Synoptic Gospels," 78–79. The kingdom parables and several of Jesus's actions (healings, exorcisms, sharing meals with sinners, etc.) anticipate a transformed world. The term *prolepsis* indicates a kind of prophetic speech that treats as past something that is yet unfulfilled, as in Amos's lamentation of the fall of Israel, which at the time of writing had not yet occurred (5:1–3), and Jesus's lamentation of the fall of Jerusalem long before 70 CE (Soulen and Soulen, *Handbook of Biblical Criticism*, 142).

assume Earth was at the center of the solar system, with other celestial bodies revolving around it, but in 1616, Galileo promoted Copernicus's earlier theory that the sun, not Earth, is at the center of the solar system. The idea met with sharp resistance because astronomers holding this view developed complicated explanations for the movements of planets. To adopt the Copernican model involved dismantling time-honored theories, and what is more, the church "objected to the heliocentric paradigm because it seemed an insult both to humanity and to Christ that they be displaced from the centre of divine creation."[47]

Looking back through the history of biblical and theological interpretation, we find numerous examples of paradigm shifts.[48] Biblical studies looks quite different in the twenty-first century than it did in earlier generations. Attention to such matters as gender and sexuality, empire and colonialism, anti-Semitism, race, socioeconomic disparities, and environmental concern, to mention only a few, involves bringing new questions and concerns to old texts. Advancements in the sciences also invite a rethinking of biblical and theological assumptions. What we need, according to John F. Haught, is "theological reflection broad enough to assimilate all that is new in scientific research without abandoning the substance of Christian teaching." Needless to say, not all quarters of Christendom are quick to embrace this idea, but Haught adds that if religion is to remain "alive and honest," there must be a combination of "deep respect for traditional creeds and biblical texts" but also a willingness to reinterpret tradition in light of ongoing scientific research.[49] Haught reminds us that Christian biblical and theological studies must not be impervious to change. New historical contexts, new information, new social and cultural realities, new methodologies, and new ethical questions all demand periodic reassessment of

---

47. Bonnycastle, *In Search of Authority*, 72. Umberto Eco offers a fascinating exploration of early theories about "the sky and the earth" and the resulting maps produced to explain them. Here we find a colorful illustration of paradigm shifts and how profoundly our current ways of looking at the world differ from those in earlier times. "Spare a thought, then, for those who fought at the frontiers of infinity and the future," he concludes. "Remember the greatness of those imaginary geographies and astronomies, and those errors that often bore fruit" (*Inventing the Enemy*, 161; full discussion, 134–61).

48. For discussion of the use of this term in biblical studies, see, e.g., Shedinger, "Kuhnian Paradigms"; and Crossan, *Greatest Prayer*, 84–85.

49. Haught, *Making Sense of Evolution*, xvii. Regarding the relationship of science to religion, see various insights in de Waal's *Bonobo and the Atheist* (from the perspective of a scientist) and Sacks's *Great Partnership* (from the perspective of a rabbi).

theological positions.⁵⁰ If Jeremiah or John are to mean anything in our day, that exercise of "translation" from past to present, from one culture to another, must be constant.

With respect to human impact on the animal world, the differences between now and then—between life in wealthy, modern, urban, Western societies and life in land-dependent, nomadic, iron age Israelite or first-century Roman ones—are as enormous as the differences between, say, communications or transportation. Think papyrus versus an iMac, or a journey from Syrian Antioch to Rome on foot or by ship compared to air travel across the northern Mediterranean. To compare one with the other is on some levels meaningless. Melting polar caps, depleted fish stocks, and a thousand other pressing concerns are obviously not ones faced by writers removed from us by two millennia and more, but that is not to say they have nothing to teach us as we grapple with them.

Some Conclusions about Reading Animals in the Christian Bible: Cat-and-Mouse Hermeneutics

In the main, writers of the Jewish and Christian Scriptures reflect a positive view of the natural world that originates in the creative acts of a loving God. This theological premise lies behind all they write, even if not always stated explicitly, and even though the great majority of their stories, poems, apocalypses, and letters principally concern human activities within that context. Nahum Sarna describes the creation narratives of Genesis as a prologue to the historical dramas unfolding in the rest of the Bible, asserting unequivocally that "the basic truth of all history is that the world is under the undivided and inescapable sovereignty of God."⁵¹ Similarly, N. T. Wright argues, "Underneath the basic Jewish praxis there lies the belief that Israel is the people of the creator god. If this were not so, the *halakah* would lose its point, or at least radically change its character. If one said to an articulate first-century Jew 'Why do you keep Torah?', the ultimate answer would be 'Because I am part of Israel, the chosen people of the creating and redeeming god' . . . The fact of the creating and redeeming god is the greater whole, which gives meaning

---

50. For a dramatic example of a paradigm shift in academic work in religion, see the various essays in *Jesus, Judaism, and Christian Anti-Judaism* (edited by Fredriksen and Reinhartz) that examine transformations in New Testament studies in the post-Holocaust era.

51. Sarna, *Understanding Genesis*, 9.

and purpose to the individual expression."[52] In light of this, there is reason to be suspicious of characters in the Bible who appear to act with indifference to the rest of creation or as if it does not have inherent value. Samson, as noted, is not an ideal Israelite.[53]

The expression "cat and mouse" indicates a playful (from the hunter's perspective) chase involving repeated capture and release. I introduce it here because I tend to land on one reading strategy before giving it up to pursue another, an approach that suits our topic because the ancient writers simply do not speak in any systematic fashion to the kinds of ethical concerns that motivate today's readers. We are on the hunt for those always-elusive moments of "prophetic suggestiveness" (Said) providing opportunities for theological reflection on the religious significance of animals. Such an approach invites criticism, to be sure, not least that it involves little more than a form of textual play, a cat-and-mouse dance of selective reading and overreaching claims motivated by an external and thoroughly modern concern. This is true. But when is this not the case for interpreters of the Bible? When does the Bible ever speak without complication to present-day readers regarding their present-day interests? There is no such thing as an uncomplicated and unembellished retranslation and reapplication of old books in new settings.

The ancient Pharisees understood this quite well, recognizing that if Moses possessed any authority or value, teachers of Torah must rethink the meaning of that ancient wisdom for their own times. As Josephus puts it, the Pharisees "have delivered to the people a great many observances by succession from their fathers, which are not written in the law of Moses" (*Ant.* 13.10.6). Their preservation and dissemination of religious ideals relied on the combination of ancient wisdom (Moses) and accompanying traditions of reading ("their fathers," codified later in the Mishnah).[54] They realized that a translation of old ideas and texts into new contexts was necessary if those writings were to remain meaningful and authoritative.

As for selectivity and a strategic placement of emphasis in my approach, there is some justification in the fact that biblical authors do the same thing. The Bible is anthropocentric, meaning writers are often more

---

52. Wright, *New Testament and the People of God*, 246.

53. Cf. Heb 11:32, which perhaps refers specifically to Samson's faith in his final prayer (Judg 16:28) without implying anything about his character as a whole.

54. For a brief overview of the Pharisees' history and beliefs, see, e.g., Ferguson, *Backgrounds of Early Christianity*, 480–85.

concerned with humans and God's relationships with them than the rest of creation.⁵⁵ We see this in Peter's brief reference to the Genesis flood narrative. As he tells the story, only "a few, that is, eight persons, were saved" thanks to Noah's ark (1 Pet 3:20). But this is clearly a selective summary of the story because of course there were representatives of "all flesh" on board, of birds and land-based creatures (Gen 6:19, 20). For Peter, the floodwaters are representative of Christian baptism. The waters saved Noah and his family by allowing the ark to float; the waters of baptism are similarly salvific. This passage illustrates how easily writers turn away from the wider implications of the events they describe and the stories they tell. The animals accompanying human passengers on the ark, not to mention those perishing in the floodwaters, vanish from the record completely along with any lessons attached to that part of the story; the ark no longer concerns all life on earth but rather a few select humans (those on the boat and the baptized Christians Peter addresses). The unintended consequence is a muting of important themes found in the precursor text, namely that God makes provisions to rescue representative members of "all flesh."⁵⁶ A similar erasure of the animals on Noah's ark occurs in 2 Pet 2:5 where again we find the omission of animal life in a brief account of the story.

Our interest in animal-aware Bible reading and hermeneutical strategies faces many obstacles. How should we proceed? Positioned between recovery and resistance⁵⁷ as hermeneutical approaches, Horrell, Hunt, and Southgate employ terms like *revision*, *reformation*, and *reconfiguration*. In

---

55. For discussion of the term as it relates to ecologically concerned readings of the Bible, see Habel, *Birth*, 8–10.

56. Added to this are two negative bestial similes in Peter's first letter (the proneness of sheep to get lost in 2:25 and the violence of lions in 5:8) that further diminish any sense of animal worth, however subtly. He also compares Christ to a lamb without defect or blemish in another simile (1:19). If Peter directs the letter to Jews (a disputed view), this possibly involves a subtle denigration of animal sacrifice because in the preceding verses he refers to the readers as "ransomed from the futile ways inherited from your ancestors" (1:18).

57. In his study of the Bible and the environment, Horrell refers to readings of "recovery" as apologetic approaches seeking "the recovery or retrieval of the Bible's ecological wisdom, a wisdom that has been hidden and obscured by interpreters who failed to see or attend to such dimensions of the text." By readings of "resistance" he indicates those by "ecological thinkers [who] have suggested that the Christian tradition cannot provide the kind of valuing of the earth that our contemporary context demands, and so [it] must be rejected" (*Bible and the Environment*, 11, 13). In their study of Paul and the environment, Horrell, Hunt, and Southgate describe their work on Paul's writings as navigating a space somewhere between "recovery" and "resistance" (Horrell et al., *Greening Paul*, 14–15, 21, 216–17, etc.).

part they build on H. Paul Santmire's remarks in *Nature Reborn: The Ecological and Cosmic Promise of Christian Theology* about the Christian tradition constantly "*re-forming*" itself,[58] and Ernst M. Conradie's idea about the use of heuristic or doctrinal "keys" to help read the Christian tradition in light of contemporary environmentalism.[59] Such a key or guiding concern shapes the way interpreters read the whole Bible, just as justification by faith shaped exegesis for Martin Luther, or various liberation agendas do for others. The image of an interpretive "key" connotes the device that "unlocks" a text, on the one hand, but also the idea "of a musical key which sets the 'tenor' in which the text is to be re-performed by the interpreter." While sympathetic to this idea, Horrell, Hunt, and Southgate prefer the image of "a hermeneutical *lens*":

> A lens—which is, of course, itself something *made*, constructed—shapes and configures what we see, bringing aspects of the object being examined into particular focus (though it may blur or otherwise distort others). And a lens can be two-way: just as a pair of glasses changes how the wearer sees those in front of her, so too the glasses change the way the wearer's eyes appear to others. A doctrinal or hermeneutical lens, then, not only shapes our view of the biblical text, but also determines how we and our context are viewed, and which aspects of our own context the biblical text relates to.[60]

By reading texts with such a hermeneutical lens in place, readers bring ancient writings into conversation with contemporary concerns, emphasizing some motifs, ideas, or themes over others.[61] Debates about what hermeneutical lenses best suit particular issues are inevitable. In the case of theological ecology, ideas like stewardship and liberation may apply. When discussing animal compassion, other concepts are available. Andrew Linzey acknowledges that the picture of animal-human relations in the Bible, complete with slaughter, sacrifice, designations of unclean, and even genocide, is one of disharmony not harmony, violence rather than peace, and yet he regularly calls attention to the biblical call to compassion and protection of the vulnerable as a guiding principle.[62] Others emphasize hospitality.

---

58. Cited in Horrell et al., *Greening Paul*, 39, italics original.
59. Conradie, "The Road," 306, cited in Horrell et al., *Greening Paul*, 40.
60. Horrell et al., *Greening Paul*, 41, 42.
61. Ibid., 47.
62. E.g., Linzey's editorial introduction to *Animals on the Agenda*, 6, and Linzey, *Creatures of the Same God*, 98–99.

Laura Hobgood-Oster, for one, notes examples of hospitality to animals in the Bible (e.g., Rebekah's care of Abraham's camels [Gen 24:19–22]) and Christian tradition.[63] She builds on Jesus's radical views of hospitality, as illustrated in his instructions to "invite the poor, the crippled, the lame, and the blind" to a banquet, not just the rich who are in a position to return the favor (Luke 14:12–14). She also cites John Dominic Crossan, who observes that the "open commensality and radical egalitarianism of Jesus' Kingdom of God are more terrifying than anything we have ever imagined,"[64] and then she asks whether this radical vision applies to human beings alone. "While that might have been the gist of the meaning in some of the parables and actions of Jesus as recounted in the early texts," she writes, "there are also passages that point to an all-encompassing reach." Examples listed in the immediate context include Matt 6:26 ("Look at the birds of the air; they neither sow nor reap nor gather into barns, and yet your heavenly Father feeds them") and Mark 7:28 ("even the dogs under the table eat the children's crumbs" [spoken by the Syrophoenician woman]). These and other passages lead her to conclude "there is ample evidence of an underlying assumption: that God opens the table to all creatures."[65]

I see no need to choose one key or lens over the other. Hospitality, protection of the vulnerable, stewardship, generosity, and self-sacrifice are all prized qualities we must aspire to, and each finds support in biblical teaching.

---

63. Hobgood-Oster, *Friends We Keep*, 116–22; Hobgood-Oster, "Christian Hospitality," esp. 77–79; Hobgood-Oster, *Holy Dogs and Asses*.

64. Crossan, *Jesus*, 73.

65. Hobgood-Oster, *Friends We Keep*, 121.

3   Recognizing the Grace of God in Animal Creation

Most High Omnipotent Good Lord, yours are the praises, the glory, the honor, and all blessing. To you alone, Most High, do they belong, and no one is worthy to mention your name. Praise be to you, my Lord, with all your creatures . . . Praise be to you, my Lord, through our Sister Mother Earth, who sustains and rules us, and produces different fruits with colored flowers and herbs.

—FRANCIS OF ASSISI (CA. 1181–1226),
"THE CANTICLE OF BROTHER SUN"[1]

FORMS OF ESCAPIST THINKING are commonplace in popular theology, often involving some version of a world-ending apocalypse preceded by the eleventh-hour escape of an elect few. This kind of thinking presents a significant obstacle for a robust animal theology because in such scenarios animals are invariably "left behind." There are even businesses catering to

---

1. Taken from McGinn, ed., *Essential Writings*, 291. For an introduction to St. Francis and his importance within Christian tradition as one modeling concern for the wellbeing of animals, see e.g., Vauchez, *Francis of Assisi*, 271–82; Bauckham, *Living with Other Creatures*, 198–212; and Warner, "Retrieving Saint Francis." Cf. Regan who finds prohibitions against animal cruelty philosophically insufficient because they fail "to address or explain . . . the obligation to *promote the good* of other animals. Perhaps no one better exemplifies what a commitment to this ideal means than St. Francis of Assisi. Merely not to hurt animals, or to stop others from doing so, is not enough for him. There is another, higher obligation—namely, to be of service to them by promoting their good, something not captured by the prohibition against cruelty" (*Defending Animal Rights*, 32–33, italics original).

those concerned about their pets in a post-Rapture world, which presupposes on the part of customers that their beloved cats and dogs have no place in heavenly bliss.[2] (The website aftertherapturepetcare.com includes a video introduction explaining this bizarre business concept. The company assures customers that their volunteers are "atheist[s] or [adherents of] another non-Christian religion" so they, like the animals, will be left behind and therefore in a position to fulfill their obligations.[3])

However, a biblical understanding of the appearing or coming of Jesus does not indicate a dualist rejection of our world but instead its transformation. Allowing this, the purpose of salvation plausibly includes stewardship of God's good world in the meantime as an activity in keeping with creation's ultimate destiny.[4] Kingdom building in the present reasonably includes care, nurture, comfort, and support for the environment and its nonhuman creatures, activities that "will find [their] way, through the resurrecting power of God, into the new creation that God will one day make." Just as in the biblical story God does not rescue Israel *from* Gentiles, but rescues them *for* Gentiles, by bringing his mercy through Israel, so too God does not rescue humans *from* creation but *for* creation. "What we do in the Lord is 'not in vain,'" Wright continues, "and that is the mandate we need for every act of justice and mercy, every program of ecology, every effort to reflect God's wise stewardly image into his creation."[5] Animals are a positive part of the biblical story and far from expendable. They are integral to

---

2. On escapist theological thinking, see Haught, *Evolution*, 146–48 (which he contrasts with the writings of Pierre Teilhard de Chardin): "Too often we have thought that Christ's salvific role is that of liberating our souls *from* the universe rather than making us part of the great work of renewing and extending God's creation" (147, emphasis original). See too Muddiman, "New Testament Doctrine"; Maier, "Green Millennialism"; and Lamp's provocative reading of Heb 11:16 in *Greening of Hebrews*, chapter 6.

3. See http://www.aftertherapturepetcare.com/.

4. Wright, *Surprised by Hope*, 142–43, 199–200. For his view that neither Jesus nor his Jewish contemporaries expected the end of the space-time universe, see *Jesus and the Victory of God*, 207–9, and *New Testament People of God*, chapter 10. Even though understanding "dominion" as stewardship is not without its problems (see e.g., Barker, *Creation*, 199–200, 215; Horrell, *Bible and the Environment* 4, 6), this oft-abused dominion concept is not necessarily as negative as many suppose. *Radah* describes Solomon's rule, for instance, and it was not marked by constant violence: "he had dominion [*radah*] over all the region . . . and he had peace" (1 Kgs 4:24).

5. Wright, *Surprised by Hope*, 208, 210. Commenting on Jas 1:18 and the renewal and completion of creation, Painter writes, "Perhaps it is even implied that the renewed humanity has a role to play in God's purpose of bringing in the transformed creation" (*James and Jude*, 76; cf. 84, 99).

the record of God's dealings with the world. This chapter explores a few key themes and passages supporting this assertion.

Looking through Animals to Hidden Realities

As described in Exodus, Israel's tabernacle includes among its materials goats' hair and rams' skins (26:7, 14; 35:6–7, 23). Animals provide the stuff out of which Moses makes this most sacred symbol of God's presence among the wandering people. In this triad, *God* resides within this tent of *animal* bodies to which the *people* come for worship, direction, sacrifice, and prayer. This idea of the material remains of animals contributing to religious life and expression has counterparts in other times and places.

Listed among the treasures in the Vatican's library in Rome since at least 1475 is one of the most famous of all biblical manuscripts. Codex Vaticanus, usually identified by the symbol B in text-critical apparatuses, is a fourth-century copy of both Testaments and the Apocrypha, with a few significant lacunae.[6] Vaticanus is one of the oldest parchment manuscripts of the whole Christian Bible, which is to say a writing surface of animal skins rather than plant-based papyrus. The use of vellum or parchment—"the skins of cattle, sheep, goats, and antelopes, and especially from the young of these animals"[7]— for writing is an ancient practice. Animals are literally part of many Bibles and sacred texts, from those produced by the Qumran community along the shores of the Dead Sea[8] to the ornate biblical manuscripts and ecclesiological productions of monastics during the Middle Ages. Even in our day this technology remains in use, as is the case with the magnificent *Saint John's Bible*: "The pages of *The Saint John's Bible* are made of calfskin vellum. The skins are soaked in lime, dried, scraped or 'scrutched,' and sanded smooth. The final product is nearly translucent, with a 'hair side' and 'smooth side.'" In addition to the pages we might also note other uses of animal byproducts

---

6. Metzger, *Text of the New Testament*, 47–48.

7. Ibid., 4.

8. In addition to the use of skins for writing surfaces (vellum), archaeologists found leather *tefillin* (Hebrew for prayers) or phylacteries at Qumran. These are small boxes containing biblical texts (often excerpts from Exod 12:43—13:16; Deut 5:1—6:9; 10:12—11:21; and verses from Deuteronomy 32). These boxes are attached to leather straps and tied to the head or left arm. Similarly, *mezuzot* are boxes with biblical passages attached to doorposts. For the reasoning behind both, see Deut 6:8–9. Regarding these discoveries at Qumran, see VanderKam, *Dead Sea Scrolls*, 33; and Hurtado, *Origins*, 35–36. For pictures and descriptions, see, e.g., Davies et al., *Dead Sea Scrolls*, 22, 50, and 51.

Recognizing the Grace of God in Animal Creation

associated with the production of Holy Scripture, like bird feathers used for quills. Here again *The Saint John's Bible* offers a contemporary example of this animal-based technology: "All the script is written using quills hand-cut by the scribes. Only the largest flight feathers, called 'primaries,' are used: goose quills for the main body of text, turkey and swan quills for heavier letterforms." Even the paints involve animal products: "Vermillion, lapis lazuli, and other cakes and powdered pigments are used for color. The materials are mixed with egg yolk and water to make paint that is thicker than the black ink and loaded onto the quills using brushes [made from animal hair]."[9] Consider also modern publishers that constantly announce the use of "genuine leather" to help sell Bibles.

These animal-based technologies illustrate in colorful fashion a principal theme explored in this chapter. Though most view these productions as nothing more than an instrumental use of animals, these creatures' bodies simply harvested as raw materials necessary to make books, pens, and a tent, I prefer to find here a symbol of the human, animal, divine triad. Animals are in these cases literally the word of God, literally the delivery systems through which God speaks to people of faith. In this role, animals are the nexus where the divine and the mundane meet. This occurs often in biblical literature, as illustrated below, but consider first a very different illustration of this idea that animals potentially point beyond themselves to something profound.

Just as some glimpse an undefined or under-defined transcendence in music or literature,[10] for others a quasi-mystical experience opening onto other realities stems from their encounters with animals. We see this in Jean-Christophe Bailly's remarkable *Le versant animal*, a delightful book that defies simple categorization. Bailly is simultaneously philosophical and poetic, blending personal encounters with the natural world with speculations on the mysteries inherent in the concurrent and sometimes overlapping existence of humanity and other-than-human beings. He begins with a fleeting, chance sighting of a deer that occurred while driving. The result is an almost mystical sense of communion between the observer and the

---

9. I take all three excerpts from the official website for *The Saint John's Bible* (http://www.saintjohnsbible.org/promotions/process/production_tools.htm). For an introduction to the project and explanation of the production techniques used, see the video content at this link, and also the fascinating 2005 documentary *The Illuminator and a Bible for the Twenty-First Century*.

10. I examine such noninstitutional, nonstructured spirituality throughout *Gods and Guitars*. See, e.g., 1–5, 45–48.

observed as they (literally) journey the same road for an "instant." Though not examining animals from a religious perspective, Bailly's reflections suit our purposes here quite nicely:

> I had touched some part of the animal world. Touched, yes, touched with my eyes, despite the impossibility. In no way had I entered that world; on the contrary, it was rather as if its strangeness had declared itself anew, as if I had actually been allowed for an instant to see something from which as a human being I shall be forever excluded, either the nameless, purposeless space in which animals freely make their way, or the other way of being in the world that so many thinkers through the ages have turned into a background against which to highlight the supremacy of humankind—whereas it has always seemed to me that this strangeness ought to be considered on its own terms, as a different posture, a different impetus, and quite simply a different modality of being.[11]

What appeals to me in this wonderful passage is the acknowledgment that animals are not mere "background" for the human story but rather imbedded in their own strange world, one people cannot ever fully inhabit or know. For Bailly, a chance meeting with a deer proves to be revelatory, "a proof that there is no supremacy, neither of humans nor of beasts, that there are only passages, fleeting sovereignties, occasions, escapes, encounters."[12] The bodies of animals make the construction of the tabernacle and Bible possible, thus allowing people to "go through them" to find God. Bailly's deer permits the poet-philosopher a glimpse into a different modality of being and another world beyond human comprehension. Both examples involve forms of revelation made possible by animals.

To translate Bailly's idea into theological terms, what if the Creator's purposes for animals are largely unrelated to humans? Bailly refers to his exclusion from the "strangeness" of the animal world, acknowledging its independence from human experience. There are momentary sovereignties—in both directions, as when human-animal encounters prove violent and one dominates the other—but one never completely inhabits the space of the other. Perhaps we do well to think of humans and those seemingly endless nonhuman species as existing in parallel, all complete in themselves ("no supremacy") and serving the Creator's purposes alone. To be

11. Bailly, *Animal Side*, 2.
12. Ibid.

sure, the borders of these parallel worlds are porous, frequently bringing their inhabitants into contact with one another, for better or worse, but this does not infringe on any individual being's standing in the eyes of God, any more than do race, gender, or social position within the community of people (cf. Gal 3:28). The usefulness of an animal to human wellbeing is not the measure of that creature's ultimate value, theologically speaking.

Exploring the Creation Stories

Can you imagine a stretch of grassy land bubbling like water in a pot? For that is really the best description of what was happening. In all directions it was swelling into humps . . . And the humps moved and swelled till they burst, and the crumbled earth poured out of them, and from each hump there came out an animal . . . And now you could hardly hear the song of the Lion: there was so much cawing, cooing, crowing, braying, neighing, baying, barking, lowing, bleating, and trumpeting.

—C. S. LEWIS, *THE MAGICIAN'S NEPHEW* (1955)[13]

The Bible includes many depictions of animals as valuable quite apart from any benefits humans derive from them. God delights in them for what they are. At the same time, the Bible includes various stories in which God chooses to bless humans through their encounters with animals. They are messengers, functioning like angels that carry the words and blessings of God to the children of Adam and Eve. We turn now to examples of both, beginning with visions of human-animal harmony that illustrate a partnership between the species as opposed to a relationship characterized by exploitation, despotism, and consumption.

---

13. Lewis, *Magician's Nephew*, 122, 123. There are various hints in this children's book of Lewis's views about human responsibility to animals. For instance, the narrator censures the villain Uncle Andrew for his cruel experimentations on animals (25–26, 139), and Aslan is clear he expects the newly appointed Kings and Queens of Narnia to treat the creatures of Narnia "kindly and fairly" (151; though possibly this indicates magical, talking animals as opposed to regular "dumb beasts," a distinction occasionally made in The Chronicles of Narnia). Animals figure prominently in Lewis's writing more broadly. For analysis focusing on his fiction, see Blount, "Fallen and Redeemed." For religious perspectives, see Linzey, "C. S. Lewis's Theology of Animals"; and Williams, *Lion's World*, 20–29.

Eden's Other Residents

Psalm 104

Obviously animals exist independently of humans. That their reason for being is not determined in any way by their usefulness to *Homo sapiens* is obvious from a scientific point of view because the latter arrived rather late in evolutionary terms.[14] This idea is also present in the theological-poetic language of the Bible. The soaring verse of Psalm 104 is a meditation on the wonders of the natural world that takes readers back to the creation stories of Genesis. The psalm begins and ends with adoration of the Creator (Ps 104:1, 35) and includes several statements revealing the divine hand behind all that exists. Certain features of this lovely passage deserve notice.

For one thing, as in Genesis 1 (vv. 24–25 cf. 26), animals appear first (Ps 104:11–12, 14a; cf. Gen 2:15–19 where the reverse is the case). This means that within the poetic-theological cosmology of Genesis 1 and Psalm 104 animals exist, however briefly, within the confines of the text, apart from humans (cf. Job 38:26). Furthermore, there is no hint in the poem of a utilitarian value in animals. They are not present to meet human needs (other than offering the poet a compelling subject). Animals are part of the worshiping and worship-inspiring world the poet sees, and they have no obvious instrumental function.[15] They exist only for God's purposes, perhaps even as God's playthings: "Yonder is the sea . . . and Leviathan that you formed to sport in it" (vv. 25, 26). The psalm highlights the shared "creatureliness" of humans and other species. All alike are dependent on God for sustenance (v. 27). Lions seek "their food from God" (v. 21), who also causes "grass to grow for the cattle, and plants for people to use" (v. 14; Gen 1:29–30).

When reading Genesis 1, Psalm 104, Psalm 148, and other visions of creation at peace and praising the Creator, we need to remember these scenes are eschatological and utopian; the writers anticipate all things achieving

---

14. I presuppose but do not discuss evolution. Despite many claims to the contrary, I do not find any threat in Darwinian evolution for Christian theology or biblical faith. As Haught puts it, "different levels of explanation are simultaneously operative without ruling one another out" (*Making Sense of Evolution*, 24). For helpful theological reflections on evolution, focused particularly on the issue of theodicy and animal suffering, see Southgate, *Groaning of Creation*. Essential reading for those exploring the relationship between science and religion is Rabbi Jonathan Sacks's *The Great Partnership*.

15. Regarding Psalm 104, Allen writes, "The psalmist is not indifferent to areas of the created world beyond man's immediate concern nor has he a selfish view of nature as being merely man's to exploit (cf. Job 38, 39). From his widened perspective he can lose a purely human fear of ferocious beasts and hear the lion's roar as a prayer (cf. Job 38:41; Joel 1:20)" (*Psalms*, 33).

their full, God-intended potential.[16] Allowing a scientific understanding of origins, there never was a time when life on earth was actually at peace with itself. "Nature, red in tooth and claw," as the oft-cited Tennysonism puts it, characterizes the evolutionary story. What Genesis and other passages offer are, on the one hand, glimpses into the world's potential from the perspective of faith (not science) and, on the other hand, prophetic critique, a means of articulating ways the world *as it is now* (from these writers' perspective) is deficient. Genesis and the Psalms are theology, myth, and poetry, but are no less true for that. It is another kind of truth compared to the ever-expanding knowledge derived from the sciences. To place the biblical writers in opposition to the work of biologists and physicists, as though one potentially rules out the other, involves absurd assumptions.

Finally, brief references in Psalm 104 to humanity's fallen state ("labor" in v. 23 recalls Gen 3:17–19; also the "sinners" and "the wicked" of v. 35) identify a notable distinction between the descendants of Adam and Eve and other species. Whereas animals are among the awe-inspiring works of creation pointing the psalmist to God ("O LORD, how manifold are your works!" [v. 24] etc.), people alone face the judgment called for at the end of the poem ("Let sinners be consumed" [v. 35]). The poet himself claims God's grace only cautiously ("May my meditation be pleasing to him" [v. 34]).

Genesis and Psalm 104 remind us of the world's inherent goodness but also that corruption and evil mar this beautiful vision. The two subjects—creation and malevolence—are inextricably linked. The world as we experience it is morally ambiguous, and biblical literature situates us in this ambivalent space and time and urges the faithful to struggle against want, cruelty, and violence through acts of generosity, kindness, and peacemaking. Too often, however, certain readings of the Bible serve to justify selfishness.

Subdue and Have Dominion

We crossed the rivulet, then rising a sloping, green, turfy ascent, alighted on the borders of a grand forest of stately trees, which we penetrated on foot a little distance to a horse-stamp, where was a large squadron of those useful creatures . . . It was a fine sight; more beautiful creatures I never saw . . . [a] useful part of the creation, who, if they are under our dominion, have consequently a right to our protection and favour.

—WILLIAM BARTRAM, *TRAVELS* (1791)[17]

16. Bauckham, *Bible and Ecology*, 82.
17. Bartram, *Travels*, 224.

Eden's Other Residents

In many respects the natural world remains completely beyond "Adam's" rule. When lecturing Job, God makes this very clear in a long list of creatures who fill land, sky, and sea and remain entirely beyond human control and comprehension: "Is the wild ox willing to serve you?" (Job 39:9). Implied answer? Absolutely not. Other passages in the Bible refer to forms of human authority. The terms usually translated "subdue" (*kabash*) and "have dominion" (*radah*) in Gen 1:26–28 are enormously consequential when considering humanity's relationship to the rest of the created order, particularly because they seem to indicate a response to nature characterized by harsh conquest, as if the world exists only to satisfy human needs and desires. Offhand appeal to this passage often serves to justify activities that harm animals and their habitats, to the point that some find the root cause of environmental devastations in the Christian Bible, owing to its foundational role in framing the narrative and worldview of Western societies. As they see it, Gen 1:26–28 (cf. Ps 8:6–8) endorses the destructive exploitation of the natural world—the case famously put forward by Lynn White Jr. in the 1967 article "The Historical Roots of our Ecological Crisis"—and presents a highly problematic obstacle for those combating an unsustainable treatment of the planet and its resources. If in fact God says, "Go ahead, do what you want with the world and all that is in it, it's yours to do with as you will," as some readers take these verses to mean, it is difficult to convince them that such crises as climate change, the collapse of ecosystems, and species loss are cause for alarm.

Others argue that the kingly rule of Gen 1:26–28 and the terms *kabash*/subdue and *radah*/have dominion are not as harsh as they appear, with the semantic range permitting notions of possession and shepherding,[18] though this approach is not without its critics.[19] At the very least, the

---

18. For examples, see Adams, "Dominion in Genesis?" 6–10. The term *kabash* plausibly indicates taking possession of the land (e.g., Num 32:22, 29; Josh 18:1; 1 Chr 22:18), which certainly carries harsh overtones of conquest over enemies but, as Bauckham points out, "the land itself has only to be possessed. It is not itself an enemy to be forcibly subjugated" (*Bible and Ecology*, 16–17). He suggests that "subdue" likely indicates agricultural activity and so carries a similar sense as Gen 2:15 (21–22).

19. On "stewardship" readings of Genesis, including objections, see Bauckham, *Bible and Ecology*, 1–36. For Barker, the concept is problematic because it introduces a business model. She prefers to view Adam as the high priest of the world, a role characterized by sacrificial self-giving that promotes the healing of creation (*Creation*, 199–200). Cf. Moritz who finds the evidence regarding the *imago Dei* in biblical, intertestamental Jewish, and early Christian literature to point to humans as priest-kings of creation, called to be God's mediators to the animal world ("Animals and the Image of God," 144).

immediate canonical context where this language appears softens the force of the subdue/have dominion mandate because whatever the terms mean, (*a*) they appear within the perfect pre-fall conditions of Genesis 1, and (*b*) not only presuppose a vegetarian diet (1:29; 3:18) but also (*c*) companionship with animals (2:18–20) and (*d*) tilling the land (2:15), the last activity meeting an expressed need ("there was no one to till the ground" [2:5]).[20] Unrestrained consumption and reckless disregard for God's good world, animate and inanimate, is obviously not in view.

At the same time, we must not overlook the heavy-handedness the Hebrew terms translated as "subdue" and "dominion" include.[21] A constructive way forward in reading Gen 1:26–28 involves consideration of the wider setting of the passage, which is to say not just the making of the world and the garden scenes of Genesis 1–3 but the larger story of creation through to re-creation in the flood (Genesis 1–9). This larger section stands as a unit framed by stories of order emerging out of watery chaos. Consideration of diet also begins and ends the unit (1:29–30; 9:3–4), as do repetitions of various key phrases and concepts, including "be fruitful and multiply" (1:28; 8:17; 9:1), "wind" (1:2; 8:1), and a distinction between domestic and wild animals (1:24–25; 8:1). There is also a sense of narrative progression away from the ideal toward the less-than-ideal. For instance, there is no meat eating in the garden before Adam and Eve's disobedience (1:29) or after (3:18). Even as Noah prepares for the flood, God distinguishes animals from food, instructing Noah to bring "every kind of food that is eaten . . . and it shall serve as food for you and for them" (Gen 6:21; i.e., animals themselves are not food and they too eat plants). But things change once the waters recede. The harmony and nonviolence of first creation no longer exist. Instead, the "fear and dread" of humans "shall rest on every animal of the earth, and on every bird of the air, on everything that creeps on the ground, and on all the fish of the sea." What is more, they are "delivered" to humans and "shall be food" for them (9:2–3).

It is essential we read Genesis 1 in light of Genesis 9, and vice versa. The shift from the harmonious garden where Adam and Eve live in peace with Eden's other residents, subsisting on a vegetarian diet (9:3 cf. 1:29), contrasts sharply with the postdiluvian reality in which humans and

---

20. "The explicit reason for making Adam is . . . clarified in Genesis 2:15, where it becomes apparent that Adam was formed in order to 'serve' and 'keep' *adamah* [the ground, land]. In other words, the first Earth being is created for the benefit of Earth, not vice versa" (Habel, *Rainbow of Mysteries*, 55).

21. E.g., Rogerson, "Creation Stories," 25; Habel, *Birth*, 40.

animals eat meat (cf. 9:5) and live in fear of one another (cf. 9:2). Some suggest the permission to eat meat was a temporary dispensation based on a few textual clues. Since the flood destroys the vegetation previously used for food, the permission, if temporary, preserves survivors during an interim time of regrowth. Furthermore, unlike the promise never again to flood the earth (9:8–17), there is nothing in the remarks about diet in 9:2–3, suggesting this too is a permanent license to eat meat as opposed to a short-term provision for Noah and his kin.[22]

While intriguing, this approach does not recognize that the writers and redactors of Genesis 1–9 as a whole are engaged in a prophetic critique of the human condition *in their own historical moment.* Their world is one of disharmony and brutality. There is no explicit indication that Gen 9:2–3 is a temporary permission to eat meat, and the story seems to indicate an entirely new order of existence for human and nonhuman animals, even if one marred by moral collapse. Genesis 1–9 presents us with a trajectory of regression away from the celebratory "very good" of first creation (Gen 1:31) to God's regret at making the world at all (Gen 6:6). Like the later prophets, Genesis presents the garden harmony between humans and animals as an ideal though not necessarily an existing reality (cf., e.g., Hos 2:18).

There are a few important observations that follow a consideration of Genesis 1 in light of the larger context of Genesis 1–9. First, the story moves quickly from the wonders of creation, to human degeneration and expulsion from the garden, to the grim pronouncement about humanity's moral state in 6:5–6, resulting in the flood (6:17–20). The salvation of a few and the receding floodwaters present a new beginning but not one with humanity returned to its prediluvian innocence. They remain outside paradise. The postdiluvian world is a damaged world from the first appearance of the rainbow. Violence, the separation of humans from other species due to fear and dread, and meat eating are characteristic of this new, non-Edenic reality.

The permission to eat meat in Genesis 9 indicates a falling away from the ideal presented in Genesis 1 and is a concession to humanity's sinful behavior.[23] As Jean Kazez puts it, the meat eating permitted in Genesis 9

---

22. For a succinct overview of this view, see Barad, "What about the Covenant with Noah?" 16–20.

23. Bauckham, *Bible and Ecology*, 25, 26, 29, etc. For a survey of Jewish commentators arguing this position, see Schwartz, *Judaism and Vegetarianism*, 1–6. Among others discussing this view, see Phelps, *Dominion of Love*, 94–97, though he does not hold the position himself. Phelps argues Gen 9:1–3 does not derive from "God's authentic inspiration" (93; full rationale, 92–94).

is "not what God originally intended. Things went downhill after a perfect beginning. It was either wipe us out or capitulate somewhat to our evil ways, and God chose the second option."[24] Genesis 1 is, therefore, part of a prophetic critique of the "actual" world characterized by the language of Genesis 9, known to the writers and editors of the Genesis material, and known to all who read it.[25] The subdue/dominion language of Genesis 1, even with its implications of coercion, belongs in its prediluvian/garden of Eden setting and points toward an ideal relationship with the rest of creation. Other Torah passages, like Exod 23:9–12, which outlines instructions about the gracious treatment of land and animals, "are arguably the best commentary on the verbs *kabash* and *radah*," according to Rogerson. He adds that such Torah regulations, far from condoning the exploitation of the natural world and life within it, call for humanity to exercise "a gracious role in an otherwise cruel world, inspired by narratives and cultural memories about God's compassionate action in freeing a people from slavery."[26]

Manna

Is the bread-like manna God gives to Israel in the wilderness an echo of the vegetarian ideal of Genesis 1? Soon after leaving slavery in Egypt, Israel laments they also left behind meat and their fill of bread (Exod 16:3). God then promises to bring bread and meat to the people from heaven (16:4, 8). It seems the provision of quail to accompany the manna mentioned in Exodus 16 is not a regular occurrence, however, because later in their journey, the people again complain, yearning for a more diverse diet: "The rabble among them had a strong craving; and the Israelites also wept again, and said, 'If only we had meat to eat!'" (Num 11:4). This time when God sends quail, however, a disaster follows: "while the meat was still between their teeth, before it was consumed, the anger of the LORD was kindled against the people, and the LORD struck the people with a very great plague," a judgment linked specifically to the "craving" noted earlier in the chapter (Num 11:33–34). Though their persistent grumbling about food is symptomatic of other issues—including trust in their leaders, Moses and Aaron,

---

24. Kazez, *Animalkind*, 14. For further comments on the diets of Genesis 1 and 9, see, e.g., Morgan, "Sacrifice in Leviticus," 34–37.

25. Rogerson, "Creation Stories," 27, and "What Was the Meaning of Animal Sacrifice?" 12–13.

26. Rogerson, "Creation Stories," 30.

trust in God, and impatience with their newfound nomadic existence—this appetite for meat and dissatisfaction with God-given non-meat provisions recalls the downward spiral of Genesis 1–9 just described. In both cases, the meat eventually provided is not God's preference for the people but rather a concession to their appetites. There are other examples of such concessions. For instance, God allows the Israelites a monarchy when they demand it, an episode reminiscent of those disgruntled wanderers in the wilderness. We even see the earlier wilderness scene recalled in that context: "they have not rejected you [Samuel], but they have rejected me from being king over them. Just as they have done to me, from the day I brought them up out of Egypt" (1 Sam 8:7–8; cf. Deut 17:14–20).

Another Gardener

I close this brief discussion about the Genesis stories of origin with a speculative aside about an unusual verse in the Fourth Gospel. According to John 20:1–15, Mary Magdalene is first to see the stone removed from the entrance to Jesus's tomb. Two angels ask why she cries, so she answers that someone took away her Lord's body. She then turns and sees Jesus but does not recognize him (cf. Luke 24:13–16). This is not remarkable in itself. It was still dark, for one thing (20:1). John also tells us she stood witness to the crucifixion just days earlier so clearly there was no doubt that Jesus actually died (19:25). No matter how strong her faith and quite apart from anything Jesus said about rising from death (cf. Mark 8:31 etc.), her presence at the tomb and assumption that someone removed the body (20:13, 15) indicate she was not expecting to find him alive. At this moment, John offers a curious detail about Mary's understandable confusion: "Supposing him to be the gardener, she said to him, 'Sir, if you have carried him away, tell me where you have laid him'" (20:15).

Why "the gardener"? Is it relevant that this is, according to Genesis, humanity's first vocation? There we read that God places Adam in the garden precisely "to till it and keep it" (2:15). Given the Fourth Gospel's rich symbolism, it is worth considering whether the introduction of this term in its culminating scene is more than bland speculation about Mary's confused state of mind. The mention of the gardener is particularly poignant given the organization of this Gospel around *semeia*, signs. The miracle of turning water into wine at Cana, John tells us, is "the first of his signs" (2:11), and the healing of an official's son "the second sign that Jesus did"

(4:54). The enumeration of these *semeia* does not continue (though cf. 20:31–32), but other dramatic ones include 5:2–9 (the healing of a paralyzed man); 6:1–14 (the feeding of five thousand); 9:1–7 (the healing of a blind man); 11:1–44 (the raising of Lazarus from death); and 19:1–37 (the crucifixion of Jesus). We have here seven signs that follow, according to N. T. Wright, "the sevenfold sequence of the old creation." The eighth sign and the climax of John's Gospel is of course the resurrection of Jesus, which occurs, John tells us twice (20:1, 19), on "the first day of the week." This new day ("Early . . . still dark") and new week (John 20:1) is the beginning of a new creation commencing with the resurrection of Christ. The sequence of signs throughout John's Gospel is "always about the new creation bursting in on the old."[27]

If we follow through on this paralleling of old and new creation in the Fourth Gospel, Jesus is the new Adam, the new gardener. Mary's confusion is, Wright suggests elsewhere, "the right mistake to make because, like Adam, he [Jesus] is charged with bringing God's new world to order."[28] If the resurrected Jesus is an echo of the Adamic gardener, however oblique, we have yet another moment of "prophetic suggestiveness," to borrow again Edward Said's phrase. Christ's resurrection marks a return to Eden, or at least the beginning of a return to Edenic paradise. Edward Said considers striking the "silence" about the horrors of slavery in Jane Austen's *Mansfield Park*. The "silence" regarding this allusion to Adam's activities in Eden is conspicuous too. John says nothing about it. He trusts readers to recognize its import. Jesus is the new Adam. For readers of the New Testament, this idea is more familiar from Paul's writings (e.g., 1 Cor 15:45–49). John's (or Mary's) contribution to an Adam Christology is a reminder of the first human vocation of gardening and the peaceful, caring connection to the land and all its diverse residents that Adamic story involves. The call for Christians to follow and imitate the risen Lord is also a call to care for (new) creation, an assignment that includes attention to all other living things (Gen 2:18–20).

---

27. Wright, *Resurrection of the Son of God*, 669.

28. Wright, *Surprised by Hope*, 239. For Wright, the coming new creation involves particular responsibilities for the people of God, including attention to ecological concerns. He refers to this in various writings. See, e.g., *Surprised by Hope*, 90, 119, 213, 221; and his article "Jesus Is Coming—Plant a Tree!"

Eden's Other Residents

Tobit: It Is Not Good for Humans to Be Alone

Of the dog in ancient story
Many a pleasant tale is told;—
As when young Tobias journeyed
To Ecbatane of old,
By the angel Raphael guided;
Went the faithful Dog and good,
Bounding through the Tigris meadows
Whilst they fished within the flood . . .

—MARY HOWITT, "TOBIAS'S DOG"[29]

A dog appears in many of Rembrandt's biblical paintings, subtly observing the events depicted even when there is no such witness in written versions of the stories. Look closely at *The Stoning of Stephen*, for instance, and you will see a dog partially hidden by the body of a stone-wielding vigilante (cf. Acts 6:8—8:1). Speculating on this distinctive canine presence in more than thirty of Rembrandt's works, John I. Durham observes there is no reason to assume the painter was particularly fond of dogs and suggests instead that the animals indicate a particular insight. Dogs have no iconographic significance here but "are one more way of presenting the Bible as a human document, albeit a document about divine reality."[30] Biblical characters are real people, interacting with the real world and "surrounded by the creatures, the vegetation, the things that made his own landscape so continuously entertaining." There are no halos on Rembrandt's saints, and he put the dogs in these paintings "because he was a human painter painting human scenes, even about divine moments, for human eyes."[31]

Dogs do not often appear in the Bible, certainly far less than Rembrandt's work suggests. Perhaps the most intriguing biblical story involving a dog is the rarely read (at least in Protestant circles) book of Tobit. This story is part of the Greek Septuagint (LXX), though not the Hebrew Bible.

---

29. Taken from Leonard, ed., *Dog in British Poetry*, 71. The full poem is on pp. 71–72.

30. Durham, *Biblical Rembrandt*, 42–43. Though she does not discuss Rembrandt's work specifically, Hobgood-Oster notes that dogs are ubiquitous in Christian symbolism: "If one begins paying close attention to the art adorning Christian churches, particularly those built during the Middle Ages and the Renaissance, dogs are everywhere" (*Holy Dogs and Asses*, 90). For further discussion about the significance of dogs in Christian art, see 90–98.

31. Durham, *Biblical Rembrandt*, 43.

It is a delightful, edifying, and even humorous tale of Jewish piety amidst oppression and deprivation that includes poignant triadic images of communion between humans, nonhumans, and a representative of the spirit world. It also takes us back to the garden of Eden, where God declares, "It is not good that the man should be alone" (Gen 2:18). According to Genesis, after speaking these words, God forms animals from the earth and the woman from Adam's rib and brings them to Adam to partner with him (2:19–20, 22). In the book of Tobit we find a repetition of these basic plot elements as the principal character, Tobias, gains both forms of companionship by the story's end.[32]

A Canine Angel

The setting of this fairy tale romance is Nineveh in the late eighth and early seventh centuries BCE where the titular character lives after the Assyrians carried Israel's northern kingdom into captivity (Tob 1:1–3; cf. 2 Kgs 17:1–6). While there, the pious Jew Tobit maintains his exemplary commitment to the God of his people, evident in his refusal to compromise his diet (Tob 1:10–11) in the same manner as Daniel and his friends during their Babylonian exile (Dan 1:5–17; cf. 2 Macc 5:27). He also cares for the poor (e.g., 1:17; 2:1–2) and ensures proper burial for the Jewish dead at great risk to himself (1:16–20; 2:3–8). The latter activity incites the ire of the king, and Tobit loses all he owns and is forced to flee with his family: "Then all my property was confiscated; nothing was left to me that was not taken into the royal treasury except my wife Anna and my son Tobias" (1:20).

At the heart of the story is a journey. After the righteous Tobit goes blind (2:9–10) and expects to die, he sends Tobias on a mission to recover money left in trust with a relative—money the young man will need to bury his father, care for his mother, and practice almsgiving (4:1–11). A lot happens during Tobias's adventure. Readers discover that a stranger offering

---

32. Composed sometime around 200 BCE, Tobit combines elements of Hellenistic romances, fairy tales, and Jewish wisdom. The plot also incorporates themes well represented in folktales, including the grateful dead (reward for proper burial) and the dangerous bride (demon-haunted woman). For helpful introductions, see e.g., Helyer, "Tobit"; Knight and Levine, *Meaning of the Bible*, 389–91; Koester, *History, Culture and Religion*, 268; and Harrington, *Invitation to the Apocrypha*, 10–26. On the dangerous bride tradition, cf. Matt 22:23–33. Hebrew and Aramaic fragments from Cave 4 at Qumran indicate a Semitic original though we only possess the complete story in the LXX (VanderKam, *Dead Sea Scrolls*, 34–35).

to accompany him is actually an angel (5:4), though characters in the story only learn his true identity later (12:15: "I am Raphael, one of the seven angels who stand ready and enter before the glory of the Lord"). Together, Tobias and Raphael recover the money (9:5) and along the way liberate a righteous woman named Sarah from the tormenting demon Asmodeus (3:8; 8:2–3). Tobias marries Sarah (7:12), and on the return journey, Raphael provides Tobias with a cure for Tobit's blindness (11:13–14). Everyone lives happily ever after, as is only fitting in a good fairy tale.

As an animal lover, with dogs a regular part of home and family life, I find two verses particularly amusing and edifying. One occurs at the outset of Tobias's travels, the other when he and his angelic companion begin the trip home:

> The young man [Tobias] went out and the angel [Raphael] went with him; and the dog came out with him and went along with them. (6:1–2; 5:16 in the RSV)

> And the dog went along behind them [Raphael and Tobias]. (11:4)

The writer tells us nothing more. Strange as it is, this dog shows up both times without any introduction and there is no further mention of it, leading readers to wonder, what dog? Is it Tobit's? The Vaticanus and Alexandrinus versions of the story offer this explanation at 5:17 (LXX), which the RSV follows (at 5:16: "the young man's dog"). Or is the animal merely a stray, a roaming scavenger belonging to no one? Codex Sinaiticus suggests this, mentioning "the dog" without any further qualification (the reading followed by the NRSV). Either way, the appearance of "the dog" (or "the young man's dog") leaves us to speculate why the animal is in the story at all and why it shows up specifically as the friends travel.

The angel Raphael is obviously a vehicle of God's grace (12:18). When Tobit comforts Anna who is concerned for her son's safety, he says, "Do not fear for them, my sister. For *a good angel will accompany him*; his journey will be successful, and he will come back in good health" (5:21–22). This is humorous, of course, because Raphael is in fact an angel (cf. 5:4), something readers know but Tobit does not at the moment he speaks these words. And there is possibly more to smile about here. Just two verses after Tobit's assertion of an accompanying angel—and without warning, and sitting oddly in its context—we learn of "the dog" that "came out with him and went along *with them* [plural, referring to Tobias and Raphael]" (6:2). Is "the dog" also an angel? The question presents itself because in his blessing on

Tobias and Raphael, Tobit says, "May God in heaven bring you [plural] safely there and return you in good health to me; and may his angel, my son, accompany you *both* for your safety" (*o angelos autou sumporeuthātō umin* [plural]; 5:17). Tobit specifically mentions *both* legs of the journey (there and back), and the mysterious dog appears each time the friends hit the road. The prayer is also for an angelic companion for *both* Tobias and Raphael. Raphael is an angel, yes, but what angel accompanies him in accordance with Tobit's blessing? The dog qualifies. This animal is a Godsend, an "angel," an answer to Tobit's prayer.[33] There is no reason to think it is not an actual dog, which is to say a non-canine angel in disguise, as Raphael is disguised as a human. The latter is explicit. By all appearances, this is an actual dog assuming the angelic function of companionship and protection in answer to Tobit's prayer.

Even if the last suggestion is off the mark, I find this appearance of a mysterious companion animal a compelling image of human (Tobias), nonhuman (dog), and divine (Raphael) harmony and fellowship. It is also a subtle reminder that we find God in, and experience God's blessings through, the wonders of the natural world, including animals. It also takes us back to the Edenic paradise with its harmony and companionship among diverse species in the presence of God (Gen 2:18–20). God specifically makes these creatures because it is not good for Adam to be alone, and apparently it is not good for Tobias to be alone either—hence the answer to his father's prayer is, in part, "the dog." Perhaps we do well to extend Hebrews' call to "show hospitality to strangers" beyond our own species; in doing so some entertained angels without knowing it (Heb 13:2). Tobias might agree, not only with reference to Raphael (an actual angel in human disguise) but also with reference to the angelic four-legged protector that accompanies him during hazardous travels.

The appearance of the dog in this fascinating story is peculiar for a few reasons. For one thing, in ancient Near Eastern cultures, dogs were not usually pets but instead were considered scavengers.[34] Even more unusual,

---

33. Cf. the assessment of *The New Oxford Annotated Bible* at RSV Tob 5:16: "The *dog* is a surprising feature of the story, but plays no special role." In the note at 11:4, the editors suggest, "perhaps [the dog's] presence in the story is a survival from an older folk tale, in which he had a real function."

34. "In the Bible and ancient Jewish tradition, dogs are not pets, beloved insiders to the household and participants in family life, but outsiders—scavengers, disdained as animals that eat unclean food" (Boring, *Mark*, 212). In light of this, Boring refers to Tob 6:2 and 11:4 as "a rare exception" indicative of a Hellenistic context (212 n. 169). See too

as noted already, is the way in which this animal simply appears without any preamble. The manuscripts reflect some uncertainty about the scene, making it explicit that it was Tobias's dog (a detail added at 5:17 in Vaticanus and Alexandrinus as a way to explain its curious entrance to the scene: *o kuōn tou paidariou met' autōn*). It is likely that the dog originated in an earlier story familiar to the author, who then absorbed it into this tale.

Regardless of where this narrative detail originates, and apart from confusions in the manuscript and translation history of Tobit, this triad of a companion animal walking along with the human Tobit and divine Raphael in the text, as we have it, offers a way of imagining the place of the nonhuman within our theological contemplation. The scene invites re-evaluation of an anthropocentric worldview. Tobias's parents are understandably concerned to see their son venture into the world alone (5:18), and when the answer to Tobias's prayer includes more than he realizes (i.e., what is presumably a caring and protective dog), it disrupts the reader's expectations of the role of animals in a religious narrative. It is much the same in this respect as the stories about Balaam's donkey or Jonah's whale. Animals are often gifts from God, and through them God often chooses to "speak" to or bless human actors in biblical dramas.

A Crazy Fish

Tobias's dog is a symbol of companionship, protection, and answered prayer, but other creatures contribute to this story of restoration and deliverance too. Here again, in accord with Gen 2:18–20, it is clear that human isolation from animal creation is not good because other-than-human creatures help carry the story to its cheerful conclusions.

Even though Tobit is a model of Jewish piety, his life is anything but easy. In addition to the deprivations and dangers endured as a result of his exile to a foreign land, Tobit becomes blind when sparrow droppings "fell into [his] eyes and produced white films" (2:10). The plight of this righteous man enduring harsh circumstances brings Job to mind, and indeed the opening section closes with Tobit's Job-like prayer from the depths of his despair.

Houston, "Classifying Animals," 22, and Hobgood-Oster, *Holy Dogs and Asses*, passim. Crossan's short article, "The Power of the Dog," is a fascinating reflection on dogs and their connection to victims of crucifixion. On pet keeping in the Bible more generally, Nathan tells a story about a man's close relationship with a lamb ("it was like a daughter to him" [2 Sam 12:3]), and in Job 41:5, God asks Job rhetorically if he intends to play with Leviathan as a bird or put it on a leash.

At this point, the author introduces the next major character. Sarah (3:7–15) resembles Tobit in certain respects, as a righteous woman who experiences horrible calamities that seem completely unjust. The paralleling of Tobit and Sarah is deliberate, something suggested by the time indication provided:

> *On the same day* [that Tobit "with much grief and anguish of heart . . . wept, and with groaning began to pray" (3:1)] . . . it also happened that Sarah, the daughter of Raguel, was reproached by one of her father's maids. For she had been married to seven husbands, and the wicked demon Asmodeus had killed each of them before they had been with her as is customary for wives (3:7–8).

She too is righteous and cries out to God for comfort in her despair (3:11–15). With readers now aware of Tobit and Sarah's unhappy circumstances (1:1—3:15), the major actions of the story commence as God answers the prayers of these righteous Jews by sending Raphael, whose name means God heals, or God is a healer, or medicine of God.[35] Raphael, with the help of a fish, supplies the cure for Sarah's demonic torments (3:16–17) and Tobit's blindness.

Almost immediately after Raphael, Tobias, and "the dog" set out on their journey to Rages (6:1–2), an unusual thing occurs to the young man when washing his feet in the Tigris River. A large fish jumps out of the water and tries to swallow his foot (6:3), but this, we quickly realize, is God's providence. Raphael instructs Tobias to take the fish's gall, heart, and liver "as medicine" (6:5), and the rest for food (6:6). The significance of the "medicine" is apparent when the two arrive in Media and stay with Tobias's relative Raguel. Tobias, Raphael explains (rather matter-of-factly), is to marry Sarah (6:13) in order to fulfill his father's wishes (4:12). Since this poor girl is the victim of a demon's torments, Raphael explains that the fish medicine is the remedy to force it away (6:17–18). The house of Raguel celebrates the nuptials (7:1–16), even slaughtering a ram as part of the feast (7:9), and when Tobias and Sarah enter the bridal chamber, the fish medicine proves effective, chasing the demon "to the remotest parts of Egypt" where Raphael binds it hand and foot (8:3). The wedding celebrations continue, and Tobias sends Raphael to Rages to collect Tobit's money and bring Gabael back to join in the festivities (9:1–6). Once the wedding celebrations are complete it is time for the journey home (10:8–13), but Raphael's work is not finished yet. As the angel, the young man, and the dog

---

35. Helyer, "Tobit," 1238; McColley, "Raphael," 655.

go their way (11:4),[36] Raphael instructs Tobias to have the gall ready and, as expected, the fish medicine cures Tobit's blindness (11:7–15). As the tale ends, Raphael reveals his identity (12:15), and Tobit's life comes to a happy conclusion full of praise and thanksgiving to God.

The crazy fish that tries to swallow Tobias's foot (6:3) facilitates this satisfying resolution. Rather than harming Tobias, this fish is the means of grace that releases Sarah from her demonic tormentor, saves Tobias's own life (as Sarah's husband; i.e., the demon killed the seven previous husbands), and gives Tobit sight. The fish's action is an act of self-sacrifice that benefits many others. Presumably this fish is relatively small, judging by the phrase "tried to swallow the young man's foot" (i.e., this was not like Jonah's fish, which swallowed the whole man), so it was obviously not a self-serving attempt to eat Tobias. Instead, in this beautiful triad, the self-sacrificing fish and the divine representative Raphael provide the man Tobias with a wonderful gift that not only brings liberation for the righteous Tobit and Sarah but also contributes to the sequence of events leading to Tobias's marriage.

Nonhuman species play a prominent part in the story directly and indirectly. References include the following:

- 1:4: sacrifice at the temple
- 1:6: first fruits of the flock, tithes of cattle, first shearing of sheep
- 1:10–11: Tobit refuses to eat Gentiles' food (presumably meat); cf. Dan 1:5–17
- 2:10: sparrow droppings blind Tobit[37]
- 2:12–14: Tobit's wife, Anna, receives a goat for a meal
- 6:2: the dog accompanies Tobias and Raphael as they leave home
- 6:3–9: a large fish tries to swallow Tobias's foot; the fish serves as both food and medicine
- 6:17–18; 8:2–3: Tobias uses the fish medicine to free Sarah from the demon Asmodeus

---

36. As the NRSV note indicates, Codex Sinaiticus reads, "And the Lord went along . . ." (not the dog).

37. The humorous quality of this scene deserves notice. For discussion, see McCracken, "Narration and Comedy in the Book of Tobit," esp. 402, 417, regarding the "remarkable double hit" and "perfectly aimed bird droppings." Referring to the book as a whole, McColley describes Tobit as "a comedic analogue of the book of Job" ("Tobit and Tobias," 769).

- 8:19: Raguel slaughters two steer and four rams for a feast in his home
- 9:2, 5: use of two camels for traveling
- 10:10: Raguel, Sarah's father, gives Tobias and Sarah oxen, sheep, donkeys, camels
- 11:4: the dog appears for a second time, joining Raphael and Tobias as they set out for home
- 11:4, 8–14: the "gall" made from the fish cures Tobit of his blindness

Sparrow droppings contribute to Tobit's blindness (though bungling physicians are also culpable [6:10]), but ultimately this trial brings greater good because it contributes to the sequence of events leading to Sarah's rescue from a demon's tyranny, her marriage to Tobias, and the recovery of the family's wealth (9:1–6). The sparrow that blinds Tobit sets in motion a sequence of events leading to a satisfying ending. The bird is no more deserving of blame than the wind that blows down Job's house. We find in the book of Tobit God's grace mediated through animal creation.

And the Greyhound Went with Him: A Biographical Tangent and God's Speech to Job

Each mortal thing does one thing and the same:
Deals out that being indoors each one dwells;
Selves—goes itself; *myself* it speaks and spells,
Crying *What I do is me: for that I came.*

—GERARD MANLEY HOPKINS,
"AS KINGFISHERS CATCH FIRE" (1877)[38]

Though writing a generation later, the Victorian poet Gerard Manley Hopkins invokes a Romantic enthusiasm for the natural world, finding in it not only artistic and intellectual stimulation but also a resource informing theological contemplation. Hopkins's art stands out in this respect, for though there are remarkable exceptions, it is generally the case that Christian thinking is anthropocentric in orientation. Perhaps fascination with postmortem destinations (heaven, hell, purgatory) in much Christian

---

38. Hopkins, *Major Works*, 129.

discourse minimizes perceived value in the material world, or maybe the tendency to stress the unique status of humans as made in the image of God (see Gen 1:26)[39] and the fallen state of the post-Edenic universe is to blame. Whatever the reason, many Christian thinkers seem reluctant to recognize anything of spiritual import in the ecological and zoological wonders that surround us. To my mind, this is a missed theological opportunity. Hopkins's willingness to see the divine purpose in each thing—"*What I do is me: for that I came*"—and his awareness that all creation is "charged with the grandeur of God," as he says elsewhere,[40] inspires a worldview that refuses to put self, and humanity as a whole, at the center of all things.

Hopkins's complex poetry gestures toward a communion with the world around him that includes other species, and I am surely not alone in saying experience resonates with this insight. Such was the case for me a few years back when we lost our spirited greyhound Tiger after a short illness. I mentioned above that I enjoy the oddly out-of-place references to "the dog" in the book of Tobit. That image of a dog and human sharing a journey is potentially enriching and instructive (cf. how traveling a river in the company of hippopotamuses going in the same direction inspired Schweitzer, or Bailly's brief encounter with a deer, both noted earlier). Such was my experience during Tiger's last days with us.

It was a heartbreaking diagnosis. Osteosarcoma is a bone cancer that leaves few viable treatment options, apart from pain management. The brief time between diagnosis and our final goodbyes was not easy. There were frequent trips to see the veterinarian and the financial costs of palliative care involving an expensive regimen of medications. Far worse was the emotional toll as we waited the inevitable but gradual progress of the disease. We wondered constantly when the quality of life ends for an animal, and whether the decision to delay euthanizing was for our own benefit or hers. In the end, a shattered leg bone, badly compromised by

---

39. For an overview of major views about what "image" means in Genesis, see e.g., Wenham, *Genesis*, 29–32. "The strongest case has been made," he concludes, "for the view that the divine image makes man God's vice-regent on earth" (31–32). However, it is incorrect to take the language in Genesis about humanity's unique role in creation as a license to ignore and exploit the rest of the natural world. Bauckham sees dominion and image as indicating a sacred responsibility and trust: "If the dominion over other creatures were merely a matter of power, it too would be only the superlative version of what other creatures have. What links it to the image of God is that it is a delegated participation in God's caring rule over his creatures" (*Bible and Ecology*, 19). See too Moritz, "Animals and the Image of God."

40. From the poem "God's Grandeur," in Hopkins, *Major Works*, 128.

the cancer, forced the decision (and also gave proof we waited too long in letting her go).

Companion animals inspire much behavior well described as spiritual in the broadest sense of the word.[41] These creatures have a remarkable capacity to disrupt self-centeredness and inspire affection and appreciation for something completely "other." Though with Hopkins I contemplate and define spirituality in light of both Christian theology and the wonders and mysteries of the natural world, there is inevitable dissonance that results from each attempt to link the two, particularly when animals are involved. The church's history boasts many teachers finding religious meaning in encounters with other sentient beings, and yet many more reflect the deeply entrenched assumption that humanity alone is all that really matters, theologically speaking. The book of Job challenges this widespread attitude.

"Is it by your wisdom that the hawk soars, and spreads its wings toward the south?" (Job 39:26). This is but one of a litany of questions God puts to Job once he responds to Job's complaints from the whirlwind. Job lost everything (1:6—2:8) and, understandably, he voices despair, sorrow, and anger over his miserable plight. Yet, God does not explain the man's losses and torments but instead directs Job to observe the world around him, including a wide array of nonhuman species (Job 38–41). Is Job 38–39 a parody of the "dominion" described in Genesis? According to Habel, the "wisdom tradition in Job 38–39 challenges and apparently subverts the so-called royal dominion tradition . . . represented in the Genesis text." The various questions God puts to Job imply a negative answer, meaning he "does not possess the knowledge, skills or power to control creation." Job 39 makes this quite clear: the wild ox refuses to serve him (39:9); the horses' might terrifies him (39:20). Habel considers Job 39:9–12, with its description of the ox, "a parody of the idea that humans should have dominion over wild beasts." In Job we find a reversal of the situation in Gen 9:2; animals do not fear humanity, but rather the reverse is true.[42]

---

41. Jay McDaniel argues that companion animals are important because most people do not have opportunities to encounter animals in natural habitats. "Thus, as a spiritual discipline for learning to listen to animals," he writes, "I recommend 'taking care of pets.'" Some find the hierarchal nature of relationships with pets problematic, he acknowledges, but adds that "for many people today, a relationship with their pets . . . is the first way, and perhaps the only way, they can learn to listen to animals" ("Practicing the Presence of God," 144; see too 134).

42. Habel, "Wild Ox," as cited in Horrell, *Bible and the Environment*, 59, 60. On this, with reference to Habel, see also Bauckham, *Bible and Ecology*, 50–51. Psalm 104 raises similar questions because it is clearly God who rules the natural world, not humankind.

Eden's Other Residents

Tiger in the foreground, with Laugh, as always, keeping an eye on her.
Photograph by Tim Henderson (Thunder Bay, Ontario)

Lions, mountain goats, wild asses, eagles, deer, oxen, ostriches, horses, and the mysterious but mighty Behemoth and Leviathan appear among the wonders God describes, and the effect on Job is striking and perhaps predictable. "I am of small account," he says to God, "what shall I answer you? I lay my hand on my mouth. I have spoken once, and I will not answer; twice, but will proceed no further" (40:4–5). The experience transforms Job. His worldview no longer centers on his own predicament. He gains perspective, acknowledging his minuteness (which is not to say insignificance) in relation to God and everything around him. Our interactions with the divine occur within a richly diverse and majestic world populated with seemingly endless species. As other writers remind us, these creatures are as dependent on God for life and wellbeing as human beings (see e.g., Pss 78:23–25;

Recognizing the Grace of God in Animal Creation

104:21; 145:15; 147:9). The animals of the forest belong to God (Ps 50:9–10; cf. 104:24) who feeds them (Ps 147:9), and the wild animals in turn praise their Creator (Ps 148:10; cf. Isa 43:20).

Caring for and grieving the loss of a dog turned my thoughts away from myself and toward an "other," and then to the ultimate "Other." My relatively short time with Tiger in life awakened compassion and celebration of God's good world, and my journey with her through the valley of the shadow of death evoked a longing to find meaning and solace in loss. Much to my surprise, this animal-human relationship reminded me that I am not at the center of a God-ordered universe. For the nineteenth-century poet Gerard Manley Hopkins, all living things reveal the Creator God, with each kingfisher and dragonfly—and let us add, presumably with Tobias's full agreement, each companion canine—offering a glimpse of the divine.

Odysseus, Lazarus, and Their Dogs

Tobias is not the only biblical character with a companion dog that is a medium of God's favor. A poor man in a New Testament parable also experiences a moment of grace in canine form. Poor, hungry Lazarus lies outside the gate of a wealthy man's home, a man with more food than he can eat. Though Lazarus is destitute and dying, a dog licks his sores (Luke 16:21).[43] As already noted, dogs do not fair well in biblical literature; often they are depicted as dangerous, dirty scavengers (e.g., 2 Kgs 9:36; Matt 7:6; 2 Pet 2:22[44]). Paul uses the term in an insult (Phil 3:2).[45] We need to see past our own cultural associations of dogs as pets and appreciate that a despised dog is the only creature aware of Lazarus's existence. This parable resembles the Good Samaritan story in highlighting how the least likely of passersby extends a helping hand (paw) to one in need. In its own way, the dog shows sympathy to Lazarus when fellow humans—Jews who are in fact religiously

---

43. Some ancient Near Eastern cultures attribute healing capacities to dogs. Perhaps this association is in view here as well. See Hobgood-Oster, *Holy Dogs and Asses*, 88.

44. On the proverbial language of 2 Pet 2:22 that combines remarks about the behaviors of pigs and dogs, see Davids, *Letters*, 251–52.

45. The insult is actually sharper than first appears on a casual reading. Whereas English speakers consider the pejorative use of the term *dog* as indicating one in some sense worthless or vulgar, for Jews like Paul the insult includes a religious sense, referring to Gentiles (cf. Jesus's use of the term to refer to a Syrophoenician woman in Mark 7:27). Paul makes a shocking claim in Phil 3:2: "the great reversal brought in by Christ means that it is the Judaizers who must be regarded as Gentiles" (Silva, *Philippians*, 169; see too 180–81).

obligated to show compassion for a hungry and poor individual in their midst—do not. This image of a caregiving dog, one that shows kindness to a man even though it is despised within that man's society, is startling. As in the book of Tobit, we simply do not expect a dog in this context.

Also significant are the Hellenistic dimensions of this story. Jesus's parable of two men dying, one carried by angels to Abraham's side (Lazarus), the other descending to Hades (the rich man, often called Dives), is reminiscent of and arguably indebted to Homer's tale of Odysseus visiting Hades in *Odyssey* 10.[46] If correct, this Homeric backdrop offers a further connection because dogs appear in both *Odyssey* and Luke's parable. Lazarus's dog is an unexpected friend to Lazarus in 16:21. So too the disguised Odysseus is a solitary figure when he first returns home after many years of war and adventure but one loyal friend recognizes him right away despite the hero's altered appearance:

> There the dog Argos lay, full of the vermin of dogs;
> And then, when he perceived that Odysseus was nearby,
> He fawned over him with his tail and dropped both his ears.
> But then he was no longer able to go closer
> To his master. The man looked away and wiped off a tear.
> He hid easily from Eumaeos, and he at once asked a question:
> "Great wonder is it, Eumaeos, that this dog lies here in the dung..."
> "Ah yes, this is the dog of a man who died far away,
> And if he were the same in body and in his actions
> As when Odysseus left him behind on his way off to Troy,
> You would wonder at once when you saw his speed and his force..."
> When he had said this [Odysseus] entered the well-situated halls,
> And he went straight through the hall to the noble suitors.
> But the fortune of black death took Argos away
> Once he had seen Odysseus in the twentieth year.[47]

Odysseus's dog sees/recognizes his master when others do not. Odysseus's dog shows kindness to his master when others do not. Odysseus's dog aligns with the story's hero when most others do not. Odysseus (disguised as a beggar) is hungry while others eat much. All of this loosely parallels the story Jesus tells. Lazarus is likewise alone and hungry, but a dog is aware of his presence and shows him a simple kindness.

---

46. I argue that Luke 16:19–31 derives in part from Homer's *Odyssey* in Gilmour, *Significance*, 137–44.

47. Homer, *Odyssey*, book 17, lines 300–305, 312–15, 324–27.

When Lazarus dies, angels carry his body away, presumably because there is no one else to offer him this dignity. This is consistent with Lazarus's name (one whom God helps). The dog in this parable is also a godsend, a means of grace. No human neighbor comes alongside Lazarus, but a despised dog does. God helps the poor man through an animal, an angel unawares, much like that unexpectedly canine answer to a father's prayer in the book of Tobit.

A Herd of Swine and a Demoniac

The brief passage about a dog licking Lazarus's sores dramatically contrasts human indifference with God's compassion, especially as mediated through a most unlikely and nonhuman character. The next scene considered is not so subtle, though it resembles the Lazarus parable in that animals are a means of divine favor. Here Jesus comes to the rescue of a distraught man who, like Lazarus, lives on the margins of human society (cf. Mark 5:3–5). Just as a dog's touch is a tangible expression of God's care to the one man, so the actions of a herd of pigs bring relief to the other.

The story of the demoniac living among the tombs and his liberation after an encounter with Jesus obviously deserves notice by those exploring the biblical presentation of animals (Matt 8:28—9:1; Mark 5:1–20; Luke 8:26–39). According to the Synoptic evangelists, Jesus and his disciples cross the Sea of Galilee and arrive in the country of the Gerasenes (Mark 5:1; Luke 8:26) or Gadarenes (Matt 8:28). Though the exact location of the town is uncertain owing to discrepancies in the manuscript tradition, that Jesus's mission shifts into Gentile territories at this point is clear (note reference to the Decapolis in Mark 5:20).[48]

A story involving a great herd of swine (5:11: *agelē choirōn megalē*)[49] inescapably has religio-cultural overtones. On the one hand, Torah regulations do not permit Jews to eat pork (Lev 11:7–8; Deut 14:8; cf. 1 Macc 1:47), and on the other, Romans and other Gentiles considered pigs sacred, "to be sacrificed to the gods and consumed in sacred meals, including at ancestral tombs on ritual occasions."[50] The scene involves a dramatic clash of religious

---

48. See e.g., Beavis, *Mark*, 93.

49. For other references to *choiros*, swine, see e.g., Matt 7:6; 8:30–32; Luke 15:15–16. One important biblical backdrop to this story is Isa 65:1–7, which links the images of dwelling in tombs and swine.

50. Boring, *Mark*, 152.

and cultural traditions. The story also alludes subtly to Rome's military occupation of the region and appears to serve as an allegory of liberation on some level. The demons identify themselves as "Legion" (Mark 5:9; Luke 8:30), a military term conspicuous since the Tenth Legion stationed in Palestine used the insignia of a wild boar on its banners.[51] While there is much to say about these literary, historical, cultural, and military links, I limit my remarks here to a few observations centered on the animals themselves.

The narrative concerns Jesus's rescue of the man wandering among the tombs, a powerful setting that reminds us that although physically alive, he is in other senses already dead. The demons recognize Jesus's authority over them, and after his repeated demands (as Mark's use of the imperfect in 5:8 suggests) they leave the man and enter the swine with Jesus's permission (Matt 8:31–32; Mark 5:12–13; Luke 8:32). Once they enter the animals, the whole herd rushes down the steep bank into the sea and drowns (Matt 8:32; Mark 5:13; Luke 8:33).

Traditionally, interpretation assigns the many animals of the story ("the herd, numbering about two thousand" [Mark 5:13]; "a large herd of swine" [Luke 8:32]) an entirely passive role. Most see their behavior as the reflex reaction of startled animals that bolt in terror when the demons enter. Responsibility for the animals' death therefore lies with the demons,[52] though Jesus gives the fateful permission to leave the man and enter the herd. As William L. Lane puts it, "What must be seen above all else is that the fate of the swine demonstrates the ultimate intention of the demons with respect to the man they had possessed. It is their purpose to destroy the creation of God, and halted in their destruction of a man, they fulfilled their purpose with the swine." Jesus permits the demons' entrance to the herd knowing the destruction of the animals "was the express purpose which lay behind the request of the demons."[53] Jesus faces a catch-22, it follows, forced to decide between the rescue of one human and the destruction of two thousand animals. As Bauckham sees it, it is ultimately "the demons who destroy the pigs, but Jesus lets them do so, presumably because the destruction of the pigs was of lesser concern than the deliverance of a man from demon-possession." Elsewhere Bauckham argues that the story

---

51. Ibid., 151.

52. E.g., Bauckham, "Jesus and Animals I," 47: "[The demons'] destruction of the pigs manifests the inherent tendency of the demonic to destroy whatever it possesses (cf. Mark 5.5, 9.22)."

53. Lane, *Mark*, 186.

shows Jesus permitting "a lesser evil" and that the destruction of the pigs "is preferable to the destruction of a human personality."[54]

To my mind, this reading is not very satisfying. For one thing, the demons did not destroy their physical host completely before Jesus's arrival (i.e., the man among the tombs was still physically alive, even if socially, mentally, and spiritually dead), and their plea to transfer from a human body to animal bodies indicates—within the logic of the story—their need of a corporeal host. If this is the case, it is not clear that their purpose was the immediate destruction of either the possessed man or the swine. They need a body or bodies to survive. Their terror at Jesus's presence in the region is clear, evident in their desperate efforts to escape their own destruction, which included assignment to "the abyss" (Luke 8:31) and "torment" (Matt 8:29; Mark 5:7). Why then would they destroy the bodies needed to avoid this miserable fate, even if temporarily?

Second, regardless of how we read the story, it is awkward to attribute this destruction of animal life to Jesus, even if it is an indirect consequence or viewed as a lesser evil. The Gospels present Jesus casting out other demons without similar collateral damage, so why does it/must it occur here?

Third, the simple causal connection of Jesus's exorcism with the death of so many animals suggests he had little regard for other-than-human life. This is out of step with the tenor of his teachings about fallen sparrows (Matt 10:29–31) and laboring animals (Luke 14:5).

Finally, if we interpret the destruction of the swine as collateral damage, an unavoidable consequence, the only way of exorcising the demons, it leaves the impression that while Jesus was able to save one life, he was not able to save others at the same time. There are limitations on his powers and authority. In the context of the Synoptic Gospels, and perhaps especially in Mark with its emphasis on Jesus as the lord of all creation and Jesus's peace with the animal world (1:12–13; cf. 16:18), this is absurd.

Several commentators appeal to a kind of greater-to-the-lesser explanation with respect to Jesus's permission to the demons and the drowning of the herd. Lane writes that "Jesus allows the demons to continue their destructive work, but not upon a man," and Witherington refers to "a matter of priorities," which guides Jesus's actions.[55] If this is the case, it diminishes the place of animals in a story about a demonic attack on creation that concerns them

---

54. Bauckham, "Reading the Synoptic Gospels," 81; cf. Bauckham, "Jesus and Animals I," 48.

55. Lane, *Mark*, 186; Witherington, *Mark*, 183.

Eden's Other Residents

as much as humans. But there is no need to find here the notion that some living things (animals) are expendable while others (humans) are not, or that Jesus's concern, authority, and ability are sufficient to attend to the plight of one created being but not others. Is it possible that the pigs play a more active role in this deliverance story than usually assumed?

I raise the question because the Bible does not present animals as mere Cartesian automatons in relation to spiritual matters.[56] We find animals crying out to God for sustenance (e.g., Job 38:41 and Ps 147:9 [ravens]; Ps 104:21 [lions]; Joel 1:20 [wild animals]), recognizing and reacting to an angelic messenger (Num 22:22–35 [Balaam's donkey]), fulfilling divinely appointed tasks (Jonah's fish; cf. Jer 8:7), accompanying an angelic healer (Tobias's dog), and as part of "the whole creation," waiting and groaning for eschatological freedom from bondage and decay (Rom 8:18–23). Animals also participate with the rest of creation in praising their Creator. There is no more striking picture of this than that offered by John the Seer, whose four living creatures—an image of animate creation in its entirety—sing without ceasing, "Holy, holy, holy, the Lord God the Almighty, who was and is and is to come" (Rev 4:8; discussed below). Perhaps the pigs in this unusual Synoptic scene are not simply victims but rather active participants, even warriors fighting against the powers of darkness bent on ruin.

If the demons have no immediate need to kill their host (they did not kill the man physically outright), and if Jesus's permission to them does not involve direct or indirect participation in the destruction of created things (difficult to reconcile with his mission), perhaps the animals themselves are the agents of their own fate. Perhaps these animals sacrifice themselves in this story of liberation, acting as willing participants in Jesus's rescue of the demon-possessed man. The devils need a bodily host and want to avoid assignment to the abyss, hence their unusual plea to Jesus. However, the demons do not anticipate creation's abhorrence of their evil presence, which through an exercise of self-sacrifice destroys them. The demons do not plunge the swine into the waters. It is the other way around. The swine hurl the demons into the "sea" using their own bodies, destroying the devils in the process.

---

56. For a helpfully distilled selection of René Descartes's influential writings on animals, see Kalof and Fitzgerald, *Animal Reader*, 59–62. For diverse reflections on Descartes's view of animals as basically machines, see Steiner, "Descartes, Christianity, and Contemporary Speciesism"; Osborne, *Dumb Beasts*, 75–79; and Derrida, *Animal*, passim.

The term *sea* is highly suggestive (and it is not named specifically as the Sea of Galilee in Mark 5:1, 13, as it is in 1:16 and elsewhere).[57] The "sea" carries mythological significance in the Bible; it precedes the act of creation as the site of primordial chaos that in Christian apocalyptic thinking ultimately disappears under the rule of God (Rev 21:1). These two thousand pigs are not the passive victims of demonic activity. Instead, they remove Legion and its corrupting and destructive presence in creation, and by this act of cleansing—one that is a prolepsis, an anticipation of the kingdom of God in its fullness—they share with Jesus a dramatic part in the rescue of a possessed man.

In the literary environment where we find this story, animals are actively in communion with their Creator. What prevents us from viewing this scene as an act of worship, one that involves the rescue of a fellow creature and, in partnership with Jesus, a reclaiming of God's good world through self-sacrifice, especially in a religious context that values martyrdom? In effect, Jesus's permission to the swine amounts to his saying, "Okay, enter the swine if you want to, but be careful what you wish for." This does not diminish Jesus's role in healing the man (he sends the demons out), but it illustrates cooperation between Jesus (divine) and the natural world (swine) that rescues and heals a troubled man in a striking example of the triadic formula. Just as he uses mud to cure blindness (John 9:6–7) on another occasion, Jesus here allows animate creation to participate with him in bringing shalom to those who need it most.

Animals as Active Participants in God's Creation

We are biased toward our own species, tending to think we alone matter among all other living things.[58] We find it difficult even to imagine other species possessing forms of intimacy with their Creator, but we find imagery to that effect in biblical poetry. In *Reasons for Hope: A Spiritual Journey*, Jane Goodall entertains the idea of something approaching a spiritual dimension in animal lives. The reactions of chimpanzees to a waterfall, observed

---

57. Boring, *Mark*, 58. Boring notes that by using the term *sea* rather than *lake*, as in "the Sea of Galilee" (Mark 1:16 etc.), Mark evokes "the chaos and anticreation motif associated with 'sea' in ancient Near Eastern imagery and the Hebrew Scriptures."

58. On this point, consider Peterson's various remarks about what he calls Darwinian narcissism, a "large-scale, species-wide" self-interest (*Moral Lives of Animals*, 37–41, 43, 128, etc.).

by Goodall during field research in Tanzania, suggest to her "feelings akin to awe," and she wonders whether "similar feelings of awe . . . gave rise to the first animistic religions, the worship of the elements and the mysteries of nature over which there was no control? Only when our prehistoric ancestors developed language would it have been possible to discuss such internal feelings and create a shared religion."[59] When later discussing this startling notion in an interview, she adds, "What I saw [when observing chimpanzees responding to waterfalls and rainfall] was an expression of what I think is a spiritual reality."[60] These are fascinating remarks coming as they do from one in the scientific community, and they resemble biblical accounts (and indeed those stemming from other religious traditions) that also describe the capacity of animals to respond to inexplicable wonders in ways usually thought characteristic of humans alone.

Is it merely a poetic fancy for the psalmist to call on sea monsters, wild animals, cattle, creeping things, and flying birds to praise God (Ps 148:7, 10), or is it possible that in their own way they actually do just that? Within the theological-poetic language of the Bible it is certainly possible for nonhumans to engage in forms of communion with their Maker. We also find them functioning on God's behalf as messengers of divine grace (Tobias's fish, Lazarus's dog, the Gadarene demoniac's swine) and instruments of God's judgment. Illustrations of both appear in close proximity in the Elijah-Elisha cycle. We learn the Lord commands ravens to feed Elijah (1 Kgs 17:4), thus saving the prophet's life in a time of drought when they dutifully bring him bread and meat (17:6). Soon after Elisha takes up Elijah's prophetic mantle, however, animals serve a shockingly different role. When "small boys" mock the prophet, he curses them in the name of the Lord, and two bears come out of the woods and maul forty-two of them (2 Kgs 2:23–24). The latter incident is disturbing, which perhaps explains its conspicuous absence from Josephus's account of Elisha in *Antiquities of the Jews*.[61] There is a similar pairing of animal-mediated mercy and judgment in the lions' den of the book of Daniel. An angel shuts the lions' mouths to rescue the blameless prophet, but later, when the king throws Daniel's accusers and their families into the pit, a leonine judgment breaks "all their

---

59. Goodall, *Reason for Hope*, 189. De Waal also observed this behavior and describes it in *Bonobo and the Atheist*, 199–200.

60. Goodall, "Dance of Awe," 654. The citation from *Reason for Hope* above also appears here, on p. 653.

61. On this omission, see Allison, "Rejecting Violent Judgment," 469.

bones" before they reach the bottom (Dan 6:22, 24).⁶² In Ezekiel the Lord announces, "I will send famine and wild animals against you" (5:17).⁶³

Such judgment stories are chilling and reflect the very real fears of the threats posed by wild animals for nomadic and semi-nomadic people and their herds and flocks. The terror presented by predators lingers long in memory: "Great and terrible flesh-eating beasts have always shared landscape with humans. They were part of the ecological matrix within which *Homo sapiens* evolved. They were part of the psychological context in which our sense of identity as a species arose. They were part of the spiritual systems that we invented for coping. The teeth of big predators, their claws, their ferocity and their hunger, were grim realities that could be eluded but not forgotten."⁶⁴

Understandably, animals frightened people in biblical cultures as they do in all times and places. David's encounters with lions and bears (1 Sam 17:34–36) are an example of the dangers facing those in open spaces. In light of this deeply rooted terror, it is not remarkable that the biblical God is one who rules and directs these same animals, often to serve God's purposes, as we see in the Elisha and Daniel stories. The prophets also help people cope. Visions of peace like those in Isaiah (11:6–9; 65:25) and Job (5:22–23), Daniel's survival in the lions' pit (Dan 6:16–24), and the story of Jesus in the wilderness "with the wild beasts" (Mark 1:13) reinforce the image of a God who is stronger than the natural world. We see a similar pattern in the Bible regarding water. For cultures living near (and often dependent on) seas, rivers, and lakes, poetry and miracle stories that depict God's absolute mastery over the elements and otherwise unruly waters

---

62. Goldingay warns against pursuing a few interpretive rabbit trails when considering this miracle story: "There is no suggestion in vv 22–24 . . . that Daniel is exercising lordship over the animal creation in accordance with the purpose envisaged in Gen 1 and that promised in Isa 11:6–9; 65:25. Nor is there any suggestion that the animals had more sense than their master (cf. Num 22:26–33; 1 Sam 6:12) or lacked spirit (like some Ignatius speaks of, *Romans* 5). It is God's act that the story relates, not Daniel's or the lions'" (*Daniel*, 129).

63. Brownlee translates 5:17 as "famine and rabid animals," noting that wild animals present no threat to those in a walled city. These are instead "'*evil* animals' not just because they are fierce," he explains, "but because they are rabid." Ezekiel describes siege conditions in 5:5–17 and the health of the people is badly compromised. When the prophet warns that pestilence and bleeding will be epidemic, the "word does not here mean 'bloodshed,' but 'bleeding' from the anemic condition of the people who are malnourished" (*Ezekiel*, 91–92, italics original).

64. Quammen, *Monster of God*, 3.

Eden's Other Residents

(e.g., Gen 1:1–10; Job 38:8–11; Pss 65:7; 74:13; 89:9; 104:5–9; 107:23–32; Jer 5:22; 31:35; Mark 4:35–41) are comforting. In the book of Jonah, God sends a great wind that threatens sailors but also calms those same waters (1:4–16). God also provides the large fish that swallows the hapless prophet, and then later speaks to that fish, directing it to vomit Jonah back onto dry land (1:17; 2:10). God is in control of nature.

The earth speaks in the Bible too. After Cain murders Abel, his brother's blood cries out "from the ground" (Gen 4:10) in a scene involving God's interrogation of the suspect, which Norman Habel describes rather poignantly: "Yhwh reveals that there is a witness to the crime and quite pointedly asks Cain to listen. Listen! There is a voice whose testimony is to be heard! Listen! There is a voice rising from a person you cannot see! Listen! There is a voice being mediated through the very *Adamah* [fertile ground] whom you are supposed to serve."[65] It is no surprise to find animals also speaking in the Bible, so I close this chapter with a few notes on triptych narratives involving God's communication to his people through animals.

This takes many forms. Job maintains that animals, birds, plants, and fish teach those willing to listen (12:7–10). The book of Numbers presents us with a donkey that literally speaks. Animals also "speak" in other ways, as we see in the story of Jesus's so-called triumphal entry. His decision to enter Jerusalem riding a donkey (Matt 21:1–11; Mark 11:1–11; Luke 19:28–40; John 12:12–19) is a highly symbolic gesture because this particular animal, as opposed to a horse, is a symbol of peacetime.[66] Once again we find a triad formula offering a meaning-rich site of convergence as the divine one "who comes in the name of the Lord" (Matt 21:9) rides an animal in the midst of a "large crowd" of people (21:8). Matthew and John explicitly connect the identity of the animal Jesus rides to the prophet Zechariah, citing Zech 9:9 with its announcement that "your king comes to you; triumphant and victorious is he, humble and riding on a donkey, on a colt, the foal of a donkey" (cf. Matt 21:5; John 12:14–15).[67] Zechariah envisions the end of con-

---

65. Habel, *Birth*, 72.

66. See e.g., Bauckham, "Reading the Synoptic Gospels," 80–81. For a wide-ranging examination of the donkey in ancient Near Eastern societies and texts, including their various symbolic meanings, see Way, *Donkeys*, esp. chapter 2. Way focuses on the Hebrew Bible in chapter 4. See too Bulliet's chapter "Early Domesticity: My Ass and Yours" in *Hunters, Herders, and Hamburgers* (143–73) for numerous connections between humans and donkeys in history and culture.

67. Matthew's story has two animals, not one as in Zechariah, which might indicate

flict and anticipates peace among the nations. According to the logic of the Gospel story, the crowds realize the import of Jesus's actions and identify him as the peace-bringing king of Zechariah, precisely because he comes to Jerusalem on a donkey. He does not come to them on a "war horse" (cf. Zech 9:10). The donkey Jesus rides therefore "speaks" to the crowds lining the road and throwing their cloaks on the ground before the arriving king.

Jesus often mentions animals, and they are actors in his ministry (as in the story of the prodigal son—the swine the young man feeds—and the story of the demon-destroying swine). In the accounts of the triumphal entry, a literal animal functions as a "text" in itself, one the crowds must interpret. They do so correctly, according to Matthew and John, interpreting the animal in a "this is a sign of that" manner that helps them recognize in Jesus the enactment and embodiment of a particular prophetic drama (i.e., the one Zechariah describes).

In this chapter, we considered positive depictions of animals in biblical literature. They are a good part of the good world God made. They contribute meaningfully to human experience, including people's spiritual awareness, something particularly evident in triadic moments in which the presence of animals accompanies revelation. The Bible regularly reveals God's grace through other-than-human beings. Why then does killing animals figure so prominently in pre-70 CE biblical religion? To this we now turn.

---

some confusion about the Hebrew parallelism in Zech 9:9. There is no confusion in Matthew's phrase "sat on them" in 21:7, however, which does not mean Jesus sat on two animals, as some suggest. The antecedent is plausibly the cloaks placed on the donkey and its colt.

4 Revisiting Animals in Religious Ritual

THE BIGGEST KNOT TO untangle when sorting out the Bible's view of animals is sacrifice. The biblical record itself is not uniform in its presentation of this aspect of ancient Israelite religion, which complicates the matter. There are those like Job who, "blameless and upright," fearing God and turning from evil, offer regular burnt offerings (Job 1:1, 5). At the same time, there are condemnations of such rituals as practiced by some (e.g., 1 Sam 2:12–17) and in other places assertions that God does not want these offerings at all (e.g., Ps 40:6). The differing attitudes toward the practice is not remarkable in itself if we recall that the biblical story spans more than a thousand years of dramatic religious, social, and political transformation. "It would be surprising," Rogerson notes, "if a single understanding of animal sacrifice had prevailed during such a period."[1]

My interest here is neither to trace the development of sacrificial worship throughout Israel's history nor to harmonize the biblical accounts. I am not even concerned to explore the meanings of these blood offerings to any great extent. Instead, I have in mind contemporary readers of the Bible trying to make sense of this material who find the very idea of killing bulls, goats, and lambs, regardless of the reason, incomprehensible and incongruous with a high view of nonhuman sentient life. Need these writings be a source of embarrassment for animal theology, or is there a way of viewing this subject that is animal affirming? Is there anything constructive to

---

1. Rogerson, "What Was the Meaning of Animal Sacrifice?" 8.

gain for conversations about animal compassion in this part of the biblical story? I suggest that there is and that effectively erasing this material from discussion, as some do, is unfortunate.

My argument takes the following form. First, I approach the disparate voices within Scripture concerning animal sacrifice, with affirmations and condemnations appearing side by side, as indication that in the evolution of the Jewish religion God permitted but never demanded animal sacrifice. I realize this is a contentious position to take, but it seems reasonable to suggest these offerings represent a human longing to find spiritual meaning using a "vocabulary" and form of religiosity widely represented in the cultures of the ancient world. This helps us understand in part the competing visions within Scripture as some link sacrifice to deeper spiritual transformations (e.g., Ps 51:16–19), while others assert blood offerings are a nonessential part of the religious life (e.g., Jer 7:21–23).

Second, though I frame sacrifice as a human initiative, part of an aspiration to seek out ineffable spiritual realties, I maintain that (*a*) the rituals involving animals were revelatory and meaningful for those engaged in them and, as a recurring subject in Scripture, have much to teach us now.[2] God allowed the widespread practice of animal sacrifice to be part of Israel's religious life but also insisted that this form of worship conform to certain expectations that distinguished Israel from its neighbors. When Israel met those obligations for approaching God, God's presence and blessing remained with the people, and offerings were acceptable. The ideal, and what is more important than particular manifestations of faith, is a people seeking God earnestly, acting on the knowledge and understanding they have, and approaching the religious life with sincerity and (from God's perspective) genuine piety. There are occasions in the Bible when God accepts

---

2. My interest is in animal sacrifice as presented in the texts, not the historical veracity of these accounts. The two are not unambiguously aligned on all occasions. Consider, to illustrate, questions raised by Rogerson ("What Was the Meaning of Animal Sacrifice?" 16), who makes the following remarks about one specific period of Israel's history: "While the Second Temple community was small, it probably lacked the economic base to support the sacrificial programme, which, in addition, was not congenial to the villagers. By the time that the territory of Judah had expanded to provide a sufficient economic base, it included many for whom the temple was remote and rarely visited . . . it may be more accurate to describe the Priestly view of animal sacrifice not as something institutionalized but as an ideology." Regarding various shifts in attitudes within and toward religious leadership and its beliefs and practices in the period between the exile and the Maccabees, often noting socioeconomic realities, see Albertz, *History of Israelite Religion*, passim. As it is the received text we consider here, not historical reconstruction, such questions, while interesting, do not matter for the argument put forward.

worshipers who act in good faith based on what they know, even if deficient in some sense. To draw on a New Testament example, Luke refers to Paul's finding "disciples" in Ephesus who, when asked whether they received the Holy Spirit, answered, "No, we have not even heard that there is a Holy Spirit" (Acts 19:1–2). Even before receiving this more complete revelation, they were already "disciples" (cf. Acts 10:1–4, 30–48).

I also maintain (b) that the biblical record of animal sacrifice is not something animal compassion advocates need despise. Though no longer practiced in Judaism, this chapter in its illustrious story serves as canonical evidence of the sacral nature of animals. This in itself is highly significant because here more than anywhere else in the Bible we find animals central to the religious life. To illustrate, while it is true that the high priest alone enters the holy of holies, and does so only once a year on the Day of Atonement (Lev 16:3–17; cf. Heb 9:7), this is actually not the full story. Animals enter that most sacred of spaces too, and indeed, the only reason high priests are in a position to do so is that the blood of those animals makes it possible. This ought to elevate our appreciation of the status of animals in the theological thinking of ancient Israel.

Like any religious ritual or praxis, abuses and pretense marred the practice, as the prophets frequently attest.[3] However, this in itself does not indicate animal sacrifice is devoid of meaning in every instance. Instead, biblical descriptions of ideal animal sacrifice provide a way for us to think about the human-caused deaths of animals in the modern world. When God allows humans to kill animals as part of worship, it requires the worshiper to be fully cognizant of God in terms of such things as time, location, and attitude. Killing animals was a serious matter, occurring in God's presence with the specific intent of giving that animal back to its Maker. Prayer and humility characterize the act, and it occurs as part of the broader community of God's people. In this deeply respectful practice of sacrifice in its ideal form, we find indirectly the Bible's most profound and unexpected condemnation of the flippant killing of animals. In this sense, Israel's animal sacrifice is prophetic, offering a biblical measure by which we might evaluate the slaughter of animals in other times and places.

---

3. Oswalt observes that in many cases the religions surrounding Israel promised automatic propitiation and blessings without demanding changes in the worshiper's behavior. It was easy, therefore, for Israelites to think that precision in ritual actions and the type and number of offerings were sufficient warrant to do whatever they wished (*Isaiah*, 97).

Moses, Pharaoh, and an Appointment with God

In the opening chapters of Exodus, with the Israelites toiling as slaves in Egypt, God through Moses informs Pharaoh that the people must travel into the wilderness to offer sacrifice (Exod 5:3), a rather bold and ambitious idea for a subjected people to put before their master. Once the plagues commence, an annoyed and frightened Pharaoh gives Moses permission for the Israelites to offer sacrifices to their God, though he adds the caveat "within the land" (Exod 8:25). This is not good enough for Moses. For one thing, the nature of the sacrifice is offensive to Egyptians, but more important still, the sacrifice to God must be "as he commands us" (8:27). Again, Pharaoh concedes, this time allowing them to go into the wilderness as required "provided you do not go very far away" (Exod 8:28). Pharaoh's response, which imposes restrictions on the Israelites' religious expression, does not impress Moses, who calls down additional plagues on the beleaguered Egyptians and their ruler.

We then learn more details about the required sacrifice shortly before the account of Israel's exodus from the land of their slavery: "You must . . . let us have sacrifices and burnt offerings to sacrifice to the Lord our God. Our livestock also must go with us; not a hoof shall be left behind, for we must choose some of them for the worship of the Lord our God, and we will not know what to use to worship the Lord until we arrive there" (Exod 10:25–26). Worship involves the whole community of people and animals, even if only some of the livestock serve for sacrifice.

This episode illustrates succinctly a key idea regarding animal sacrifice in the Bible. Our larger topic is animal compassion in biblical perspective so the slaughter of animals as part of religious expression is counterintuitive. My concern is that the widespread references to animal sacrifice throughout the Bible, including the New Testament in its employment of sacrificial imagery to understand the meaning of Christ's death, contribute to an assumption or attitude that considers animals expendable. In fact, it is just the opposite. My focus here is not the theological meanings of blood offerings (notions of substitution, etc.), but rather what the practice reveals about the value of animals and their presence in the religious life of the people of God. When viewed this way, the diverse biblical texts that speak of the presence of animals at the very center of worship in this way reveal that irreverent or unconsidered killing of animals is an offense to God and his prophets.

Eden's Other Residents

With respect to animal sacrifice, I propose we consider briefly a series of guiding questions: *Who? What? Where? When? Why? How?* In the exodus story, we see that the death of animals is no casual activity open to negotiations with a headstrong ruler concerned to protect his interests. If we bring these guiding questions to this particular story, some preliminary perspectives on sacrifice emerge.

- *Who?* God calls the Israelites to offer sacrifice (Exod 5:3). The Egyptians are not invited.

- *What?* Israel's religious rituals, unlike those of their neighbors, are distinctive and very specific with respect to the demands placed on worshipers. The surrounding cultures offer gifts to their gods too (e.g., Judg 16:23; 1 Sam 6:4; 2 Kgs 3:27; 5:17), but Moses makes it clear that the sacrifices demanded by his God are unique, even offensive to Egyptian sensibilities (Exod 8:26). At this stage, Moses is not exactly sure what animals qualify, which explains why he rejects Pharaoh's demand that the animals remain in Egypt (Exod 10:24–26). Moses anticipates regulations clarifying what qualifies as an acceptable offering.

- *Where?* God makes it clear that geography matters, specifying exactly where the people must go to worship their God (Exod 5:1, 3). Offerings within the land of Egypt or close to it do not meet God's standards (Exod 8:25, 28). Location is an important consideration.

- *When?* Pharaoh's unwillingness to let the people go delays the fulfillment of their obligations to God and brings harsh judgments on Egypt (i.e., more plagues). Moses explains to Pharaoh that the Israelites must "go a three days' journey into the wilderness" (Exod 5:3), which is a measure of distance but also a measure of time, a recurring concept throughout laws about sacrifice elsewhere in Scripture. Time often regulates ritual: hours, days, weeks, seasons, and so on. Animal sacrifice is not haphazard in this respect.

- *Why?* Simply put, Israel offers sacrifices, Moses explains, to "celebrate a festival" to the "God of the Hebrews [who] has revealed himself to us" (Exod 5:1, 3). Sacrifice is a form of worship.

- *How?* Moses is not sure what offering animals to this newly revealed God involves, and admits as much to Pharaoh (Exod 10:26: "we will not know what to use to worship the LORD until we arrive there").

I will return to these guiding questions momentarily.

Sacrifice as Concession

Is animal sacrifice a concession, as suggested above, reflecting a stage in the religious development and understanding of God by the people? When Moses first speaks to Pharaoh, he presents God's words to him as "Let my people go, so that they may celebrate a festival to me in the wilderness" (Exod 5:1) without clarifying what the festival involves. *Notice there is no reference to animal sacrifice in this verse.* When Pharaoh refuses, Moses explains further that the God of the Hebrews "has revealed himself to us; let us go . . . to sacrifice to the LORD our God" (Exod 5:3). God demands celebration (5:1), but it is Moses who adds the agenda for that festival of celebration (5:3). Is the "sacrifice" of 5:3 part of the "Thus says the LORD" of 5:1? That gap, that silence between 5:1 and 5:3, is suggestive, perhaps indicating what *Moses understands celebration of a newly revealed god to entail*, an assumption derived from the widespread contemporary religious practices he sees all around him. Jeremiah offers some support here: "in the day that I brought your ancestors out of the land of Egypt, I did not speak to them or command them concerning burnt offerings and sacrifices. But this command I gave them, 'Obey my voice, and I will be your God'" (7:22–23). Sacrifice is something Moses assumes to be a requirement, though I suggest God still allows the people to explore their religiosity in this way, even if it is, for lack of a better term, a human initiative. Animal sacrifice is a concession from God.[4] God permits the practice and even chooses to meet the people in this form of worship, but God also controls the who, what, where, when, why, and how of the rituals, placing considerable restraints on blood offerings in the process. This worship still reveals God and, significantly for our purposes, brings together animals, the community of God's people, and the Creator of those animals and people into a profound, triadic communion.

The permission to kill animals ritually is a concession from God to those living in a less-than-ideal world. We see this elsewhere. It is analogous to the permission to eat meat in the Noahic covenant that within the context of the mythology of Genesis 1–11 stands in sharp contrast with the Creator's original intent (Gen 9:3; cf. 1:29). In both cases—meat eating and sacrifice—regulations qualify the permission. With respect to diet, humans are not to eat flesh with blood still in it (Gen 9:4), and only certain animals

---

4. According to Schwartz, Maimonides (1135–1214) "states that the biblical sacrifices were a concession to the primitive practices of the nations at the time" (*Judaism and Vegetarianism*, 8). See too 106–9.

are ritually clean and therefore suitable for food, prohibitions that limit the permissible diet considerably.[5]

The divine concession to sacrifice is also analogous to Israel's demand for a king, motivated by a desire to be like other nations (1 Sam 8:5). God reluctantly allows this, telling Samuel, "Listen to the voice of the people . . . they have rejected me from being king over them" (1 Sam 8:7; cf. Deut 17:14–20), thus countenancing their monarchy just as God countenanced a carnivorous diet after the flood, despite the plant-based diet offered in the newly created world. Another example of such concession to human shortcomings appears in legislation concerning divorce (Deut 24:1–4) as interpreted by Jesus:

> Some Pharisees came, and to test him they asked, "Is it lawful for a man to divorce his wife?" He answered them, "What did Moses command you?" They said, "Moses allowed a man to write a certificate of dismissal and to divorce her." But Jesus said to them, "Because of your hardness of heart he wrote this commandment for you. But from the beginning of creation, 'God made them male and female.' . . . Therefore what God has joined together, let no one separate" (Mark 10:2–6, 9).

As with the diet given in the Noahic covenant and the permission to have a monarchy, a sanctioned behavior (divorce; cf. Deut 24:1–4) contrasts with an ideal that God ultimately prefers (union).

If there is any merit to this view of sacrifice as concession, there are a few general observations to make. First, understanding sacrifice this way does not rule out the possibility that the triadic meeting of God (through a priest), animal, and human worshipers has value and speaks profoundly of the importance of animals in the religious life, a theme I return to below. Second, it allows us to contextualize the Bible's many criticisms of animal sacrifice (e.g., 1 Kgs 15:22; Prov 21:3; Isa 1:11–15; Hos 6:6; 8:13; Amos 5:21–25). Some failed to meet the high ritual demands of cultic regulations, a breakdown perhaps including a loss of respect for the dignity of animals. These critiques also indicate failures to fulfill other covenantal obligations. The prophets called instead for people to repent and reassess their commitment to the Creator, demonstrating faithfulness through acts of justice and prayer and genuine acts of piety. "Sacrifice and offering you do not desire . . . Burnt offering and sin offering you have not required," the psalmist writes, and against these external, ritual-based signs of religious

---

5. Webb, *On God and Dogs*, 22.

expression the poet declares, "I delight to do your will, O my God; your law is within my heart" (Ps 40:6, 8). Psalm 141 also illustrates this shift away from an emphasis on blood offerings and toward other forms of worship: "Let my prayer be counted as incense before you, and the lifting up of my hands as an evening sacrifice" (v. 2).

Various Objections to Animal Sacrifice

Before proceeding further, an important digression is in order. To discuss animal sacrifice, especially from a Christian perspective, requires caution owing to a long history of anti-Jewish prejudice linked to this facet of ancient Israel's religious life. In her fascinating study of theological folklore titled *The Singular Beast: Jews, Christians, and the Pig*, Claudine Fabre-Vassas observes that during the Middle Ages, Christian critique of Jewish animal sacrifice fuelled anti-Semitic rhetoric, with sermons and diatribes reviving and adapting the commentaries of the church fathers: "while Jews circumcise their bodies, Christians 'circumcise their hearts.' While the former sacrifice 'victims of flesh and blood,' the latter, by the New Covenant, rise to the spiritual sacrifice." In later times, Fabre-Vassas notes that kosher slaughter of animals for food was "regularly condemned and stigmatized by Christians" as well, something that intensified between the world wars. Animal protection organizations from the mid-nineteenth century to the mid-twentieth century were often particularly guilty of this, mixing racism with the pursuit of their mandates.[6]

Also challenging are modern sensitivities to the very idea of ritual slaughter. Many find the notion repugnant.[7] Such revulsion to the idea of killing animals as a religious act not only contributes to theological biases

---

6. Fabre-Vassas, *Singular Beast*, 148, 140–41.

7. I have in mind here those in the industrialized world who rarely, if ever, see animals killed for their own food, let alone those that die as part of religious or other cultural rituals. Sport hunting and fishing are an exception for some. Few, however, see what goes on inside abattoirs. The blood and violence involved in the killing of animals for any reason are obviously disturbing (which explains why PETA and other animal advocacy groups often circulate videos as part of their campaigns). As we think about the diverse cultures of the ancient Near East, it deserves notice that animal sacrifice, at least in part, served as an alternative to human sacrifice. The latter clearly terrified the prophets, who urgently warned Israel against imitating their neighbors in this respect (see e.g., Lev 18:21; Deut 18:10; 2 Kgs 3:27; 21:6; Jer 31:7). This backdrop is also pertinent when reading the Akedah, the story of the binding of Isaac, where Abraham offers a ram in place of his son (Gen 22:1–19).

but hampers efforts to understand animal sacrifice within the context of biblical literature, something true of both Jews and Christians. Klawans states the problem this way:

> The imbalanced moral disgust (that scholars often don't bother to conceal) toward sacrifice in general finds two accomplices in the religious agendas of many who set out to study sacrifice in ancient Israel in particular. Christian theology predicates itself on the idea that the self-sacrifice of God's son supersedes the presumably flawed system of ancient Israelite ritual sacrifice that preceded it . . . But religious opposition to ancient Israelite sacrifice is not distinctly Christian. It is less well known but no less significant that the movements of Judaism that advocate modernizing reforms . . . assert with an equal determination that animal sacrifice will remain a thing of the past.[8]

Schwartz illustrates the latter category by agreeing with Rabbi Yochanan Ben Zakkai, who, after the destruction of the temple, taught that prayer and good deeds now replaced temple sacrifice. Schwartz also draws on a tradition of Jewish teaching that maintains there will be no need for sacrifices during the messianic period owing to improvements in human conduct.[9]

Others, as noted, relegate sacrifice to the margins of theological significance. Hyland argues that "sacrifices and ceremonies were man-made substitutes for the true worship of God," and Phelps maintains that biblical passages referring to these rituals (e.g., Exod 29:15–18; Lev 1:5–9, 14–17; 8:22–28) describe "superstitious practices that the Israelites borrowed from the pagan religions" they encountered on their journeys.[10] I am sympathetic to the values these two writers share and their high regard for animals but wonder what we lose by turning away too soon from these texts in our search for a robust, biblically rooted perspective on animals. Nowhere else in biblical literature do we find animals so profoundly a part of religious praxis than in the sacrificial system, so to gloss over this aspect of ancient worship too quickly is misguided. What is more, there is a strategic consideration worth making. Those who write about animal ethics in relation to faith communities usually want to motivate those same communities toward advocacy and inclusion. Avoiding or denigrating or excising sec-

---

8. Klawans, "Sacrifice in Ancient Israel," 65–66. Cf. Morgan, "Sacrifice in Leviticus," 32–33, 40; Knight and Levine, *Meaning of the Bible*, 188.

9. Schwartz, *Judaism and Vegetarianism*, 107, 121.

10. Hyland, *God's Covenant with Animals*, 11; Phelps, *Dominion of Love*, 76.

tions of the Bible is problematic when dealing with those who maintain its authority as canonical Scripture.

There is no animal sacrifice in Judaism anymore, and as we have seen, at least some Jews do not expect it in future with Messiah's coming. At the same time, sacrifice is not part of Christian teaching (though its symbolism is prominent in New Testament Christology), so there is no value in attacking these rituals, as though pushing to end a brutal treatment of animals.[11] It does not happen anymore and there are plenty of other places to direct our ire and energy in defense of animals, but since the temple sacrifice ended two thousand years ago, a more constructive way forward is to contemplate what animal sacrifice reveals about the triadic animal-human-divine nature of worship in its *still present* canonical form. In doing so, I believe we have a basis to respond to those who defend killing animals, citing the sacrificial system as partial justification. We find such reasoning in, to illustrate, *The Christian Hunter's Guide to Survival*, a popular-level devotional writing that presents sport hunting as a spiritual exercise. Here we find its clergyman author appealing to Israel's blood offerings as part of a biblical rationale justifying the activity: "Whether man was killing a sacrificial animal or game that God provided in the field, it was all part of God's system."[12]

---

11. It is likely that Jewish Christians who maintained connection to the temple still participated in sacrifice (Acts 2:46; 3:1; 5:12, 21, 42; 21:17–26; note esp. the reference to sacrifice in 21:26). Of course, animal sacrifice was prevalent among pagans throughout the Roman Empire in the early Christian centuries. For descriptions, see e.g., Lane Fox, *Pagans and Christians*, 69–72, 90, 219–22.

12. Ammon, *Christian Hunter's Guide*, 62, as cited in Regan, *Defending Animal Rights*, 129. For a thorough discussion of Ammon's book, see Linzey, *Animal Theology*, 115–24. A web search reveals that Christian hunting organizations are widespread, often citing such motivations as evangelism, male bonding, or spiritual growth resulting from a "return to nature." From what I can see, there is rarely any acknowledgment that sport hunting raises ethical questions. When the websites include a rationale, the evidence on offer tends to be rather thin. The Christian Bowhunters of America, for instance, provide the following in their statement of faith: "Creation and View of Hunting: We believe God created the cosmos and the planet earth as a beautiful habitation for mankind. We believe man, God's special creation, was given dominion over the earth, to partake of, and govern all its resources wisely. We further believe that the art of hunting with the bow and arrow is a time proven means of human survival and resource management and that it is in harmony with the divine plan. Gen. 1:1–3, 9:2–3, 10:9, 27:3" (see http://www.christianbowhunters.org/StatementofFaith).

Sacrifice and the Evolution of Religious Praxis

"What to me is the multitude of your sacrifice?" God declares. "I have had enough of burnt offerings of rams and the fat of fed beasts; I do not delight in the blood of bulls, or of lambs, or of goats" (Isa 1:11). Isaiah writes that slaughtering an ox is equivalent to killing another person,[13] though it deserves notice it is not blood sacrifice alone that comes under such scrutiny; plant-based offerings are likened to idolatry at the same time (Isa 66:3). There is a larger critique of Israel's cultic life at play here, and it is not necessarily animal sacrifice specifically that is the target of the prophets' ire here and elsewhere.

It seems likely that in many such criticisms of blood offerings it is breaches of cultic protocol (i.e., not performing these rituals according to God's instructions and with appropriate humility and reverence) that is at issue more than the act itself. This is certainly the issue troubling Malachi: "'How have we despised your name?' By offering polluted food on my altar . . . When you offer blind animals in sacrifice, is that not wrong? And when you offer those that are lame or sick, is that not wrong?" (1:7–8). Postexilic Judaism was very diverse and far from uniform in its assessment of the temple and its priesthood. Groups such as the Essenes living near the shores of the Dead Sea illustrate the ability of sectarians to redefine their religious life without close association with the temple and its sacrifices.[14] It is too simplistic, however, to conclude that a shift away from animal sacrifice is specifically an act of resistance to the violence inherent to the practice, as some do.[15]

---

13. On the unjustified killing of animals as murder, cf. Barth, *Church Dogmatics*, III/4, 355.

14. It appears the Qumran sectarians understood animal sacrifice in itself as ineffectual unless accompanied by prayer (Wise et al., *Dead Sea Scrolls*, 126). Important evidence in this regard is 1QS 9:4–5: "They shall atone for the guilt of transgression and the rebellion of sin, becoming an acceptable sacrifice for the land through the flesh of burnt offerings, the fat of sacrificial portions, and prayer, becoming—as it were—justice itself, a sweet savor of righteousness and blameless behavior, a pleasing freewill offering" (cf. 3:11). Whether they actually engaged in animal sacrifice is unclear. Some believe the animal bones found at the site are the remains of meals, not evidence of offerings (e.g., VanderKam, *Dead Sea Scrolls*, 116–17).

15. As Schwartz puts it, animal sacrifices "were not the primary concern of God. As a matter of fact, they could be an abomination to God if not carried out together with deeds of loving kindness and justice" (*Judaism and Vegetarianism*, 108). Similarly, Wirzba notes, "Sacrifice is readily turned into a tool that degrades creatures and oppresses people when self-assertion is confused for self-offering. This is why the prophets

Some texts of the Second Temple period reflect a trend away from blood sacrifice in favor of new emphases like prayer and almsgiving, and for Christians, of course, the efficacy of Christ's sacrifice provided the theological basis to cease the practice, a theme treated most thoroughly in the New Testament by the author of Hebrews.[16] Again, looking at this issue from the vantage point of Christian faith requires caution. Overemphasis on prophetic critiques of sacrifice (e.g., Isa 1:11-17; 66:3; Hos 6:6; 8:11-13; Amos 5:21-24; Mic 6:6-8; Jer 7:3-7, 20-25; cf. Prov 21:3: "To do righteousness and justice is more acceptable to the LORD than sacrifice") is one concern, easily giving the impression that all cultic ritual and sacrifice is meaningless or (for some animal advocates) immoral. Add to this the New Testament teachings about the efficacy of Christ's death that makes animal sacrifice redundant (e.g., Heb 10:4, 10: "it is impossible for the blood of bulls and goats to take away sins") and together these two themes combine to generate a deep prejudice against the practice. This line of thought involves overstatement. Joseph and Mary do not appear to be evil people because they offered animals according to the law (Luke 2:22-24).

The first canonical reference to the death of an animal on a human's behalf is Gen 3:21 where we read that God made clothing for Adam and Eve out of skins. Throughout the prehistory of Genesis 1-11, including the stories of Abel (4:4) and Noah (8:20-21), and the later stories of Israel's patriarchs (e.g., Gen 15:7-17; 22:13-14), we read about animal offerings. Later, the consumption of a lamb and the spreading of blood on the doorposts in each household are central to the events of the exodus (Exod 12:3-13), and to commemorations of that occasion in perpetuity (Exod 12:14; Lev 23:5; Num 9:1-5; Deut 16:1; *m. Pesaḥ* 9:5: "the Passover observed by succeeding generations"). Eventually, with the construction of the tabernacle and temple, along with the establishment of the Aaronic priesthood, animal sacrifice becomes an institutionalized and regulated part of Israel's religious

---

railed against those who used sacrifice to improve their own standing. They directed attention to the incongruity in people who promote or demand sacrifice *without offering themselves* at the same time" (*Food and Faith*, 122, italics original).

16. See e.g., Lamp, *Greening of Hebrews*, 22. His chapter "What's with Cutting Up All Those Animals?" is a helpful overview of the christological critique of animal sacrifice in Hebrews, esp. 9:11—10:18. Christ's death means animal sacrifice is no longer necessary for the author of Hebrews. About this, Lamp writes, "The sacrifice of Christ . . . secures the benefits of forgiveness of sins and a perfected conscience for human beings. However, the animals may well note that by virtue of Christ's sacrifice, the blood sacrifices of animals are no longer necessary. In effect, those animals whose blood would have been required to perpetuate the sacrificial cult have had their lives spared by Christ" (30).

life (see esp. Leviticus 1–7). Sacrifice is a subject addressed by some of the prophets and is also an issue of concern during reconstruction efforts in the postexilic period (e.g., Ezra 3:1–6; 6:16–22; 8:35–36).

The Bible, therefore, reflects the evolution of religious thinking over many centuries and the literary records themselves involve layers of tradition redacted over a long period of time. This means that sacrifice as described in some parts of the Bible does not resemble the practice as it appears elsewhere. For instance, the occasions and places of sacrifice during the patriarchal period often occurs at the discretion of the worshiper, as appears to be the case with Israel/Jacob who offers sacrifices before his journey to Egypt in search of his son (Gen 45:28—46:1), presumably as a way of seeking God's favor for the undertaking. Later on, there are restrictions on the times of sacrifice and its location (usually in the tabernacle or temple). For most Jews, Jerusalem would become the only legitimate place for blood offerings.[17] There were daily (Exod 29:38–43), weekly (Num 28:10), monthly (e.g., Num 28:11–15), as well as seasonal offerings, and yearly festivals. Jews occasionally offered sacrifices on behalf of pagan rulers,[18] and at other times they were part of celebrations marking special occasions (e.g., the dedication of the temple [1 Kgs 8:62–64]).

Also important to note is that the biblical texts do not necessarily originate in the period of history they describe. Stories appearing early in the narrative chronology of Israel's history and/or early in the canonical arrangement are often quite late in terms of composition history. Much of the Priestly material in the Old Testament, including the first creation story (Gen 1:1—2:4) and much of the literature concerned with cultic and ritual activities likely derives from, or involves editorial activity occurring during the exilic and postexilic periods (ca. 550 BCE and later), even though it may include earlier sources. This opens up the possibility that writers represent the past in an idealized or critical manner as a form of commentary on present conditions (i.e., their own time, the time of writing).

The details of sacrificial legislation outlined in various parts of the Scriptures are complex. For the purpose of this short consideration, there are aspects of the practice I highlight because it serves my principal purpose, which is to argue that the ritual killing of animals in ancient Israel,

17. See e.g., Hurtado, *Origins*, 19, 30. Regarding notions of sacred spaces/places, see too 19–21 (regarding the Roman world) and 36.

18. E.g., Ezra 6:10; 1 Macc 7:33; Josephus *Ag. Ap.* 2.6.77. "From the time of the old Persian empire sacrifices were offered at the temple in Jerusalem on behalf of the reigning king as a token of Jewish loyalty" (Goldstein, *I Maccabees*, 340).

Revisiting Animals in Religious Ritual

or more widely in other religious traditions, is unlike the killing and consumption of animals in our day. Said differently, just because the Bible documents a period of Judaism's history during which sacrifice was central to its religious expression does not mean we have a license to kill indiscriminately now. Biblical sacrifice is profoundly unlike modern behaviors like sport hunting, research in laboratories, and industrial farming, and we must be careful not to read about blood offerings and assume it indicates that animal life is expendable and only instrumental in its value.

Guiding Questions

With respect to sacrifice, Torah describes various conditions that must apply, that effectively place strict limits on the practice. To return to our earlier questions, I offer here a few notes on animal sacrifice considering *Who? What? Where? When? Why?* and *How?* as a way to tease out a few pertinent themes illustrating how this aspect of biblical religion shows high esteem for animals among the ancient community of faith, which in turn encourages modern readers of the Bible to find in these bygone activities a much-needed esteem for nonhuman creation.

Who?

The actual performance of animal sacrifice is sometimes a private or family matter (as with Passover; see e.g., 1 Sam 20:6) but typically involves priests, selected by God to mediate on behalf of worshipers. In Lev 17:1–5, Moses warns that if anyone slaughters an ox or lamb or goat but does not bring it to the tent of meeting as an offering, "he shall be held guilty of bloodshed" (Lev 17:3–4). Not only do the priests have a role to play in the ritual death of the animal (v. 6), this legislation also serves to keep people from worshiping false gods (v. 7). These verses help us appreciate the seriousness of animal sacrifice, at least as presented in this context. Torah regulates the killing of animals and it is only permissible in particular situations involving an appropriate place, here the "tent of meeting," and as part of the worshiping community in the presence of the priests, who mediate between God and the people. Furthermore, the very fact that God (through Moses [v. 1]) speaks these words involves a refusal to permit a breaking of the sacred tripartite convergence of animal, human, and the divine. In its ideal form,

Eden's Other Residents

the tabernacle/temple is the place where God dwells, and the priesthood mediates between that God and the people.

What?

Leviticus insists on the participation of the worshiper with the animals involved ("you shall bring" and equivalents, as in Lev 4:32; i.e., it is the worshiper who brings/supplies the animal). Deuteronomy 12:15–28 distinguishes wild animals (gazelle, deer) from those of "your herd or your flock" suitable for offerings, which links the idea of personal property to sacrifice. Fish and wild animals do not qualify for sacrifice because the worshiper does not own them.[19] They already belong to God. An incident involving David illustrates the importance of this principle of costly sacrifice. When the king builds an altar to avert a plague, he insists on buying the threshing floor and the oxen used for the burnt offering despite the generosity of Araunah who wants to give them to David: "the king said to Araunah, 'No, but I will buy them from you for a price; I will not offer burnt offerings to the Lord my God that cost me nothing'" (2 Sam 24:24). Highlighting the significance of this principle, which says much about the sincerity of the one presenting these animals, the author adds that God approved and responded to David's prayer (2 Sam 24:25).

Where?

Space is meaningful in the religious worldview depicted in the Hebrew Bible. Consider the instructions to face the temple for prayer, or repeated references to land (promise of, exile from, return to) in so much biblical discourse. For many contemporary Bible readers, notions of sacred space have all but vanished, replacing forms of worship engaging all the senses for a largely internalized and individualized spirituality. As a result, it is difficult to comprehend how profoundly religious experience attaches to physical places in biblical religion. The careful organization of the tabernacle and temple and various prohibitions and regulations regarding the worshipers' approach helps us appreciate the sense of sacred space. There are prescribed behaviors for most animal sacrifices, which includes regulating location, and there are dire consequences for breaches in protocol.

---

19. On this point, see e.g., Klawans, *Purity, Sacrifice and the Temple*, 85.

When Jerusalem's temple fell to the Romans in 70 CE, sacrifice ended, which gives some indication of this respect for spatial and geographical dimensions of religious rites. According to Deuteronomy, God restricted sacrifice to "the place that the LORD will choose," and only there "you shall offer your burnt-offerings" (12:13–14). Before its destruction, the temple represented the symbolic and geographical center of Judaism's religious life and their view of the world more broadly. Worshipers faced the city and its temple to pray. Solomon asks that God "heed the prayer that your servant prays toward this place" (2 Chr 6:20; cf. 6:32), and Daniel illustrates this practice, praying near a window in an upper room facing Jerusalem three times a day (Dan 6:10). Restrictions on the location of sacrifice and appreciation for holy sites mean pilgrimage was part of Israel's religious life after the establishment of the temple (Deut 12:5–6: "You shall go there, bringing there your burnt offerings"; cf. Deut 12:20–22). The sense of a geographical focus of worship is further evident in the language of the second century CE Mishnah: "The land of Israel is holier than all lands . . . Within the wall [of Jerusalem] is more holy than [other cities] . . . The Temple mount is more holy than it" etc. (*m. Kelim* 1:6–9).

When?

There are glimpses of the centrality of Jerusalem and its temple for Jewish worship in the New Testament, linked particularly with the time-sensitive rhythms of religious life. Luke writes of devout Jews from all nations converging on Jerusalem (Acts 2:5; cf. 8:27), and pilgrimage and worship at the temple during regular festivals involved animal sacrifice. The holy family itself worshiped in this way, connecting time, place, and sacrifice: "When the time came for their purification according to the law of Moses, they [Mary and Joseph] brought him [the infant Jesus] up to Jerusalem . . . and they offered a sacrifice according to what is stated in the law of the Lord, 'a pair of turtledoves or two young pigeons'" (Luke 2:22, 24; cf. Lev 12:8). Like Luke's birth narrative, which links Jesus to the animal world through his presence in the manger (Luke 2:7) and the witness of area shepherds (Luke 2:8–20), his parents' participation in this aspect of temple worship, though brief, signals his connection to animals through ritual (cf. the holy family's participation in Passover celebrations in Jerusalem [Luke 2:41–42]).[20]

20. His later cleansing of the temple (Luke 19:45) involved a temporary disruption of activities associated with the sacrificial cult. This action is symbolic. Turning over

Notions of sacred time originate with Sabbath (cf. Gen 2:2–3) but they regulate other areas of life too. It is evident in Judith's behavior in prostrating herself and putting ashes on her head at the very time when priests offer incense in the house of God in Jerusalem (Jdt 9:1).[21] Josephus writes of the priests who during the Roman siege of Jerusalem "were not at all hindered from their sacred ministrations, by their fear during the siege, but did still twice each day, in the morning and about the ninth hour, offer their sacrifices on the altar" (*Ant.* 14.4.3). Animal sacrifice incorporates this sense of sacred time. The regular activities in the temple included daily sacrifice of two male lambs accompanied by recitation of the Shema and the Ten Commandments (Exod 29:38–46; Num 28:1–8; cf. *m. Tamid* 4:1—5:1). Priests burned incense as part of this practice (Exod 30:7–8; Jdt 9:1; Luke 1:8–11), which is symbolic of prayer (see e.g., Luke 1:8–10).

Why?

If we allow that Israel's sacrificial system is a concession to those seeking to approach and understand God, the simplest answer to this question from the worshipers' perspective is spiritual longing, and indeed we find this sentiment in many passages. Furthermore, if we allow that Israel's sacrificial system is a concession to those seeking to approach and understand God, it follows that God chooses for the ritual to be revelatory. As seen, sacrifice and offerings are part of the rhythms of personal and community life so the spectrum of occasions involving sacrifice ranges from private matters like giving birth (Lev 12:6–8) to public events like the celebration of the ark's arrival to Jerusalem (2 Sam 6:12–13). Some sacrifices occurred regularly, as during the Day of Atonement (Leviticus 16), and others were less predicable, as with offerings made before battles (1 Sam 13:8–10), times of national penitence (Judg 20:26; 1 Sam 7:1–11), or at the dedication of the temple (1 Kgs 8:5). In these cases,

---

the tables of the moneychangers (Mark 11:15) anticipates the overturning of the temple and the activities associated with it a generation later, when the Romans under Titus destroyed the city in 70 CE.

21. For other references to regular prayer, see e.g., Ps 55:18; 119:164; Dan 6:11–16. For prayers coinciding with offerings, see e.g., Exod 29:38–39; 1 Chr 23:30; Ezra 9:5; Ps 141:2; Dan 9:21; Acts 3:1; 10:3, 30; cf. 1QS 10:1–3: "[With pray]er shall he bless Him at the times ordained of God: when light begins its dominion—each time it returns—and when, as ordained, it is regathered into its dwelling place; when night begins its watches—as He opens His storehouse and spreads darkness over the earth—and when it cycles back, withdrawing before the light" etc.

the offerings are an invitation to God to meet the people and to look favorably on them in times of celebration, crisis, or mourning. The frequency and regularity of many of these rituals serves to remind the worshipers constantly that they are the people of the one true God.

How?

For those worshipers offering animal sacrifice, obedience is costly. Though in some cases the worshiper consumes the meat, the general pattern involves giving to God the whole animal, something with economic value. There are accommodations for those with fewer resources (Lev 5:11–13), but this provision calls attention to the dynamics of animal sacrifice, namely that it is not an exercise in the indiscriminate, impersonal killing of an animal. It is a religious benefit the worshiper seeks, as opposed to food, sport, entertainment, or knowledge, the reasons for the vast majority of human-caused animal deaths today. For the ancients, an animal is a gift given to God out of one's own resources, an acknowledgment of one's dependence on God's grace and a ritual intended to maintain one's proper status before God and the community of God's people.

No sacrificial rite is effective in the case of deliberate sin (Num 15:30). This is a safeguard against frivolous offerings or hypocrisy, though despite the complex regulations outlining its practice, it is clear that irreverence occurred frequently (cf. e.g., Amos 5:21–24; Isa 1:10–17). All forms of sacrifice require an acceptable attitude (Philo *Spec. Laws* 1:53; cf. Matt 5:23–24). Killing animals, even in circumstances involving a desperate need for food, is a serious matter as 1 Sam 14:31–35 demonstrates. King Saul receives a report that troops are "sinning" because of a lack of attention to religious sensitivities and ritual procedures. They slaughter the animals "on the ground," which is to say apart from proper ritual procedures, and they eat the meat "with the blood" (1 Sam 14:32). According to Lev 17:11, "the life of the flesh is in the blood" and, God says, "I have given it to you for making atonement for your lives on the altar; for, as life, it is the blood that makes atonement." At its simplest, this statement concerning the blood speaks of the high value God places on all living things.

Saul reprimands the soldiers for eating meat with blood still in it and then proceeds to build an altar for the slaughter of more animals. The latter is not necessarily a sign of his piety; in the wider context, we read that the fast imposed on the soldiers stemmed from a "very rash act" by Saul (1 Sam

14:24) so the author does not view him as a model of propriety. The point remains, however, that 1 Samuel views the soldiers' behavior in killing sheep, oxen, and calves as unlawful. The author stresses the fast imposed on the soldiers and their subsequent hunger ("the troops were very faint" [1 Sam 14:31]), which results in killing animals merely to satisfy human appetites without consideration of the gravity of the act. God has no place in the soldiers' actions, so it is a human-animal connection devoid of a sacred presence. The triad is broken.

Sacrifice and Reverence for Animals

In the worldview of Leviticus, animals are members of the community and as such are not merely disinterested victims. They are among the "inhabitants of the land" (Lev 18:27) and as part of the community would suffer were God to leave the sanctuary/land/earth (see e.g., Lev 18:24–28; 26:19–33; cf. Ezek 8:12 and 9:9: "the Lord has forsaken the land"). Furthermore, it is "only by virtue of being a member of the (covenant) community that desires the presence of God and would suffer from its withdrawal, but *not* a member of the community of (immediate) culpability for sin that the animal can play this vital role. Therefore, far from being a poor substitute, the sacrificed animal is a holy thing that performs a role on behalf of humans which they could not and could never perform for themselves."[22] Again, though the logic and practice seems foreign to modern readers, looking at the biblical material on sacrifice in this light demonstrates a profound respect and elevated status for animals. The one approaching the altar is aware the offered animal originates in the creative acts of God, still belongs to God, and returns to God.[23] The animals sacrificed are innocent of corruption. Morgan suggests that "rather than being a cruel, wasteful practice emanating from the logic of human domination, animal sacrifice can be seen to function in priestly thought as an act of humility, deriving from a keen sense of human perpetuation of, and culpability for, violence and corruption. In the light of this, I also question traditional assumptions regarding the substitutionary function, passivity and victimhood of the sacrificial animal."[24]

---

22. Morgan, "Sacrifice in Leviticus," 40, 42 (emphasis original).
23. Moritz, "Animals and the Image of God," 137.
24. Morgan, "Sacrifice in Leviticus," 42, 33.

Concluding Thoughts

This short survey only scratches the surface of an extremely challenging subject within religious and biblical ethics. I end by stressing again the need for caution in blanket condemnations and criticisms of ritual animal killing in the Bible. Like any ritual, it is open to abuses, and such abuses clearly occurred, as evident from the actions of Eli's priestly sons who consumed sacrificial meat with an apparent disconnect to the profound sacredness of the animals and rituals involved: "the sons of Eli were scoundrels; they had no regard for the LORD or for the duties of the priests to the people." They apparently consumed more than was their proper share and "treated the offerings of the LORD with contempt" (1 Sam 2:12, 17). Perhaps the description of Eli as "heavy" (1 Sam 4:18) indicates he committed similar offenses.

The critiques of animal sacrifice in the prophets and elsewhere confront those of us who recognize the Bible's authority with pressing ethical questions. The ritual killing of animals, at least as ideally presented in texts defining it, restricts the practice to sacred times and spaces, involves the sincere longing of the penitent worshiper, and demonstrates a cognizance of a mystical communion between humanity, animals, and the divine. Such reverent treatment and high esteem of animal life rarely occurs in contemporary religious life. Too easily Christian readers pass over the cultic material in Torah as though it has nothing to contribute to Christian thought and doctrine. Those same readers may also subtly dismiss any consideration of animal ethics as a Christian obligation *a priori* based on "all that sacrifice stuff" that occurred in the past. Since God permitted the killing of animals then, it must be morally neutral now. The problem is that there is no basis for the comparison when putting the altars of ancient Israel (with its relatively few animal sacrifices) alongside laboratories and the killing floors of the modern abattoir where millions of animals endure horrific sufferings and premature deaths.

Ultimately we are in no position to evaluate the motives of religious ritual, then or now. Hypocrisy is always a possibility in public expressions of piety, and clearly, as we see in 1 Samuel and elsewhere, the sacrificial system involved abuses. However, it is also likely that for many people, this practice represented a profound (triadic) harmony between God, the people of God, and the world God made. Yes, there was violence involved, but there is violence in our world too, though often hidden away in the clandestine activities of illegal poaching, or behind the locked doors of research laboratories, or in the machine-driven abattoirs of the modern food industry. We might not understand it but the sacrifice of animals in ancient Israel shows high esteem

Eden's Other Residents

for the animals in question. They are innocent in a world where humans are not, and so their blood is efficacious. They enter sacred spaces (altars, tabernacle, temple) where humans—save the priests—do not/cannot go. They die surrounded by prayer, worship, and deep respect. And most profound of all, God recognizes their death. The odor of offerings rises to heaven and pleases the Lord (Lev 1:9, 13, 17). God is as near to the death of these sacrificed animals as each falling sparrow (Matt 10:29).

It is admittedly difficult to see past ritual killing as a mere act of violence. Quite naturally, we puzzle over why God makes "good" animals only to find pleasure in their destruction (Gen 8:21; Lev 1:9, 13, 17). It makes no sense to imagine God taking pleasure in the death of an animal. But maybe there is no destruction of the animal? The institution of animal sacrifice means giving back to God something valuable to the worshiper, an animal without blemish (Lev 1:1–3). The worshiper gives back part of creation to the Creator. The emphasis falls on that act of giving and receiving, not the death of the creature, as many suppose. If there is nothing left but blood, smoke, and ashes, what "transaction" (for lack of a better word) actually occurs? What does God actually receive from the worshiper?

What if the offering of an animal for the ancient Israelites was just that, the giving of an animal to God that God in turn receives? Eugene Masure insists it is not the destruction of the animal that gives the practice meaning but the gesture of returning the animal to God: "the return of the creature to him who has made it for himself so that it may find its end and therefore its happiness in him and for his glory . . . Sacrifice is the movement or action by which we try to bring ourselves to God, our end, to find our true beatitude in our union with him. To sacrifice a thing is to lead it to its end."[25] Linzey adds that "the tradition of sacrifice is best seen as the freeing of animal life to be with God, an acknowledgment that it (as with all creatures) belongs not to humans but to God and that God is able to accept and transform its life."[26] Linzey adds that following the animal sacrifice of Gen 8:20, God affirms the value of human and animal life, promising never again to destroy all living creatures (8:21). Animal sacrifice does not indicate a low value placed on animals but rather the reverse. For Christians, this is a familiar idea because in Christ's death we see the higher sacrificed for the lower.[27]

---

25. As cited in Linzey, *Animal Theology*, 104; cf. Webb, *On God and Dogs*, 151–52. For a summary of key themes in Masure's 1943 book *The Christian Sacrifice*, see too Wirzba, *Food and Faith*, 122 n. 28.

26. Linzey, *Animal Theology*, 105.

27. Ibid., 103–5.

5   Responding to the Groaning Creation

THE NINETEENTH-CENTURY AMERICAN POET Oliver Wendell Holmes Sr. poses some questions considered in the present chapter.

> Is there not something in the pleading eyes
> Of the poor brute that suffers, which arraigns
> The law that bids it suffer? Has it not
> A claim for some remembrance in the book,
> That fills its pages with the idle words
> Spoken of man? Or is it only clay,
> Bleeding and aching in the potter's hand,
> Yet all his own to treat it as he will,
> And when he will to cast it at his feet,
> Shattered, dishonoured, lost for evermore?
> My dog loves me, but could he look beyond
> His earthly master, would his love extend
> To Him who—hush! I will not doubt that He
> Is better than our fears, and will not wrong
> The least, the meanest of created things.[1]

Holmes speculates whether it is right to consider an animal mere clay, vulnerable to the manipulation of its "earthly" master. The fate of clay is determined by the "potter's hand." Is this potter free to treat the clay/animal any way he chooses, or is there another, higher claim on those creatures than those earthly masters? Holmes uses the lower case for the term "potter's

---

1. I take this excerpt from Leonard, ed., *Dog in British Poetry*, 272–73.

hand," which contrasts with the capitalized "To Him," a clear reference to God. The lower case indicates a human/earthly master/potter with authority over an animal, such as a pet cat or workhorse, and the poet wonders about the relationship between them. Is that relationship merely an amoral one that leaves the potter free to impose his will on a "bleeding and aching" beast without consideration for its suffering?

The image of the clay manipulated by the potter is in fact a biblical one. In Jer 18:1–11 it refers to God chastising and refashioning the people of Israel. Paul uses it in a similar manner (Rom 9:19–24). However, Holmes's use of this biblical language to indicate a beast suffering by a man's hand is ironic. The prophet Jeremiah and the Apostle Paul introduce the metaphor to depict moral failures among the people of God. But human ill treatment of animals ("his own to treat it as he will") is never properly characterized as an effort to improve an animal's moral standing. Animals do things people do not like but these are not moral failings. The natural world is not fallen in any sense, like the children of Adam and Eve.[2] God curses the ground in response to human disobedience (Gen 3:17) but that is punishment on them, not the innocent land itself. (Later, God promises never to repeat this [8:21]).[3] For better or worse, the fate of everything that lives is linked to the fate of the earth; animals suffer because of human actions but they also anticipate eschatological release from this condition, according to Paul (Rom 8:18–23).[4]

Holmes further develops this contrast between human potters/masters and the divine when speculating about his dog's capacity to love "Him," God, a thought the poet is unable to articulate fully—"would his love extend / To Him who—hush!"—for fear it appears an outrageous notion, perhaps irreverent, flippant, or even blasphemous. It need not. We

---

2. This raises questions for traditional theological thinking that tends to link human suffering to moral failure. As C. S. Lewis puts it, "the Christian explanation of human pain cannot be extended to animal pain" because "so far as we know beasts are incapable either of sin or virtue: therefore they can neither deserve pain nor be improved by it" (*Problem of Pain*, in *Complete C. S. Lewis*, 628; see full comments 628–37). Linzey discusses Lewis's views on animals and their suffering in "C. S. Lewis's Theology of Animals" (on the remark by Lewis just cited, see p. 62). On the challenges of contemplating animal suffering in light of the Christian doctrine of the fall, see too Southgate, *Groaning of Creation*, 28–35 and throughout.

3. Cf. Habel, *Rainbow of Mysteries*, 84.

4. See *Jub.* 5:27–30 for the curious idea that in Eden animals possessed speech. With the fall of Adam and Eve, God not only sent animals out of the garden along with the first humans but also took their capacity to speak.

find animals actively calling out to God in the Scriptures. Lions roar and young ravens cry out, seeking their food from God (Ps 104:21; 147:9). At times this is a language of prayer, as we see in the throne room described by John the Seer where the four living creatures, representatives of all sentient beings, sing, "Holy, holy, holy, the Lord God the Almighty, who was and is and is to come" (Rev 4:8; discussed below).

Holmes's poem moves toward an exercise of faith. The poet trusts the maker of animals to do right, which in the poem indicates a form of remembrance and an assurance that suffering does not go unnoticed. Perhaps Holmes finds a basis for this sentiment in God's awareness of fallen sparrows (Matt 10:29), an enormous comfort for anyone disturbed by the plight of suffering animals.

The present chapter examines similar themes. It argues that indifference to animal suffering, particularly suffering we inflict, is an ethical matter those who take biblical literature seriously need to face. We are all in various ways "potters," consciously or not, who determine the fate of "poor brutes," whether we keep animals as pets, eat them, use them for entertainment and sport, wear their skin as clothing, benefit from their torments in biomedical research, contribute to the pollution that damages their habitats, or benefit economically in regions where industrial farming is a major employer and exporter. I consider here a simple idea, namely that animal existence is an existence within the presence of God. Throughout the Bible we find assurances that God is immanent, always near, always present to the people of God: "Where can I go from your spirit? Or where can I flee from your presence?" (Ps 139:7). The same is true of animal creation, something that introduces a theological dimension to animal existence. They too exist constantly within the presence of their maker. This ought to give pause for earthly masters who assume the bleeding and aching of brute creation is of no concern or moral relevance to them. If all animals live and die in the very presence of God, it is difficult to characterize their ill treatment as amoral and inconsequential.

Four Living Creatures

The Lord instructs John the Seer to write down what he sees for delivery to seven churches in western Asia Minor (1:11). John dutifully does so, opening his spectacular visions with seven letters from Christ himself (2:1—3:22). Immediately afterward, John sees an open door in heaven and

Eden's Other Residents

hears a voice calling him up so he can learn what is to come (4:1). John finds himself standing in the throne room of God (4:2–3), seeing the one sitting on the throne looking like "jasper and carnelian" (4:3). The one on the throne is not alone. Twenty-four elders dressed in white with crowns on their heads surround it (4:4), and in addition to that distinguished group, "on each side of the throne, are four living creatures, full of eyes in front and behind" (4:6). These are very unusual creatures. One resembles a lion, another an ox. The third has "a face like a human face," and the fourth is like an eagle. Each has six wings with "eyes all around and inside," and they sing without ceasing: "Holy, holy, holy, the Lord God the Almighty, who was and is and is to come" (4:6–8).

As we consider the scene, it helps to distinguish what the creatures *are* from what they *represent* and *do*. John certainly draws here on Ezekiel's vision of "four living creatures" (Ezek 1:5–28) as well as various noncanonical apocalyptic traditions such as those reflected in *1 Enoch*. With respect to their song, the words of the seraphim in Isa 6:2–3 are clearly in view: "Holy, holy, holy is the Lord of hosts; the whole earth is full of his glory." In Ezekiel and Revelation, the four living creatures are angels, cherubim protecting the throne of God, an image concretized in the architecture of ancient Israel's tabernacle (Exod 25:18–20) and temple (1 Kgs 6:23–28).

If that is what they *are*, what they *represent* is particularly pertinent for our purposes here. The similes used to describe these cherubim offer clues: one like a lion, which is chief among wild animals; one like an ox, the most powerful of domesticated animals; one like a man, who has dominion over all creatures (cf. Gen 1:26; cf. Sir 17:2–4; Wis 9:2–3) though being derived from dust (2:7, 19) on the sixth day with other animals (Gen 1:24–28), and like them given the breath of life (Gen 1:30; 2:7; 7:15, 21–22; cf. Job 12:10); and one like an eagle that rules the skies. This imagery suggests that the four living creatures represent the totality of sentient creation in all its diversity.[5] This use of a spectrum of animal types resembles the creation story that uses sweeping categories to encompass the whole. The authors behind Genesis refer to all creatures of the water, sky, and land, including

---

5. According to Harrington, they are "the four angels responsible for directing the physical world; therefore they symbolize the whole created cosmos" (*Revelation*, 80). For similar numerical symbolism with reference to animals cf. Bauckham's interesting observation that the inclusion of seven specific species in Psalm 104 is possibly deliberate, with these identified animals "representative of the whole" (*Bible and Ecology*, 69). Seven, like four, suggests completeness, as in the six days of creation followed by the seventh day Sabbath rest.

Responding to the Groaning Creation

both domestic and wild animals, as well as humans (Gen 1:20–28). Similarly, John's throne room scene with its living creatures depicts all sentient life submissive and joyous in the presence of the one sitting on the throne.[6]

There are four living creatures, and as elsewhere in Revelation, the number is significant. The number four often represents totality, as it does in Rev 7:1 where we read about four angels standing at the four corners of the earth holding back the four winds, which betrays "a mythically conceived flat earth (cf. Isa 11:12; Ezek 7:2); the entire world is under their regulatory purview."[7] In Rev 20:8, we again find the familiar expression "the four corners of the earth" as a roundabout way to represent totality.

What the creatures *do* is not at all ambiguous. They exist to worship the one sitting on the throne. "The ceaseless worship of the four living creatures," Hughes notes with reference to Rev 4:8, "does not imply that this worship is their sole activity, but rather that it is their constant disposition; their every action is an expression of adoration; praise is ever on their lips."[8] This is quite evident in John's descriptions of these four living creatures:

> whenever the living creatures give glory . . . the twenty-four elders fall before the one who is seated on the throne (4:9–10)

> the four living creatures and the twenty-four elders fell before the Lamb (5:8; cf. 5:11, 14; 7:11)

> the twenty-four elders and the four living creatures fell down and worshiped God (19:4)

Notice in each case the four living creatures appear in tandem with the twenty-four elders. This is an illuminating detail because the twenty-four elders are human in form and distinguished from other angels and the four

6. It is helpful to consider the worship depicted in Revelation 4–5 as a kind of cosmic map. "The most detailed attention is focused on the activity around God's throne," explains David A. deSilva, but significantly, "John's readers find themselves located in the picture as well, among the creatures 'on earth' (5:13)." John's vision therefore "articulate[s] a model *of* a well-ordered cosmos in which all created beings in every region of the map turn toward this one center—the throne of God and of the Lamb—to offer their grateful adoration. In doing so, they also articulate a model *for* the orientation of the congregations in the seven churches, whose setting presents them with several options for where to turn their attention and offer grateful adoration" (*Seeing Things John's Way*, 97–98, italics original).

7. Blount, *Revelation*, 141.

8. Hughes, *Revelation*, 75. Cf. Harrington: "The whole creation, animate and inanimate, hymns the Creator" (*Revelation*, 82).

living creatures in 5:11.[9] The number twenty-four may allude to the divisions of the priestly descendants of Aaron described in 1 Chr 24:1–19 or perhaps combines the number of patriarchs with the number of apostles, symbolically representing the totality of the faithful in a way analogous to Rev 21:12–14, which refers to "the twelve tribes" plus "the twelve apostles." According to Rev 1:6, Jesus Christ has "made us to be a kingdom, priests serving [Christ's] God and Father, to him be glory and dominion forever and ever. Amen." The twenty-four elders reflect this status. They sit on thrones and wear crowns (and hence "a kingdom"), and throughout the book, the elders have a cultic function,[10] as in 4:9–10; 5:8–11; 11:16–18; 19:4 (and so they are "priests"). Their final words are "Amen. Hallelujah!" which recalls the celebratory language that opens the book (19:4 cf. 1:6).

What John presents us in this remarkable throne room scene, with its mysterious coupling of living creatures and elders, is the Bible's most vivid depiction of "humans" and "animals" celebrating and worshiping together in complete unity. All living things, symbolized by these angelic representatives, sing and worship together, kneeling before the Creator God.

Viewed this way, John's Apocalypse invites Christian readers to understand their worship of the Creator as part of a larger collective response. We lend our voice to a greater whole, singing alongside all life on the planet. In some mysterious sense we are co-participants with all creation in praise of God. What is more, given the high honor of the four living creatures (both in Ezekiel and Revelation) that enjoy such distinguished proximity to the throne of God Almighty, it behooves us to evaluate whether we show appropriate dignity and respect for nonhuman members of this all-inclusive choir. The throne room scene parallels worship on earth—the scene is not some cryptic forecast of a remote future—so even now, animate creation, in its own way, joins its voice with all God's people on earth.[11] The human voice is only one among many because "every creature in heaven and on earth and under the earth and in the sea" sings to God, in a way acceptable to God (Rev 5:13).

---

9. Mounce describes them as "an exalted angelic order" (*Revelation*, 121).

10. See Harrington, *Revelation*, 79, 82.

11. Cf. Wright: "As we read Revelation, we must not allow the wonderful heavenly vision in chapters 4 and 5 to lull us into imagining that this is the *final* scene of the story, as though the narrative were simply to conclude (as in Charles Wesley's hymn) with the redeemed casting their crowns before the throne. This is a vision of *present* reality, seen in its heavenly dimension" (*Surprised by Hope*, 281, italics original).

Reading Revelation 4 this way makes cruelty or indifference to animals indefensible for Christians. Animals are not inferior beings in this scene but rather co-celebrants, co-worshipers, equally part of the unceasing praise John witnesses in heaven. Indeed, the (human-like) elders themselves reinforce the all-encompassing, comprehensive representation of creation in this scene, acknowledging that their Lord and God "created *all* things" (Rev 4:11), and to the extent that animals are part of that wholeness, their voices mingle with those of humankind. Christian congregations often echo the song of the four living creatures, knowingly or not, each time they sing the well-known hymn "Holy, Holy, Holy" (1826), by Reginald Heber, which includes the words "all thy works shall praise thy name in earth and sky and sea." John's vision of harmonious worship imagines an all-encompassing community, and the peaceful coexistence of all life.

The Son of God in a Manger

Slipping back from the heavenly throne room to earth, we find another scene of animals in the presence of the Son of God, this time in Luke's Gospel. Luke alone includes the charming detail that after giving birth to her son, Mary laid the newly born Jesus in a manger (2:7). The term *phatnē* appears only in Luke's Gospel among New Testament writings—at 2:7, 12, 16 in the birth narrative, and then 13:15, on the lips of Jesus himself in a harsh rebuke of some of his critics: "You hypocrites! Does not each of you on the Sabbath untie his ox or his donkey from the manger, and lead it away to give it water?" Luke's use of the term therefore presents a neat pair of images capturing positive relationships between Jesus and the natural world. The latter involves affirmation of Torah instructions regarding the humane care of domesticated animals in one's possession. (Recall the Hebrew phrase *tsa'ar ba'alei chayim*, which indicates the tradition of showing kindness to animals, or causing no discomfort or pain to other living creatures, discussed earlier). This is in keeping with Jesus's teachings elsewhere concerning animal care on the Sabbath (Matt 12:11–12; Luke 14:4; alluding to Exod 23:4–5; Deut 22:1–4) where we find lesser-to-the-greater forms of argumentation. Of course you care for your animals during the Sabbath, so extend similar generosity to people. Though Jesus's rebuke in Luke 13:15 concerns the healing of a disabled woman (13:10–13), he equates her well-being with the needs of animals when defending his actions.

Eden's Other Residents

Luke's other and better-known manger reference is even more illuminating as we consider the explicit and implicit presence of animals in early Christian writings. As the familiar story goes, Joseph travels with the pregnant Mary from Nazareth in Galilee to his ancestral home Bethlehem in Judea as required by a census (Luke 2:1–5). By including the incident in his Gospel, Luke accomplishes a few things. He affirms Jesus's Davidic ancestry (cf. Luke 1:69; 2:4) and invites readers to recall Bethlehem's significance in prophetic literature (i.e., from that town comes a ruler [Mic 5:2; cf. Matt 2:6]). More to the point, Luke's detail about the manger anticipates the rejection of Jesus during his later ministry (and the rejection of his followers as illustrated throughout the book of Acts). After taking his first breaths, Jesus is not welcome in the more natural setting of an inn where we expect human babies to sleep. Instead, he is in the equivalent of a stable where animals reside.

The no-vacancy inn and assignment to a manger prefigures his rejection by the very people he comes to rescue. This is a recurring theme throughout all the Gospels. He comes to his own, a Jew among Jews, a human among humans, but the people do not welcome him (John 1:11). Repeatedly Jesus's opponents doubt his claims and misunderstand his teachings and actions. They libel and ridicule him, though sometimes it is ironic, as in the account of Herod Antipas's soldiers who dress him up in an elegant robe (Luke 23:11). Presumably they do this in mock acknowledgment of reports about the man being an awaited royal figure (Luke 23:2), but Luke's readers recognize the soldiers' foolishness in light of revelations earlier in the story. They know full well that Jesus is an ancestor of David, born in the city of David (2:4; cf. 1:69; 2:11). He really is a king.

The manger story functions in a similar way to the "elegant robe" draped over Jesus's shoulders by the soldiers. There is no sense of humiliation for the child here. Rejected by human society, yes—"no place for them in the inn"—but as Luke tells the story, the image of Jesus sleeping in a manger is entirely suitable. If humankind does not welcome him (cf. John 1:11), the lord of all creation is equally at home among other members of the earth community (cf. Mark 1:12–13).

Luke's entire birth narrative involves numerous examples of the miraculous interventions of God. There are two miraculous births (the other being the child born to Elizabeth and Zechariah [1:24, 57–58]), angelic visits (1:11–20, 26–38; 2:9–15), the fulfillment of ancient promises (1:68–71; 2:28–32), and the infliction and restoration of a physical impediment

Responding to the Groaning Creation

(1:20 cf. 1:64). In the narrative world of Luke's Gospel, there is no doubt about God's abilities to enable events to unfold according to plan. Even the mighty Roman emperor himself fulfills an assigned role in the story, complicit along with the actors directly involved (see 2:1–2). The point is that Jesus's physical proximity to animals, or at least a space reserved for them—there are no direct references to them, despite their inevitable inclusion in artistic depictions of the nativity scene—is not something abhorred in the incarnation story Luke tells. Of course it is within God's ability to secure a more suitable lodging for a royal, human baby, but Luke's God chooses not to do so. By their attempt to mock Jesus with a robe, the soldiers affirm the prisoner's royal status. By assigning the miraculously born child to a manger-crib, the world of human society attempts to humiliate or denigrate his divine mission but instead affirms the incarnational scope of that mission. There is no protest in Luke's brief mention of exclusion from human lodging, and as if reinforcing the appropriateness of the Davidic child's association with animal space, the first to visit him are shepherds, people who live with and care for animals, directed to the "child wrapped in bands of cloth and lying in a manger" by no less than an angel of the Lord (2:8–16). This is all entirely appropriate to mark the birth of David's son because David himself, after all, was once a shepherd (1 Sam 16:11; 17:14–15, 34–35).

Mark's Snakes

We read of Jesus's direct contact with animals elsewhere in the accounts of his life and ministry, and frequently the presence of these often overlooked characters is theologically significant. In Mark's version of the wilderness temptation, Jesus is "with the wild beasts" (1:13). This brief reference to unlikely companions, a scene in which animals do not fear him and he does not fear them, echoes the peaceable kingdom. There is no enmity between predator and prey, humans and animals: "[you] shall not fear the wild animals of the earth . . . the wild animals shall be at peace with you" (Job 5:22–23; cf. Isa 11:6–9).[12] The incident suggests a reversal of the fear and dread animals experience in the post-flood world (see Gen 9:2).

---

12. For a thorough discussion of Mark 1:13 and its rich significance, see Bauckham, "Jesus and the Wild Animals," which also appears as chapter 5 in *Living with Other Creatures*.

Mark's Gospel (as it appears in modern translations) also closes with a possible vision of harmony between animals and humanity. According to Mark 16:17–18, various signs accompany those who believe: they cast out demons, speak in new tongues, and heal the sick. If they drink poison, it does not harm them and, curiously, the same is true when they pick up snakes. This unusual remark appears in a later addition to the original form of Mark's Gospel (i.e., 16:9–20),[13] which explains why it sits awkwardly within the wider context of the book and indeed the New Testament as a whole, but there are a few intertextual echoes perhaps underlying the author's thinking. Luke announces snakes are no longer a threat (Luke 10:19) and also reports that Paul's encounter with a snake causes him no injury (Acts 28:3–6). In both passages, overcoming snakes demonstrates the authority of the kingdom of God.

Perhaps the author of Mark 16:18 also has in mind the consequences of Adam and Eve's disobedience, which includes the enmity between the serpent and the woman's offspring: "he will strike your head, and you will strike his heel" (Gen 3:15). What "Mark" indicates here is that the resurrection and the proclamation of the gospel inaugurate a reversal of the curses of Genesis and an undoing of the damage resulting from this "enmity" between humanity and the rest of creation (Gen 3:17–18 cf. Rom 8:19–22). When Isaiah represents the restoration of peace in the world, he envisions a nursing child playing over "the hole of the asp," and a weaned child putting "its *hand* on the adder's den" (Isa 11:8–9). "Mark's" strange image of interspecies peace (*handling* snakes without harm) reveals an early Christian expectation that eschatological transformations are manifest in present realities.

The tendency is to read the passage with its Genesis overtones as a victory over evil, the serpent typically understood in Christian tradition as an incarnation of the devil.[14] If we take the passage as a sign of transformation rather than conquest/defeat, it represents a return to innocence, a realization of an Edenic ideal. Said differently, the author of 16:9–20 understands the implications of the story told in 1:1—16:8 as a liberation and renewal of all things. Jesus is lord of creation, a role that involves healing and restor-

---

13. For an overview and evaluation of the text-critical evidence, see Metzger, *Textual Commentary*, 122–28. According to Henderson and Warren, "The resurrection narrative in Mark 16:9–20, though canonical and ancient, is a later compilation reflecting ancient readers' discomfort with the intensity of Mark's non-ending" (324).

14. For brief discussions, see Walker-Jones, "Serpent/Snake," 478–79, and Farrell and Karkov, "Serpent," 693–95.

Responding to the Groaning Creation

ing what is broken. At the beginning of the Gospel, Jesus lives in peace with the wild animals (1:12–13), and at the end, his followers do the same, handling snakes without harm (16:18), thus forming an *inclusio*[15] in the longer (and canonical) version of Mark. Snake handling is a sign of the kingdom alongside other miracles like healing.[16] The miraculous activities described in Mark 16 are nonviolent. The reference to poison presumably indicates an attempt to harm the followers of Jesus,[17] so it seems unlikely that the snake-handling image involves a form of aggression on the part of Jesus's followers, a sort of symbolic attack on the Genesis serpent. Instead, the image is one of peace, analogous to Jesus's being "with the wild beasts" in Mark 1. Mark 16:18 enacts Isa 11:8, reverses the enmity between humanity and nature (not the devil) in Gen 3:15, and depicts a new harmonious relationship with nonhuman species like that modeled at the outset of the Gospel (Mark 1:12–13).

The Bible's Nonhuman Stories

Just as Anne Brontë uses the Bible in novels and poetry creatively to bring animals to the fore, so too does the German painter Michael Sowa in the print hanging in my office. From across the room as I type this I see a dark, menacing sky and churning sea whipped up by powerful winds. There is a ship tossed around in these chaotic waters, but even though it is at the center of the work, it is small against the stormy backdrop, heightening the drama and reinforcing the isolation of its passengers during a threatening tempest. The turbulent sky and waters dominate the painting and so overwhelm the ship that it almost appears the scale of the work is out of proportion.

---

15. The term refers to the repetition of a phrase or idea at the beginning and ending of a passage. For a brief definition with examples, see Soulen and Soulen, *Handbook of Biblical Criticism*, 85–86.

16. As a point of interest, there is a tradition in some areas of the American South that takes the language of passages discussed here literally. As a contemporary movement, snake handling involves "physical handling of snakes as a means of demonstrating the truth of Mark 16:18; Luke 10:19, and Acts 28:3–5. The practice is limited to Pentecostal communities in some southern U.S. states. Sometimes, the practice extends to fire contact and drinking of poison" (Kurian, ed., *Christian Dictionary*, 711).

17. Cf. Eusebius *Hist. Eccl.* 3.39.9, which relates the story of an attempt to poison Justus Barsabbas (mentioned in Acts 1:23) foiled by divine intervention (Beavis, *Mark*, 248; Schweizer, *Good News according to Mark*, 377–38).

Eden's Other Residents

People rarely take a second look when they see the painting from a distance, as I see it now. It is unremarkable because it appears to be little more than a black blob with a splash of color in the middle. But when they move closer they inevitably smile, as I do each time I consider the details in the print. To their surprise they find there are no human passengers on this ship. Instead, it is a bizarre menagerie traveling the high seas. There is, among several other animals, a camel, a monkey, and either an ostrich or an emu. But that is not the end of it. Look closer still and you notice the boat is not the only thing in the water. An elephant leans over the stern of the vessel holding a rope. Holding on to the other end are two dinosaurs on water skis sliding across the waves. This is not a terrifying scene at all but rather a witty and whimsical one of animals at play, perfectly at home in this wild environment. (Is the picture of waterskiing dinosaurs an etiological myth? Now we know why the dinosaurs disappeared. Either they or the elephant let go of the rope!)

Clearly the painting evokes the biblical story of the great flood with its sailing animals, but there is one conspicuous omission. Noah and his family are nowhere present. Just as St. Peter fails to mention the animals on the ark in 1 Pet 3:20 and 2 Pet 2:5, Michael Sowa fails to include humans in his painting. These animals are on a journey by themselves and humans know nothing about it (cf. Job 38:26).

There is more to observe in the picture. We find in this small waterborne community a celebration of difference. There appears to be only one representative of each species, for one thing, which further distinguishes this seafaring crew from those aboard Noah's ark (Gen 7:2–3). Sowa's playful scene includes animals that transgress the boundaries of time (dinosaurs riding along with more recent species), geography, and preferred habitat. The land-based giraffe and zebra stand alongside an alligator and camel, and the unlikely avian passengers sharing the scene include a vulture, a peacock, a toucan, an ostrich, and a seagull. With a playful wink, Sowa also alludes to Isa 11:6 as a lion and a lamb sit side by side, foregrounded as they look out over the dark waters and toward anyone viewing the picture.

Sowa's work disrupts expectations in all kinds of ways. We do not expect to see such unlikely pairings and friendships. We do not expect to see such a terrifying scene juxtaposed with the playful antics of representatives from the Triassic period. We do not always expect adaptations of familiar stories to omit their central characters (here, Noah and his family along with the animals' mates). This is what makes the work so charming and potentially illuminating. In a chapter considering animals in the presence of God, it serves as a reminder that God's relation to the natural world is not necessarily something we comprehend in its fullness because we are not part of the picture. Like Bailly's deer discussed earlier, we are not permitted to intrude on those other "fleeting sovereignties."

At the same time, as I consider this painting with reference to the Bible, my mind turns to definitions of community and the borders of inclusion and exclusion. There are many occasions in biblical literature when the embrace of Otherness is a prized virtue, and when we act according to this virtue, new definitions of community emerge. Even with Israel's highly regulated boundary markers that ordered and distinguished its way of life from the surrounding nations, the prophets depict the nation with permeable borders inviting Gentiles to stream into Jerusalem (e.g., Isa 2:2–4). The teachings and actions of Jesus in the Gospels also reflect an expanding vision of hospitality and community. Embracing the unlovely and unexpected means that others also become beneficiaries of the blessings of the kingdom of God. We see this defiance of traditional boundaries illustrated memorably, to give but one example, in the story of a generous Samaritan's care of a Jew (Luke 10:25–37). The question is whether this expanding vision of community and concomitant call to hospitality and grace reaches beyond our own kind, and whether generosity of spirit and compassion motivated by our experience of God's grace reaches out to embrace not only family, friends, and others of the same species but also animals. Reinforcing this demand are glimpses of the eschatological fullness of the kingdom that encompasses all creation, and therefore all species.

Responding to the Groaning Creation

Frequently, religious people speak of the specialness of human beings, how we are made in the image of God, or blessed by the Spirit; but so often they fail to point out the equal truth that humans are also the most unlovely species in the world—the species capable of degrading itself beyond that of any other creature. Unique we may be, but unique also in our violence, our wickedness, our capacity for evil. Alone among all beings in the universe we are capable of the best—and also the very worst.

—ANDREW LINZEY[18]

---

18. Linzey, *Creatures of the Same God*, 3.

Eden's Other Residents

In his remarkable autobiography *Bound for Glory* (1943), the renowned folk singer Woody Guthrie recalls a disturbing incident that happened during a childhood visit to relatives on a farm. The young Woody and Lawrence quietly enjoy spending time with a mother cat and her new kittens and try to hide them from an older farmboy known for his cruelty. "Warren kills all th' new little baby cats that gits born'd on th' place," Lawrence explains. "I had these hid out under th' barn. Don't let 'im know we're here."[19] Readers experience the story through a child's eyes, which heightens the pathos and sense of helplessness that follows. The bully Warren finds the younger boys and the cats, and Woody and Lawrence watch helplessly as he proceeds to kill all seven kittens and injure their mother with great violence ("threw," "squeezed," "swung," "kicked," "booted," etc.).[20] The two boys and the mother cat do their best to protect the kittens, the latter "clawing at Warren's arm," though their efforts fall short. Warren physically assaults all three, and insults and spits on the younger "Cat-lovin' bastards," his brother Lawrence and nephew Woody.

Woody's sense of powerlessness against a stronger, cruel opponent is disturbing, and there is an alignment of this boy's ineffectual attempts to intervene and the mother cat's futile efforts to protect her offspring. After the assault, there is a further paralleling of this boy and cat as they both share in their grief. Woody finds the nearly dead mother cat "making her way out where Warren had slung her little babies," and he joins her in mourning the dead:

> . . . she took the dead baby in her teeth, carried it through the weeds . . . She laid the baby down when she come to the edge of a little trickling creek, and held up her own broken feet when she walked around the kitten again, circling, looking down at it, and back up at me. I got down on my hands and knees and tried to reach out and pet her . . . I took my hand and dug a little hole in the sandy creek bank and laid the dead baby in, and covered it up with a mound like a grave. When I seen the old Mama Maltese holding her eyes shut with the lids quivering and smell away into the air, I knew she was on the scent of her second one. When she brought it in, I dug the second little grave.[21]

---

19. Guthrie, *Bound for Glory*, 77.
20. Ibid., 80.
21. Ibid., 81.

The incident evidently put the young Woody Guthrie in a philosophical frame of mind. At the close of this section, he writes, "And I was thinking: Is that what crazy is?" Guthrie does not talk often about animals in *Bound for Glory*, so it seems reasonable to suggest that the events occurring at his grandmother's farm are emblematic of other concerns. What manner of craziness occupies his thoughts as he buries these mangled kittens?

Guthrie's *Bound for Glory* recalls a lifetime of encounters with the poor, the unemployed, the marginalized, and society's most vulnerable. "I know you people I see here on the Skid," he announces to an audience in a shabby venue later in life, "where the working people come to try to squeeze a little fun and rest out of a buffalo nickel." The group includes "hoss wranglers, dead enders, stew bums; stealers, dealers, sidewalk spielers; con men, sly flies, flat foots, reefer riders; dopers, smokers, boiler stokers; sailors, whalers, bar flies, brass railers; spittoon tuners, fruit-tree pruners," and many more.[22] What concerns Guthrie and inspires his writing and singing are those most vulnerable to society's bullies, the Warrens of this world, whether heartless landlords and landowners, indifferent politicians, or abusive employers. Just as Guthrie the child fights, however feebly, on behalf of defenseless, endangered kittens, so Guthrie the man brings whatever resources he can muster to the aid of the poor. Guthrie's story about an attempt to protect kittens and the subsequent sympathy shown for their grieving mother prepares readers for the adult Guthrie's compulsion to give a voice to the voiceless.

For Woody, coming to the aid of the weak against the attacks of the strong is a way of life. As mentioned, though he does not speak often of animals, he gives no indication that his concern for the poor as an adult invalidates his childhood attentions to the animal victims of a vicious butcher. Guthrie recalls the scene with the kittens toward the end of his story in a way that suggests the memory of that long ago act of violence is one and the same with forms of mistreatment witnessed as an adult: "I drug my thumb down acrost the strings of the guitar. In the river waters at my feet, I could see the reflection of fire and kids fighting their gang wars and a right young kid up a tree and a mama cat hunting the squeezed-out bodies of her kittens . . . I seen the Redding jungle camp reflected there too, and the saloons along Skid Row."[23] Past and present mingle, as do the stories of

---

22. Ibid., 258.
23. Ibid., 308.

helpless animals and struggling people. Without fail, Guthrie chooses to stand with the weak, regardless of species.

The issue is not that Guthrie was a "cat-lovin' bastard" in one stage of life and a friend of folk on Skid Row in another, but rather that he sides with the downtrodden and friendless no matter where he finds them, no matter who they are. It is all one and the same to him. A story of animal compassion in *Bound for Glory* illuminates stories of compassion for the people he meets while riding in boxcars during the Dust Bowl era. This slippage across species deserves emulation and is consistent with biblical values.

Interconnectedness

"You see," Father Worm began, "Harriet loved Nature. But loving Nature is not the same as understanding it. And Harriet not only misunderstood the things she saw—vilifying some creatures while romanticizing others—but also her own connection to them." Father Worm paused, his eyes narrowing. "Ah, connections, Son. That's the fateful key that Harriet missed, the key to understanding the natural world."

—GARY LARSON, *THERE'S A HAIR IN MY DIRT! A WORM'S STORY*[24]

We find assumptions about the interconnectedness of all life throughout Scripture. God creates land animals and humans on the same day (Gen 1:24–28) and gives them the same food (Gen 1:29–30). God makes them all out of earth (Gen 2:7, 19) and gives them all the breath of life (Gen 2:7 with 7:21–22; cf. Job 12:10). Their divinely given mandates overlap, as in the command to be fruitful and multiply (Gen 8:15–17; 9:1). Qoheleth observes that both animals and people return to dust (Eccl 3:19–20; cf. Job 12:10). All creation awaits liberation from decay, a cryptic remark from Paul that at the very least makes clear that the destiny of animals is in some inexplicable way linked to the destiny of the human children of God (Rom 8:18–23).

Animals suffer the consequences of the garden rebellion (Gen 3:14; 6:7, 13, 17; 7:21; 9:2–3) and other judgments (e.g., 1 Sam 15:3; Jer 7:20;

---

24. Larson, *There's a Hair In My Dirt!*, n.p. This is part of a story Father Worm tells his son, who is distressed to find a hair in his dinner. Spoiler alert: the hair comes from (the dead) Harriet. I confess to finding all manner of insights and pleasures about animals and theology in Gary Larson and his *Far Side* cartoon panels. See Gilmour, "Far Side of Religion."

Ezek 32:13; Jonah 3:7–8; Hab 2:17; Zeph 1:3), though they are not morally culpable. At times animals die side by side with people, as in Jericho where all living things face the sword (Josh 6:21). In the Red Sea, six hundred horses pulling the Pharaoh's chariots drown along with their drivers (Exod 14:6–9, 23–28; 15:1, 19, 21), a story reminding us that human behavior has consequences for nonhuman life. All share the same fate.[25] The land, animals, birds, and fish—all mourn the absence of faithfulness among the people of God (Hos 4:1–3). Perhaps their innocence explains in part their role in various judgments God brings on humanity. When godless nations function as the instruments of God's judgments, God still punishes those nations (e.g., Jer 51:20–24). When animals are the means of judgment, God does not condemn those creatures (though cf. Gen 9:5). Examples of punishment meted out through nonhuman creation include Moses's frogs and gnats (Exod 8:1–6, 16–17; cf. Pss 78:45; 105:30), Elisha's bears (2 Kgs 2:24), and Jeremiah's dogs, birds, wild animals, and snakes (Jer 15:3, 17; cf. Ezek 5:17; 14:21; 29:5).

Peter's Unclean Animals and Jonah's Fish and Cows

Though on first glance it seems an unusual choice of passages when exploring the interconnectedness of all life, I turn now to Peter's strange vision in Acts 10:9–17 (also reported in Acts 11:4–9). I say unusual because this human (Peter), animal (vision), divine (heavenly voice) triad involves animals seen in a "trance," for one thing, as opposed to actual animals. What is more, the story is not directly concerned with animals but rather with the inclusion of Gentiles to the largely Jewish community of Jesus's followers. The lesson Peter learns from the vision is clear from his words to Cornelius and his household: "I truly understand that God shows no partiality, but in every nation anyone who fears him and does what is right is acceptable to him" (Acts 10:35).

The incident follows a series of dramatic events, including a second report of Jesus's ascension (1:6–11; the first is Luke 24:50–52); the arrival of the Holy Spirit and Peter's explanatory sermon to a culturally diverse

---

25. E.g., Habel, *Birth*, 56–57; "Earth," 124: "Domains of Earth are frequently destroyed when God liberates Israel or punishes a nation." Byrne notes that "when human beings fail, that failure redounds negatively upon creation ... Conversely, human restoration will be reflected in a transformation of the non-human created world" ("Ecological Reading," 88). See too Linzey, *Animal Theology*, 23.

Eden's Other Residents

audience (2:1–36); and the persecution and expansion of the Jesus movement (e.g., 7:54—8:3). There is also the well-known account of Saul's/Paul's encounter with the risen Jesus and his transformation into a witness of the resurrection (9:1–30; cf. 22:3–16; 26:12–18). The story of Peter's vision of the animals is particularly important to Luke's introduction of Paul. The apostle's proclamation to the Gentiles eventually receives the support of the Jewish Christian leadership in Jerusalem because of Peter's arguments about their inclusion among the people of God (15:6–11). Peter reaches this conclusion only after the dramatic animal episode occurring on a rooftop in Joppa (10:9; cf. 10:34–35; 11:17).

Though not mentioned often in the Bible, Joppa is yet familiar to many readers because of one particularly memorable story. The book of Jonah begins with the Lord instructing the prophet to preach against the wickedness of Nineveh (1:1–2). Jonah understands this is not an announcement of inescapable doom (a sermon he would gladly deliver to the hated Assyrians, one suspects) because later he complains that God relents in bringing judgment. He knows God is merciful, slow to anger, and loving, ready to forgive the penitent (4:2). In order to avoid this calamitous (!) outcome, he climbs aboard a ship in Joppa to escape "the presence of the LORD" (1:3). The rest of the story is well known.

To come across the name of Joppa in the book of Acts, in a story involving another kind of reluctant prophet to the Gentiles, is surely more than coincidence. Peter, of course, is reluctant in a very different sense. He does not hate Gentiles, as appears to be the case with Jonah. Instead, the issue is Jewish-Gentile relations as they concern dietary regulations and ritual purity. Peter is unsure where Gentiles fit in with the Jewish Christian gospel and fellowship among the people of God. Peter announces the dilemma directly when he first meets with Cornelius: "You yourselves know that it is unlawful for a Jew to associate with or to visit a Gentile; but God has shown me [in the animal vision he just experienced] that I should not call anyone profane or unclean" (10:28; cf. 10:34–35). Peter's associates in Jerusalem struggle with the same questions: "the circumcised believers criticized him, saying, 'Why did you go to uncircumcised men and eat with them?'" (Acts 11:2–3; Gal 2:11–14).

It is particularly noticeable that Luke repeats the place name Joppa often (Acts 10:5, 8, 23, 32; 11:4, 13), perhaps to jog the reader's memory of that other reluctant prophet to the Gentiles. One possible reason Luke finds the Jonah story useful for his purposes is its emphasis on God's

Responding to the Groaning Creation

determination to show grace despite human resistance. God gets Jonah to Nineveh quite apart from the prophet's intentions, and so too, in the book of Acts, nothing hinders the will of God. As the wise Pharisee Gamaliel puts it, with reference to the early Jesus movement, "if this plan or this undertaking is of human origin, it will fail; but if it is of God, you will not be able to overthrow them—in that case you may even be found fighting against God!" (Acts 5:38-39). Throughout Acts, we find God's authority over all realms of human experience; religious opposition, the political machinery of the Roman Empire, and even the natural world in the form of a storm causing a shipwreck (23:11; cf. 27:13-44) cannot thwart the divine plan.

Animals figure prominently in these stories about Jonah and Peter, and there are similarities between them worth observing. To begin with, both include miraculous interventions involving animals ("the LORD provided a large fish to swallow up Jonah" [Jonah 1:17]; "[Peter] saw the heaven opened and . . . all kinds of four-footed creatures and reptiles and birds of the air" [Acts 10:11-12]). In both stories, God's use of these bestial forms of communication prove effectual, leading Jonah and Peter to preach in Nineveh and Caesarea respectively (Jonah 3:1-5; Acts 10:30-48). The results in both stories are positive. Nineveh repents (Jonah 3:6-10) and the Gentile mission proceeds (Acts 11:18; 15:13-20; etc.), an outcome that reaffirms that God's concern for humanity extends to all people (Jonah 4:11; Acts 11:18).

The stories also present us with animal-affirming themes. As with other triadic stories in the Bible, God uses nonhuman beings to reveal insights or truths in dramatic fashion. We find inclusiveness at the heart of both triadic stories, and in the case of Jonah this is particularly striking. After Jonah preaches, the king of Nineveh calls for a fast as a mark of penitence. What is surprising is the extent of the king's decree: "No human being or animal, no herd or flock, shall taste anything. They shall not feed, nor shall they drink water. Human beings and animals shall be covered with sackcloth, and they shall cry mightily to God" (Jonah 3:7-8). This is a remarkable example of humans and animals engaging their Creator together. The practice of animals "repenting" alongside humans is not an Israelite one but a Persian one; however, Bauckham points out that Israelite readers of this story "were presumably not to think it ridiculous. These animals were part of the human world and shared, to some extent at least, its relationship with God."[26] A similar sentiment closes the book in a clear statement of God's concern for humans and nonhuman species. God puts the following question to Jonah: "should I

---

26. Bauckham, *Bible and Ecology*, 110.

not be concerned about Nineveh, that great city, in which there are more than a hundred and twenty thousand persons who do not know their right hand from their left, and also many animals?" (Jonah 4:11).

The central message in Acts 10 is also inclusiveness and the extent of God's love. Peter sees a variety of creatures, "all kinds of four-footed creatures and reptiles and birds," accompanied by the voice of God inviting Peter to "kill and eat" (Acts 10:12–14). Surprisingly, Peter refuses to do what God commands because the animals in question are ritually unclean.[27] The point of this object lesson immediately follows, namely that Peter must not declare something unclean if God declares it clean (10:14–15).

The logic and praxis behind Jewish dietary regulations often puzzle readers of Torah, but it is important to remember that ritual impurity is not synonymous with sin. When the authors and editors of Leviticus explain that animals with divided hoofs that chew the cud are appropriate to eat (Lev 11:3–4), whereas others—for example, the camel—that chew the cud but do not have divided hoofs are not, it has nothing to do with the latter being evil or somehow inferior. We must read Leviticus 11 and other passages regulating the ancient Israelite diet alongside the creation stories, where God pronounces all living things "good." The issue is community definition, boundaries that define Israel over and against other nations.[28] The connection between identity and diet is evident in Lev 20:24–25 where the separation of the people from their neighbors serves as explanation for laws concerning consumption: "I have separated you from the peoples. You shall therefore make a distinction between the clean animal and the unclean, and between the unclean bird and the clean." Clearly it is about more than animals or food. When Peter refuses to eat the animals presented to

---

27. On clean and unclean animals, see Douglas, "Forbidden Animals in Leviticus"; and Houston, "Classifying Animals."

28. For discussion on purity laws and an introduction to the literature on the subject, see Knight and Levine, *Meaning of the Bible*, 181–88, and Neyrey, "Clean/Unclean." With respect to ancient Israelite diets more generally, blanket statements are not possible. Efforts to reconstruct eating habits must take into account such variables as climate, warfare, regional disparities, and uneven distribution among the populace. The archaeological data provides only partial glimpses into this aspect of the ancient world, owing to the fragile nature of agricultural and animal remains. Furthermore, biblical references to land and food (e.g., the familiar phrase "land of milk and honey") are ambiguous because they often "have a particular rhetorical and theological purpose. Only with care and with some qualification can they be used to understand the actual experience of the land by the ancient Israelites" (MacDonald, *Ancient Israelites*, 8). On meat consumption specifically, see esp. chapters 5, 10, and 11, and also Reed, "Meat Eating."

him, it is a statement of his Jewish identity, not a value judgment about the four-footed creatures, reptiles, and birds presented to him.

The "punch line" in Peter's visionary lesson is that Gentiles are no less valuable in God's sight than Jews, no less beneficiaries of the momentous work of Christ. The Jewish Peter is free to proclaim the gospel to the Gentile Cornelius. As we read the story, it is important to remember the same is true of all nonhuman beings as well. For the lesson to make sense, if Jews and Gentiles are alike acceptable before God, so too are all creatures, whether clean or unclean in terms of Jewish dietary regulations. They are all "good" (Genesis). Said differently, all of these unclean animals appear to Peter only after "heaven opened and [they were] lowered" (Acts 10:11). Are there animals in heaven? Apparently there are. Even unclean ones.

Also worth noting is Peter's religiously motivated decision not to eat meat. Luke tells us that Peter was hungry and yet even when the divine voice commands (!) him to kill and eat three times, the apostle refuses (Acts 10:10, 14, 16). Christians easily fall into the trap of thinking diet plays no part in the Christian life. Here is an interesting example of an apostle suggesting otherwise. Or is Peter's Judaism sufficient reason to dismiss the example presented by the story? Most assume this, though it deserves notice that leaders in Jerusalem welcoming Gentiles into fellowship with the Jewish Christian community—an outcome stemming in part from Peter's vision of animals—recommended they too consider diet as a religious matter. The Jerusalem church urges them to avoid "things polluted by idols and from fornication and from whatever has been strangled and from blood" (Acts 15:20). This combination likely indicates that avoidance of pagan temple practices is the issue here, not Jewish regulations. As we know from Paul's letters, meat associated with pagan worship proved divisive in some settings (see, e.g., Rom 14:1–6; 1 Cor 8:1–13; 10:23–33). But regardless of the historical and cultural backdrop behind these passages, it is clear that in the first century at least, diet is not a neutral matter for at least some Christians, despite Mark's interpretation of Jesus's teachings ("he declared all foods clean" [Mark 7:19]) or Paul's similarly liberal views (1 Cor 8:8).

Are there equivalent situations in modern churches in which diet needs to be evaluated in ethical terms? Consider that food reflects our values and potentially either reinforces or disrupts fellowship among the community of God's people. Church fellowships usually (ideally) bring together a variety of people with different backgrounds. When food is involved, competing needs, values, cultural expectations, and preferences inevitably clash. Socioeconomic disparity is an obvious and perennial issue, and one that is potentially divisive (cf. 1 Cor 11:21–22). No one quibbles about abstaining from certain food and drink out of respect for those struggling with allergies, alcoholism, or efforts to lose weight. But what about more fundamental changes to our relationship to food as faith communities? At the very least, should the issue of animal compassion warrant discussion in these circles? Is it appropriate for God's human representatives on earth to eat steaks and chicken wings produced under the barbaric conditions of factory farms? Raising such queries in Christian circles (in my experience, anyway) rarely results in meaningful dialogue, if the issue is acknowledged as a legitimate one for consideration at all. Though modern diets in wealthy societies are unlike anything described in the Bible, food choices, I submit, are not morally neutral for Christians, for many reasons.[29]

Christian Ethical Vegetarianism: A Modest Proposal

To me, cruelty is the worst of human sins. Once we accept that a living creature has feelings and suffers pain, then if we knowingly and deliberately inflict suffering on that creature we are equally guilty. Whether it be human or animal we brutalize *ourselves*.

—JANE GOODALL[30]

Though not mandated for Christians, a vegetarian diet does not conflict with any biblical teachings. Paul does not condemn those in the Roman church who prefer to avoid meat (Rom 14:2, 21), though it was a fear of idols, not concern for animals, that motivated their choices. As seen, the Bible does not speak often about human obligations to other species, though it clearly does not condone cruelty (see e.g., Gen 49:6–7; Prov 12:10) and certain regulations in Torah serve to alleviate undue distress for vulnerable creatures (e.g., Exod 20:10; 23:5; Deut 22:4, 6–7, 10; 25:4). These concerns deserve consideration as we contemplate food choices.

What troubles me in thinking about this topic is the ubiquity of meat in the diets of the developed world, and the enormity of the meat processing

---

29. Though he does not discuss animals or meat eating, Resseguie's study of the Gospel of Luke includes several insights on the symbolic importance of food within the community of faith. See his chapter "Meals: Spirituality of Hospitality" in *Spiritual Landscape*, 69–87.

30. Goodall, *Reason for Hope*, 225.

industries required to support it. Cruelty and inhumane treatment are inevitable in such massive operations. Should Christians be conscientious objectors to an industry that cannot care properly for animals?

References in the Bible to the slaughter and consumption of animals usually occur in relation to ritual activity, as is the case with Passover celebrations that require the consumption of a lamb (Exod 12:3–10). The Bible also serves as witness to other cultures that sacrificed animals as part of religious expression (e.g., Paul refers to meat sacrificed to idols in 1 Cor 8:1–13). Occasionally, the killing of animals proves something about human characters in stories. Samson burns three hundred jackals or foxes alive in an act of revenge, thus proving his strength over the Philistines (Judg 15:4–5). David kills bears and lions as evidence of his courage (1 Sam 17:34–37). Elijah shows himself to be a true prophet of a superior God through a contest involving the death of two bulls (1 Kgs 18:22–23). In other stories, meat eating provides evidence of prosperity and God's blessing, or indicates generosity and hospitality (e.g., Abraham serving a calf to guests [Gen 18:7–8]).

There are references to devout individuals in the Bible choosing to refrain from eating meat, usually involving efforts to avoid ritual defilement (Dan 1:5–16; Tob 1:10–13; Jdt 10:5; 12:2; Rom 14:2), and in other cases as an act of self-denial or a vow to God (e.g., Num 6:3; Judg 13:4, 7, 14). These, however, are exceptions to usual practices. Though some maintain Jesus was vegetarian,[31] others insist this was not the case.[32]

At the very least, meat eating was not widespread in the Jewish world around the turn of the era. Ben Sira, writing in the second century before Christ, observes, "The basic necessities of human life are water and fire and iron and salt and wheat flower and milk and honey, the blood of the grape and oil and clothing. All these are good for the godly, but for sinners they turn into evils" (Sir 39:26–27). The omission of meat from this list suggests that most did not rely on it as a staple of their diet. This means that meat eating in the ancient biblical contexts is wholly unlike the situation in the

---

31. For discussion, see e.g., Webb, "Didn't Jesus Eat Lamb?" and *On God and Dogs*, chapter 7; Phelps, *Domionion of Love*, 88–89; A. Alexis-Baker, "Didn't Jesus Eat Fish?" Though many of his views are tendentious and not representative of conclusions reached by most historians of earliest Christianity, Eisenman's *James, the Brother of Jesus* discusses much of the evidence for vegetarianism in the Second Temple period, including the Dead Sea Scrolls, and the early church; see esp. his chapter "James' Vegetarianism, Abstention from Blood, and Consuming No Wine" (258–309).

32. E.g., Bauckham, "Jesus and Animals II," 51–52.

societies of the developed world today. In Roman-period Judaism, "Meat and poultry were expensive and rarely eaten by peasants. Most people ate it only on feast days or holidays, though temple priests ate it in abundance."[33]

It also deserves repeating that almost all references to meat eating in the Bible (and decisions to abstain from it) are associated with cultic activity and religious expression in some form or other. This is rarely true in the modern world. As a result, there is arguably little conscious respect for the animals sacrificed for food, research, or entertainment, and no serious reflection on the sacredness of blood and death, such as discussed in the previous chapter. Many (most?) are cavalier in their attitude toward animal-based diets, quickly adopting the biblical language of "dominion" but dismissing its language of the solemnity of ritual, sacrificial death (e.g., Lev 16:1–34), and respect for the blood of all living things (e.g., Lev 17:10–14).

It is easy to trivialize meat eating in overfed societies. We now view meat eating as normative, a part of all meals. We eat for pleasure, not for religious purposes or subsistence or as an occasional luxury. This trivializing of sentient creation is theologically problematic, if Karl Barth is correct. He recommends that Rom 8:18–19 be written "in letters of fire . . . across every hunting lodge, abattoir and vivisection chamber," and maintains that the killing of animals in obedience to God as a blood offering was only possible "as a deeply reverential act of repentance, gratitude and praise on the part of the forgiven sinner."[34] Is there such reverence for nonhuman, sentient life in contemporary Christianity, which typically allows little or no meaningful place for animals in its worldview, liturgies, and ethical discourse?

How Should We Proceed?

Most agree that wanton abuse of animals is immoral, quite apart from anything the Bible says, so how do we reconcile divine concern for animals with the often cruel meat processing industry? Our society breeds and slaughters far more animals for food than we actually need, and the factory farm system places enormous strains on the environment. The combination of a

---

33. Neyrey, "Meals," 165. For general remarks about meals and the food eaten in the Roman-era Mediterranean world, see Jeffers, *Greco-Roman World*, 38–42. With respect to meat eating among the Romans, he notes the lower classes "could only afford small fish preserved in brine" (41).

34. Barth, *Church Dogmatics*, III/4, 355. On Barth and nonhuman creation, see Southgate, *Groaning of Creation*, 117–19; Webb, *On God and Dogs*, 130–35; Thompson, "'Remaining Loyal to the Earth.'"

high demand for cheap meat and a concomitant loss of respect for animals (now just commodities) encourages tolerance for a system that largely dismisses the wellbeing of chickens, cattle, pigs, turkeys, ducks, geese, fish, and more as a serious concern.

Scripture is ambiguous regarding animals, but that does not give us license to ignore the issue. The Bible is ambiguous about many issues, and we frequently reread it in light of contemporary sensitivities and cultural preferences. Consider that the Bible includes imperatives that do not indicate universal or timeless demands placed on all believers. Most Christians do not think New Testament instructions about greeting one another with a kiss (1 Thess 5:26) or concerns about hair length for men and women (1 Cor 11:14–15) constitute enduring ethical imperatives. Neither do they read passages referring to the silence of women in the church (1 Tim 2:11–12) or slavery (Eph 6:5) as normative. Obviously, many of the Bible's teachings are context specific, reflecting their historical moment and cultural setting. If Christians do not have theological obligations requiring animal sacrifice or meat eating, there is no reason not to reexamine and recontextualize biblical statements touching on animals and diet. A first step is awareness that the Bible simply does not speak about meat eating in terms even remotely resembling the situation in our day, and for this reason, even if Jesus ate meat and/or fish, that does not necessarily justify meat eating now.

The Bible does address gluttony, concern for the poor, and respect for animals. Stephen A. Reed closes his reflections on diet in the Hebrew Bible by pointing out that permission to eat meat does not put an end to moral dimensions of the issue. "Humans ought to pause when they casually take the lives of animals for their food," he writes.

> Americans [and I would add those in the developed world more widely] consume much meat, just as they consume other natural resources in large quantities. In the light of limited resources in the world and the fact that these resources are not equally distributed to all people in our world, Americans should reflect upon their consumption patterns. What we eat and how much we eat are not simply matters of personal preference. They are ethical concerns.[35]

At the very least, we must not make our decisions to kill animals for food lightly.

I noted earlier that the Mishnah refers to making a fence for the Torah, a concept responding to the ambiguity of ethical teachings.

---

35. Reed, "Meat Eating," 294.

> Moses received Torah at Sinai and handed it on to Joshua, Joshua to elders, and elders to prophets. And prophets handed it on to the men of the great assembly. They said three things: "Be prudent in judgment. Raise up many disciples. Make a fence for the Torah" (*m. 'Abot* 1:1).

What does it mean to take the Lord's name in vain? What does it mean to keep the Sabbath holy? Ambiguities abound in any attempt to apply ancient teachings to new settings. Some understand the Mishnah here to recommend safeguards against unintended violations on the laws of God. We avoid breaking Torah's mandates by limiting our opportunities to do so. If you do not want to use the divine name in vain, do not say that name at all. If you do not want to profane the Sabbath, expand the definition of what constitutes work.[36] Here we have a useful model to consider with reference to religious obligations to diet and nonhuman, sentient creation. If we want to avoid cruelty and irreverent treatment of other living things—an inescapable and inevitable outcome in the processes of meat production—vegetarianism is a step in that direction.

Alternatively, consider the Christian discipline of the Lenten fast, a willingness to give up certain foods or activities for a brief time. As with hedges or fences around Torah, this involves going beyond the minimum requirements of biblical teaching.[37] Like Zacchaeus's generosity noted at the outset, gratitude and the desire to celebrate grace received with grace given is a model of piety worth emulating. Fasting and hedging with respect to our diets out of concern for animal wellbeing means going beyond the minimum required, choosing self-sacrifice over the sacrifice of others, and making every effort to honor Torah by avoiding cruelty (cf. Prov 12:10). A

---

36. Cf. Johnson, with reference to this rabbinic principle and the requirement not to work on the Sabbath: "But what is the meaning of 'work'? Midrash located every mention of the term 'work' in Torah and came up with a comprehensive list of thirty-nine activities that were designated work-related and thus to be avoided (*Mishnah Shabbat* 7.2). To the outsider, refusal to light a fire or to tear a thread might seem trivial. But such lists 'put a hedge around the Torah' in order to ensure that the central commandment itself ('keep the Sabbath holy') would not be broken. The method and its results are open to debate, but the strong religious motivation is not" (*Writings*, 57). C. K. Barrett also comments on *m. 'Abot* 1:1: "Make additional commandments in order to safeguard the original commandments; for example, certain acts should be avoided towards the approach of evening on Friday lest one should forget and inadvertently continue to do them on the Sabbath" (*Selected Documents*, 177–78).

37. On this idea of doing more than Torah demands, see Schwartz, *Judaism and Vegetarianism*, 194.

vegetarian diet is also a way to reach back to the harmonious conditions of Eden, as it were, and ahead to the peaceable kingdom envisioned by the prophets. We live as witnesses to the coming new creation by embodying its ideals in the present. "Thy kingdom come, thy will be done on earth as it is in heaven." Hedging and fasting provide ways to think about Christian ethical vegetarianism. By voluntarily choosing not to eat animals or animal products, Christians build a fence as part of their effort to avoid treating God's creatures cruelly or frivolously.

Passages like Lev 17:3–7 tie the killing of animals to sacred ceremonies, but nothing of the kind is possible, of course, in factory farming. For most there is an enormous distance between the farms, transportation systems, and abattoirs where millions of animals live and die, and the kitchens and dining rooms where the devout give thanks for their daily bread. Most have no contact with their food before they set foot in the grocery store, which means those animals are outside "the camp" (to borrow the language of Leviticus) of God's people. By this, I mean these creatures are effectively out of our circle of community, and therefore beyond the reach of our hospitality, advocacy, and even prayer, as much as they are literally out of our sight. The machinery of the modern food industry does not—indeed cannot—treat animals with anything resembling the respect and dignity evident in biblical literature, or value their true worth as part of God's good creation. Those who recognize the religious authority of the Bible ought to evaluate their food choices in light of this and consider how to bring animals into the life-affirming community, how to complete the animal-human-divine triad.[38]

---

38. On Christians and diet from a Roman Catholic perspective, see Rubio, "Toward a Just Way of Eating," 360–78. Murti (*They Shall Not Hurt*) offers a short overview of sacred texts sympathetic to vegetarianism in various religious traditions. Kemmerer's thorough and scholarly *Animals and World Religions* does the same, though here it is veganism, not vegetarianism, that is promoted as an ideal consistent with the religious teachings explored (e.g., 8–9, 10, 286–87).

6   Returning to the Garden: *The Writings of William Bartram*

Having considered briefly a few biblical passages and themes touching on animals in previous chapters, I turn now to an example of applied Bible reading, by which I mean an embrace of Scripture's vision of creation that shapes and informs one reader's experience of the world around him. William Bartram is not widely known, perhaps, but I attempt to demonstrate how this remarkable individual allows the Bible to enlighten his perceptions about life on this planet. He sees the Creator and the Creator's handiwork in everything around him, and from this foundational premise recognizes the responsibilities this involves for the children of Adam. Bartram is not perfect, by any means, nor do his views align with mine in all instances, but I suggest that in his story we find a model worthy of emulation in many respects as we contemplate the moral implications of sharing the garden with other living things.

A Good Book, and *the* Good Book

In 1791, the American naturalist William Bartram (1739–1823) published a travelogue documenting his journeys through the Carolinas, Georgia, east and west Florida, and beyond. This remarkable text combines scientific reporting, complete with Linnaean taxonomies of excruciating detail, and surprising poetic flourishes. One quickly grows accustomed to reading of palm trees described as pompous, or the plumage of Spanish curlews that are "white as the immaculate robe of innocence," gleaming in the cerulean skies.[1]

Bartram left his native Pennsylvania in April 1773 to discover "rare and useful productions of nature, chiefly in the vegetable kingdom," returning home in 1777 to write his famous book.[2] He was born in Pennsylvania in 1739 to John Bartram, also a well-known horticulturalist and traveler, a founding member of the American Philosophical Society, and botanist for the British holdings in North America appointed by King George III in 1765. The younger Bartram was also artistically inclined, something evident from drawings that grace the various editions of his book. In 1765–1766, William accompanied his father on a botanical expedition in South Carolina and Georgia, reaching to the headwaters of Florida's St. Johns River, though it was not until 1772, when family friend Dr. John Fothergill, an English botanist and plant collector, commissioned William to return to the South, that his most famous work commenced.

William Bartram has a remarkably diverse readership in our day. Because he wrote about the people and cultural productions of the region, he is valuable to historians of revolutionary-era settlement and Indian life in southeastern North America. Because he wrote about flora and fauna, weather and waterways, landscapes and Linnaean taxonomies, he is of interest to all manner of scientists and environmentalists. And because he was a poet, with a skill in language easily overlooked amidst long lists of technical Latin and Greek designations of classes, orders, families, genera, and species, readers past and present celebrate his literary prowess. Proof of this poetic competence is most obvious in his influence on the English Romantic poets. In "Kubla Khan," Coleridge's "incense-bearing trees" and "mighty fountains" recall the writings of the famous American traveler, and the "glorious world" of the idealized America in Wordsworth's "Ruth" also draws on his vivid depictions of nature's wonders. A few decades later, in correspondence with Ralph Waldo Emerson, Thomas Carlyle refers to the "wondrous kind of floundering eloquence" in Bartram's writing.[3] The setting of novels by Charles Brockden Brown and James Fenimore Cooper, and the nature writings of Thoreau, owe much to Bartram's *Travels* as well.[4]

1. Bartram, *Travels*, 32.
2. Ibid., 1.
3. Smith, "Stone Blind," 511.
4. Slaughter, *Natures of John and William Bartram*, xv–xvi.

Eden's Other Residents

Bartram also incorporates intriguing theological and biblical reflections, though this facet of his work generally receives less notice. Perhaps this is so because he is primarily a man of science, meaning that the religious dimensions of his work tend to fade into the shadows of his analytical study of nature in much the same way as the poetic qualities of his writing. Yet, Bartram was clearly a man of faith—a Quaker in background, though perhaps not a traditional one in all respects[5]—and his occasional remarks about religion present an intriguing glimpse into Bible reading habits of late eighteenth-century America. In Bartram's 1791 publication *Travels*, it is Genesis in particular that informs the writer's understanding of the natural world he describes.

Palimpsests and the Blurring of the Species in Bartram's *Travels*

Before looking at his use of Genesis, however, I note briefly a curious stylistic habit in Bartram's writing, namely, a tendency to align human characters with nonhuman ones. When reading about an insect, bird, or animal, there is often someone in the near context who resembles that creature in one way or another. The opposite is also true, as his scientific reporting on nonhuman species and other natural wonders often sounds vaguely familiar because similar phrasing, value judgments, even narrative settings repeat. Bartram liberally recycles words and ideas. Said differently, he populates his writing with anthropomorphic animals and zoomorphic people.

He also develops parallels between human beings and plants. For instance, he observes several trees and shrubs along the "sequestered" St. Mary's River but singles out one in particular, "the great evergreen Andromeda of Florida, called Pipe-stem Wood," adding with an Adamic tone, "I gave [this tree] the name of Andromeda formosissima, as it far exceeds in

---

5. The local Quaker fellowship disowned William's father, John Bartram, because he did not believe in the divinity of Christ, though he continued to attend weekly meetings (Slaughter, *Natures of John and William Bartram*, 14, 15, 58). Slaughter links John's conclusions to his inability to accept the occurrence of miracles. Regarding John's distrust of clergy and his willingness to question the Bible, see too Slaughter's comments on p. 59. The extent to which the father's theological reflections informed the son's is not always clear, yet several values evident in William's writing are consistent with his religious upbringing. For instance, "As a Quaker, [William] Bartram believed in the worth of all creation, regarding Indians and whites as equals, and followed the Quaker tradition of tolerance and pacifism" (Fradkin and O'Connor, "Before Bartram," 107).

beauty every one of this family." According to a legend about the St. Mary's, which he then relates in the next paragraph, the source of the river is a lake, "a most blissful spot of the earth . . . inhabited by a peculiar race of Indians, whose women are incomparably beautiful."[6] Here are two instances of unparalleled beauty in near context, one of plant life and the other of people, serving to link the natural world with some of its human inhabitants. On this occasion, the pairing is conspicuous because females do not appear often in Bartram's narrative. The image of a protected paradise out of the reach of travelers—as a legend about the place goes—also recalls the garden of Eden, protected as it is from intruders after the fall (Gen 3:24).

This alignment of humans with the natural world occurs with various creatures he sees as well. On one occasion, immediately after his description of the great land-tortoise that "issue[s] forth in the night, in search of prey," Bartram reports an encounter with a lone Seminole Indian occurring, he says specifically, at "the close of day." He fears this man intends to kill him, but Bartram manages to assuage his violent intent. As it turns out, Bartram's initial suspicions were accurate. A chief later informs him that this Seminole warrior was one of the greatest villains on earth, an outlaw who recently escaped justice from his own people, stole a rifle, and vowed "he would kill the first white man he met."[7] Note the parallels between these two episodes. A hunting tortoise leaves his home, at night, in search of prey. A human hunter also leaves his home (his people), at night, in search of prey (a white man). Both stories appear in close proximity.

Or consider the vivid scene involving the exploits of a spider attacking a bee. He refers to the arachnid as a "cunning intrepid hunter," adding that it "conducted his subtil [sic] approaches with the circumspection and perseverance of a Siminole [sic] when hunting a deer." Here commentary on the natural world aligns artistically with proximate human characters because, at this point in the narrative, Bartram is in the company of a hunter said to be "an excellent marksman."[8] They come across two bears, and this hunter shoots one of them, but to Bartram's surprise the other does not run off. The remaining bear "approached the dead body, smelled, and pawed it, and appearing in agony, fell to weeping and looking upwards, then towards us, and cried out like a child." As Bartram's hunter companion prepares to shoot the cub, the writer is conflicted: "I was

6. Bartram, *Travels*, 17, 18.
7. Ibid., 12, 15, 16.
8. Ibid., xxxvii, xxxv.

moved with compassion, and charging myself as if accessary [sic] to what now appeared to be a cruel murder, endeavoured to prevail on the hunter to save its life, but to no effect! for by habit he had become insensible to compassion towards the brute creation."[9]

We move quickly from the bear story, which highlights the hunter's skill as an expert shooter, his violence, and his lack of compassion, to the spider story. Both narratives use the terms "hunter" and "prey," both emphasize the predators' prowess, and both comment on the victims' distress. Whereas the bear cub cries like a child, the bee (Bartram refers to it as "he") endeavors to extricate itself from the web, becomes fatigued and then exhausted by his struggles, and suffers "the repeated wounds of the butcher."[10] It is difficult not to read the story of the human hunter in light of the story of the spider, with the result that Bartram most resembles the bear cub in its tender childlike grief for the fallen dam, and his companion the butchering arachnid.[11] Like a palimpsest, stories about the natural world lurk in the background of those about human activity.

Is Bartram deliberately aligning human and nonhuman species for some artistic or rhetorical purpose or is this phenomenon more akin to a habit of the mind? Subconscious repetition of terms, phrases, and ideas is natural enough and hardly remarkable in itself. If this were the case with Bartram, what I observe in these passages is no more than an unintended drifting of his thought. Like a palimpsest, one story lurks in the background of another, unintended, without any connection between the two. Furthermore, even though we know Bartram occasionally shapes his narratives for ideological purposes,[12] it remains plausible that he actually observed a spider killing a bee on the very day his hunter-guide shot a bear. How else could he describe the actions of that spider? An arachnid is a hunter, a bee

---

9. Ibid., xxxv–xxxvi.

10. Ibid., xxxvii.

11. Kornegay also observes an alignment of human and insect, though he suggests it occurs with Bartram, not the bear hunter. Bartram appears in this episode hunting flowers, the spider appears hunting a bee; Bartram spies the spider and draws back, the spider sees Bartram and draws back; Bartram returns to observe the spider, the spider returns to the hunt, still keeping an eye on Bartram ("Nature, Man, and God," 85). Either way, the point stands. Bartram blurs descriptions of humans with nonhuman species.

12. E.g., he appears to adjust his narrative to coincide with certain momentous events of the American Revolution. On this, see Anderson, "Bartram's *Travels*." I return to Bartram's perspective on the American Revolution below.

in a web is a victim, and so the alignment of these ideas is not necessarily significant.

Still, I remain impressed by the sheer number of times we find anthropomorphic and zoomorphic language in Bartram's travelogue and cannot resist the suspicion there is more going on here than a mere coincidence or a trick of the mind. I also want to keep the term *palimpsest* in play. Usually, erased pencil markings on a page serve no purpose in relation to the text placed over them. However, Linda Hutcheon uses the term *palimpsestuous* of texts that linger, however faintly, in adaptations. Adaptations are deliberate rewritings of earlier texts. Palimpsestuous works are "haunted at all time by their adapted texts. If we know that prior text, we always feel its presence shadowing the one we are experiencing directly."[13] Bartram's impressions of the people he meets haunt his descriptions of the natural world, and those animals, birds, and insects he observes cast shadows on the human beings introduced to his travelogue.

Animals lurk in the background as Bartram describes human characters, and the reverse is equally true. The presence of palimpsests in Bartram's *Travels*—these overlapping narratives about humans and animals—allows the reader to see the interrelatedness of all life. The drifting of imagery across the species defies the rigidity of Linnaean taxonomy, suggesting animals are quite human and humans quite bestial.[14] For Bartram, humans are not untouched by animal life, or independent.

Science Meets Theology and Advocacy

This poetic blurring of the species is a by-product of a key theological assumption, namely, his repeated insistence that all living things originate in the creative acts of God. All living things populate the "glorious apartment of the boundless palace of the sovereign Creator."[15] In some ways, the language of Genesis suggests the relationship of animals to the first man is a functional one. Adam needs companionship in Eden, so God makes animals from the very same dust from which he makes the first man (Gen 2:18–19; cf. 2:7). All species share a common origin in dust and the creative acts of God. They inhabit the same space (Eden) and are mutually beneficial. Adam needs their companionship, and they come to him for their

13. Hutcheon, *Theory of Adaptation*, 6, 22.
14. Cf. Kornegay, "Nature, Man, and God," 84.
15. Bartram, *Travels*, xxix.

names. Similarly, Bartram's American Eden reveals an interconnectedness of plants, animals, and humans, and he frequently offers accounts of their various functions in the broader ecosystem (though *ecosystem* is not a term he uses). "In every order of nature," he writes, "we perceive a variety of qualities distributed amongst individuals, *designed for different purposes and uses*," which ultimately "manifest the divine and inimitable workmanship."[16]

One of the purposes he sees himself fulfilling is advocacy for nonhuman creatures. Animals might serve human needs on occasion,[17] but Bartram also advocates for them, urging others against unnecessary killing. He even writes of human obligations to other living things, writing about "our duties to each other, and all creatures and concerns that are submitted to our care and controul [*sic*]." Soon after this acknowledgment of human obligation to animals, he writes of "horned cattle, horses, sheep, and deer,"[18] a list that distinguishes domestic from wild animals just as we find in the book of Genesis (1:26; cf. 2:20: "The man gave names to all cattle, and to the birds of the air, and to every animal of the field"). Bartram resembles his father, John, in his pity for animals and their suffering. "As for the animals and insects," John Bartram writes, "it is very few that I touch of choice and most with uneasiness. Neither can I behold any of them that have not done me a manifest injury in their agonizing mortal pains without pity."[19] There is an awareness of human obligation in William Bartram's writing that stems from a keen sense of *where he is* ("Eden," God's creation) and *who he is* (a dominion-granted Adam, with all the responsibilities that entails).

Genesis as Palimpsest

As already noted, there are subtle but frequent echoes of Genesis throughout Bartram's *Travels*, commencing in the opening pages in his account of a storm. He arrives in the South by ship, sailing through a "furious gale" that "spread[s] terror and devastation," followed immediately by "the gentle moon rising in dignity from the east, attended by millions of glittering orbs," the sequence here resembling the great lights appearing in the sky when God subdues the primordial chaos (Gen 1:16). Bartram then writes

16. Ibid., xxx. Emphasis added.
17. For instance, Bartram hunts and eats meat (e.g., raccoon; ibid., 40).
18. Ibid., 36, 37.
19. Taken from Slaughter, *Natures of John and William Bartram*, 66.

of "the sudden appearance of land from the sea," with its echo of Gen 1:9–10.[20] It is as though Bartram's journey from the settled Northeast to the comparatively unsettled Southeast, from Philadelphia to "the Floridas, and the western parts of Carolina and Georgia," involves a journey back to the garden of Eden. It is a step back into a prelapsarian space. The "amplitude and magnificence" of the scenes that appear after his arrival in the South and emergence from the great storm that opens his narrative were, as he puts it, "great indeed, and may present to the imagination, an idea of the first appearance of the earth to man at the creation."[21] The implication is that Bartram, throughout all that follows, aligns himself with Adam and the largely pristine lands[22] he visits with the garden of Eden. He seems to reinforce this view in a number of ways.

The garden-lands he travels occasionally reveal an unexpected, even unnatural peacefulness. On one such occasion, he describes a particularly beautiful pool of water, so clear that fish of prey cannot take advantage of the element of surprise as they do in murky waters. For Bartram, "this paradise of fish [seems] to exhibit a just representation of the peaceable and happy state of nature which existed before the fall." Here it is a trout that "freely passes by the very nose of the alligator" instead of a wolf and a lamb feeding together, but the echo of Isa 66:25 and other depictions of nature at peace with itself are unmistakable (cf. Job 5:22–23; Isa 11:6–9; Hos 2:18).[23]

Bartram's advocacy for animals also gestures back to Eden's peaceful state. His reportage is realistic, so he does not depict a utopian new world where violence is completely absent, but he certainly strives to minimize it by restraining human indifference to the natural world. In this sense, he is simultaneously in Eden and urging a return to Eden. He describes himself as an "advocate or vindicator of the benevolent and peaceable disposition of animal creation in general, not only towards mankind, whom they seem to venerate, but always towards one another, except where hunger or the rational and necessary provocations of the sensual appetite interfere." Animals kill only as necessity dictates. Perhaps the most memorable illustration of

20. Bartram, *Travels*, 1–2.

21. Ibid., 2. Cf. 32, which refers to nature unmodified by the hand of man. For other Adam-like language, see 121.

22. I use the term *pristine* loosely because by the time of Bartram's visits, trade and cultivation as well as the introduction of plants, animals, and people not native to southeastern North America contributed much to the world he encountered. See e.g., Braund, "William Bartram's Gustatory Tour," 46.

23. Bartram, *Travels*, 105.

his point is a story concerning a rattlesnake discovered near a campsite, along the path to a nearby spring. Bartram only discovers the "hideous serpent" in the morning, noting that he and his companions passed close to it several times during the night, oblivious to the danger lying "within six inches of the narrow path." Bartram credits their safety in the face of such danger to both God and the morality of the natural world, referring to the snake's dignity and generosity. Bartram is so moved by the incident that he "protect[s] the life of the generous serpent," adding, "I am proud to assert, that all of us, except one person, agreed to let him lie undisturbed, and that person was at length prevailed upon to suffer him to escape."[24] This story about saving a rattlesnake resembles views held by William's father, John, who opposed sport hunting "and the wanton killing of rattlesnakes." John Bartram "resisted killing any creature unless for a good cause. Defense and hunger were high on his list of reasons to slay."[25]

This assessment of the restraint displayed by the natural world, which refrains from unnecessary violence against other living things, stands in sharp contrast with various incidents involving the wasteful killing of animals by humans. As noted earlier, the senseless killing of two bears disturbs him. He also reports his efforts to protect a herd of deer: "I endeavoured to plead for their lives . . . unfortunately for their chief . . . the lucky old hunter fired and laid him prostrate upon the green turf."[26] On another occasion, his traveling companions "roused a litter of young wolves" and, after giving chase, "we soon caught one of them, it being entangled in high grass, one of our people caught it by the hind legs and another beat out its brains with the but [sic] of his gun." The scene clearly disturbs Bartram: "barbarous sport!—This creature was about half the size of a small cur-dog, and quite black."[27] Elsewhere he describes "a rare piece of sport" among his travel companions, who torment an alligator that approached their camp. Some wanted to put an end "to his life and sufferings with a rifle ball, but the majority thought this would too soon deprive them of the diversion and pleasure of exercising their various inventions of torture."[28] Bartram does not participate in this grisly behavior, which includes thrusting fire-hardened

24. Ibid., 168, 169.
25. Slaughter, *Natures of John and William Bartram*, 66, 138.
26. Bartram, *Travels*, 128.
27. Ibid., 253.
28. Ibid., 159.

javelins down its throat. His use of the harsh term "torture" suggests he found the behavior at least gratuitous and distasteful, if not immoral.

Such incidents contrast sharply with sites where nature appears in an almost unnatural state of harmony. He describes one such place as a "blessed unviolated spot of earth," a "blissful garden," and when the moment comes for him to move on—and in case you missed the echo of Eden—he says he "at last broke away from the enchanting spot, and stepped on board my boat, hoisted sail and soon approached the coast of the main, at the cool eve of day."[29] Here he is not just Adam in the garden but arguably like the Lord God himself, "walking in the garden at the time of the evening breeze" (Gen 3:8). We also find Bartram naming some of the natural wonders he encounters in Adam-like fashion, including a bird on at least one occasion, as well as various species of plants, among them one in honor of family friend Benjamin Franklin.[30]

We find another echo of Genesis in a long taxonomical list of regional vegetation with a note about *Triticum Cereale*, which, he observes, "affords us bread, and is termed, by way of eminence, the staff of life, the most pleasant and nourishing food—to all terrestrial creatures."[31] The language here recalls the vegetarian diet mentioned in Gen 1:29–30. Bartram clearly does not mean this literally, referring to animals in the same context as "sustenance" and throughout to animals eating animals, but this makes the comment all the more conspicuous as a deliberate allusion to Genesis and the garden of Eden.

All through his book he refers to the Supreme Creator, the Author of Nature, or equivalents, terms recalling the creation narratives,[32] but there are other hints of Genesis such as the words *firmament, Sabbath, the breath of life*, and "the ruin or dispersion of the ancient Babel."[33] Bartram describes a man who witnessed a spring of water bursting from the ground; this man thought that "the fountains of the deep were again broken up, and that an universal deluge had commenced." Bartram also gives an account of unusual "swelling hills" comprised of "fossil oyster shells," which includes his obser-

29. Ibid., 98.

30. See e.g., ibid., 93, 297 n. 57. The Franklin plant is a "flowering shrub" resembling a gardenia that, he says, "we [including here is father] have honoured with the name of the illustrious Dr. Benjamin Franklin, Franklinia Alatamaha" (296 n. 56). Cf. ibid., 71, referring to a nut his father named on an earlier expedition.

31. Bartram, *Travels*, xxx.

32. Ibid., e.g., 145, 169, 286, 299, 308.

33. Ibid., 216, 289, 314, 248.

Eden's Other Residents

vation that they are "very ancient or perhaps antideluvian."[34] In both cases, of course, the descriptions take the mind back to the Genesis flood story (see Gen 7:11, 18–24). Elsewhere he describes plants' ability to transplant and colonize "almost over the surface of the whole earth," which resembles the language of the Priestly creation story.[35] There are other allusions to biblical literature in Bartram, including the story of Nebuchadnezzar's humiliation and Jesus's golden rule,[36] but Genesis is by far his most important biblical resource, beginning with a carefully structured introduction that rehearses the Priestly creation narrative's major categories: vegetation (cf. Gen 1:11–12); animals (cf. Gen 1:24–25); insects (cf. Gen 1:25); birds (cf. Gen 1:20); humans (cf. Gen 1:26–28); and moon and stars (cf. Gen 1:16).

If indeed Bartram is Adam, and the southeastern territories are Eden, what are the implications of this symbolic use of the Bible? On one level, Bartram's *Travels* offers a commentary on Gen 1:28 and the meaning of humankind's "dominion" over the fish of the sea, the birds of the air, over the cattle, the wild animals, and over every creeping thing. Bartram encounters seemingly endless species falling into each of these categories during his years of travel, but his attitude toward them is remarkably progressive and for this reason seems oddly out of step with his contemporaries, at least as he describes them. A remark about horses illustrates. After a description of what he calls this "useful part of the creation," he adds a comment about human responsibilities: "if they are under our dominion," they "have consequently a right to our protection and favour."[37]

On another occasion, a prayerful outburst reflects Bartram's religious assumptions about humanity's high station in a hierarchal creation:

> O sovereign Lord! since it has pleased thee to endue man with power, and pre-eminence, here on earth, and establish his dominion over all creatures, may we look up to thee, that our understanding may be so illuminated with wisdom and our hearts warmed and animated, with a due sense of charity, that we may be enabled to do thy will, and perform our duty towards those submitted to our service, and protection, and be merciful to them even as we hope for mercy.[38]

---

34. Ibid., 152, 201.
35. Ibid., xxxiii; cf. Gen 1:28–29.
36. Ibid., 227 (cf. Dan 4:28–33), 312 (cf. Matt 7:12).
37. Ibid., 224.
38. Ibid., 63.

Returning to the Garden: The Writings of William Bartram

It is true that Bartram seems to include within the category of "those submitted" more than just the variety of species listed in Genesis. He mentions slaves occasionally, supplied by various landowners to assist the naturalist in his work. He even owned slaves briefly during an ill-fated agricultural venture. At the same time, it deserves note that he was progressive in many respects. The Clemson University ecologist J. Drew Lanham observes that Bartram

> often seemed to see his fellow humans beyond their race, in a refreshingly liberal and humane light for the period . . . A little research into his life beyond the wilderness travels shows that his father, John, had freed his black slaves and paid them wages. William's sentiments followed this humanitarian legacy. Indians weren't always savages, and the slaves he encountered he saw as more than chattel. The man in many ways was a social trailblazer, at least in spirit, going against the grain of the prevailing culture.[39]

The American Revolution and a Vision of a Humane World

Finally, given that the events depicted in Bartram's writing span the years 1773–1777, the absence of any explicit reference to the American Revolution is conspicuous, especially since it appears he had some minimal involvement in the conflict.[40] There is much speculation on this glaring omission. Some point to his Quaker pacifism as a possible explanation[41] and find in his silence a commentary on military actions. One historian notes,

> By the time Bartram published the *Travels* in 1791, the contrast between his own distinctively pacific activity of thirteen years earlier and that of his politically active contemporaries must have seemed even more pronounced as the events of the Revolution began to cohere into a triumphant mythology, with Valley Forge serving as the point of moral and spiritual crisis, the dark night of the soul before salvation.[42]

Perhaps, then, Bartram's weaving of Genesis into his narrative is partly an act of mythmaking, the construction of an alternative (way of being in

---

39. Lanham, "Bartram on Blacktop," 407.
40. See e.g., Slaughter, *Natures of John and William Bartram*, 196.
41. See e.g., Smith, "Stone Blind," 507.
42. Anderson, "Bartram's *Travels* and the Politics of Nature," 4.

Eden's Other Residents

the) world, wild but natural, contrasting with the new republic, emerging as it did out of conflict.

Historian Edward J. Cashin offers a way forward in this direction of interpretation. Though most readers focus on the beautiful, poetic accounts of the nearly pristine lands, Cashin reminds us that it was simultaneously a dangerous world of political upheaval, with tensions among Native Americans competing for hunting grounds, tensions between Europeans and Native Americans, tensions between slaves and slave owners, and tensions between Britain and the New World settlers. So why did Bartram choose to omit the violence of the Revolutionary War? Cashin suggests we find a clue in a remark Bartram made to a friend in 1791, the same year as the publication of *Travels*: "I foresee the Magnificent structure [referring to America] and would be instrumental in its advancement—tools and instruments you know are as necessary as materials in the hand of the Architect."[43] Bartram understood his book to be an instrument in the hand of God, one helping shape an America intended by Providence. Cashin concludes that Bartram

> depicted an America *as he hoped it would be*, purged of wars and ugliness, filled with wonderful plants and animals for the betterment of mankind. If his countrymen treated Native Americans with the respect they deserved; if they ended the evil of slavery; if Americans responded to the innate moral laws endowed by their Creator, and lived in communion with nature, the "Magnificent structure" might be realized.[44]

But perhaps we can push Cashin's insight even further and suggest that Bartram's evocation of Eden is more than poetic flourish but instead an evidence of his belief that a literal recovery of paradise and retreat from the wilderness of corrupt civilization is within reach. Bartram's Bible-informed travelogue is a political tract. If we take Bartram's comment about contributing to the magnificent structure that is the fledgling, independent country seriously, we have in *Travels* a self-conscious use of the Bible with high, if somewhat dreamy, expectations. It attempts nothing less than the rebuilding of Eden.

---

43. As cited in Cashin, "Real World," 12.
44. Ibid. Italics added.

Closing Thoughts

Genesis and animals lurk in the background as Bartram describes a specific historical moment and the human characters he encounters, and the reverse is equally true. To return to Hutcheon's term, the presence of palimpsests in Bartram's *Travels*—these overlapping narratives about humans and animals—allows the reader to see the interrelatedness of the natural world. The drifting of imagery across species defies the rigidity of Linnaean taxonomy, suggesting animals are quite human and humans quite bestial.[45] Wendy Doniger argues that anthropomorphism and zoomorphism "are two different attempts to reduce the otherness between humans and animals, to see the sameness beneath the difference."[46] For Bartram, his poetic resistance to rigid demarcation of the species is a by-product of a key theological assumption, namely, his repeated insistence that all living things originate in the creative acts of God. All living things populate the "glorious apartment of the boundless palace of the sovereign Creator,"[47] as he puts it. Almost seventy years before *On the Origin of Species*, Bartram wrote eloquently of the interrelatedness of the natural world, and out of this flowed concern to limit the suffering of nonhuman species. Though less familiar to most than St. Francis or Albert Schweitzer among luminaries in the Christian tradition whose biblically informed visions of the world invite celebration of animals and advocacy on their behalf, the Quaker William Bartram stands as part of this noble heritage, inspiring and challenging us to immerse ourselves in the wonders of creation while refusing to direct unnecessary violence toward it.

---

45. Cf. Kornegay, "Nature, Man, and God," 84.
46. Doniger, "Zoomorphism in Ancient India," 34.
47. Bartram, *Travels*, xxix.

Bibliography

Adams, Carol J. "What about Dominion in Genesis?" In *A Faith Embracing All Creatures: Addressing Commonly Asked Questions about Christian Care for Animals*, edited by Tripp York and Andy Alexis-Baker, 1–12. Peaceable Kingdom Series 2. Eugene, OR: Cascade Books, 2012.

Albertz, Rainer. *A History of Israelite Religion in the Old Testament Period*. Vol. 2, *From the Exile to the Maccabees*. Translated by John Bowden. OTL. Louisville: Westminster John Knox, 1994.

Alexis-Baker, Andy. "Didn't Jesus Eat Fish?" In *A Faith Embracing All Creatures: Addressing Commonly Asked Questions about Christian Care for Animals*, edited by Tripp York and Andy Alexis-Baker, 64–74. Peaceable Kingdom Series 2. Eugene, OR: Cascade Books, 2012.

Alexis-Baker, Nekeisha. "Doesn't the Bible Say That Humans Are More Important than Animals?" In *A Faith Embracing All Creatures: Addressing Commonly Asked Questions about Christian Care for Animals*, edited by Tripp York and Andy Alexis-Baker, 39–52. Peaceable Kingdom Series 2. Eugene, OR: Cascade Books, 2012.

Allen, Leslie C. *Psalms 101–50*. WBC 21. Waco, TX: Word, 1983.

Allison, Dale C., Jr. "Rejecting Violent Judgment: Luke 9:52–56 and Its Relatives." *JBL* 121 (2002) 459–78.

Ammon, William H. *The Christian Hunter's Guide to Survival*. Old Tappen, NJ: Revell, 1989.

Anderson, A. A. *2 Samuel*. WBC 11. Dallas: Word, 1989.

Anderson, Douglas. "Bartram's *Travels* and the Politics of Nature." *Early American Literature* 25 (1990) 3–17.

Austen, Jane. *Mansfield Park*. Oxford World's Classics. Oxford: Oxford University Press, 1990.

Bailey, Kenneth E. *Paul through Mediterranean Eyes: Cultural Studies in 1 Corinthians*. Downers Grove, IL: IVP Academic, 2011.

Bailly, Jean-Christophe. *The Animal Side*. Translated by Catherine Porter. New York: Fordham University Press, 2011.

Barad, Judith. "What about the Covenant with Noah?" In *A Faith Embracing All Creatures: Addressing Commonly Asked Questions about Christian Care for Animals*, edited by

Bibliography

Tripp York and Andy Alexis-Baker, 13–22. Peaceable Kingdom Series 2. Eugene, OR: Cascade Books, 2012.

Barker, Margaret. *Creation: A Biblical Vision for the Environment.* London: T. & T. Clark, 2010.

Barrett, C. K., ed. *The New Testament Background: Selected Documents.* Rev. ed. New York: HarperCollins, 1989.

Barth, Karl. *Church Dogmatics*, III/4. *The Doctrine of Creation.* Edited by G. W. Bromiley and T. F. Torrance. Translated by A. T. Mackay et al. Edinburgh: T. & T. Clark, 1961.

Bartram, William. *Bartram's Living Legacy: The Travels and the Nature of the South.* Edited by Dorinda G. Dallmeyer. Macon, GA: Mercer University Press, 2010.

Bauckham, Richard. *The Bible and Ecology: Rediscovering the Community of Creation.* Waco, TX: Baylor University Press, 2010.

———. "Jesus and Animals I: What Did He Teach?" In *Animals on the Agenda: Questions about Animals for Theology and Ethics*, edited by Andrew Linzey and Dorothy Yamamoto, 33–48. Urbana: University of Illinois Press, 1998.

———. "Jesus and Animals II: What Did He Practise?" In *Animals on the Agenda: Questions about Animals for Theology and Ethics*, edited by Andrew Linzey and Dorothy Yamamoto, 49–60. Urbana: University of Illinois Press, 1998.

———. "Jesus and the Wild Animals (Mark 1:13): A Christological Image for an Ecological Age." In *Jesus of Nazareth: Lord and Christ: Essays on the Historical Jesus and New Testament Christology*, edited by Joel B. Green and Max Turner, 3–21. Grand Rapids: Eerdmans, 1994.

———. *Living with Other Creatures: Green Exegesis and Theology.* Waco, TX: Baylor University Press, 2011.

———. "Reading the Synoptic Gospels Ecologically." In *Ecological Hermeneutics: Biblical, Historical and Theological Perspectives*, edited by David G. Horrell et al., 70–82. London: T. & T. Clark, 2010.

Beavis, Mary Ann. *Mark.* Paideia. Grand Rapids: Baker, 2011.

Benson, A. C., ed. *Brontë Poems.* New York: Putnam's, The Knickerbocker Press, 1915.

Berkman, John. "Are We Addicted to the Suffering of Animals? Animal Cruelty and the Catholic Moral Tradition." In *A Faith Embracing All Creatures: Addressing Commonly Asked Questions about Christian Care for Animals*, edited by Tripp York and Andy Alexis-Baker, 124–37. Peaceable Kingdom Series 2. Eugene, OR: Cascade Books, 2012.

Blomberg, Craig L. *Jesus and the Gospels: An Introduction and Survey.* 2nd ed. Nashville: B & H Academic, 2009.

Blount, Brian K. *Revelation: A Commentary.* NTL. Louisville: Westminster John Knox, 2009.

Blount, Margaret. "Fallen and Redeemed: Animals in the Novels of C. S. Lewis." In *C. S. Lewis*, edited by Harold Bloom, 11–29. Bloom's Modern Critical Views. New York: Chelsea, 2006.

Bok, Hilary. "Keeping Pets." In *The Oxford Handbook of Animal Ethics*, edited by Tom L. Beauchamp and R. G. Frey, 769–95. Oxford Handbooks. Oxford: Oxford University Press, 2011.

Boling, Robert G. *Judges.* AB 6A. Garden City, NY: Doubleday, 1975.

Bonnycastle, Stephen. *In Search of Authority: An Introductory Guide to Literary Theory.* 3rd ed. Peterborough, ON: Broadview, 2007.

Boring, M. Eugene. *Mark.* NTL. Louisville: Westminster John Knox, 2006.

Bibliography

Branigan, Cynthia A. *Adopting the Racing Greyhound*. 3rd ed. New York: Howell, 2003.
———. *The Reign of the Greyhound: A Popular History of the Oldest Family of Dogs*. New York: Howell, 1997.
Braund, Kathryn E. Holland. "William Bartram's Gustatory Tour." In *Fields of Vision: Essays on the Travels of William Bartram*, edited by Kathryn E. Holland Braund and Charlotte M. Porter, 33–53. Tuscaloosa: University of Alabama Press, 2010.
Bray, Gerald, ed. *1–2 Corinthians*. ACCS 7. Downers Grove, IL: InterVarsity, 1999.
Brontë, Anne. *Agnes Grey*. Edited by Angeline Goreau. London: Penguin, 2004.
———. *The Tenant of Wildfell Hall*. Edited by Lee A. Talley. Peterborough, ON: Broadview, 2009.
Brownlee, William H. *Ezekiel 1–19*. WBC 28. Waco, TX: Word, 1986.
Brumble, H. David. "Cock." In *A Dictionary of Biblical Tradition in English Literature*, edited by David Lyle Jeffrey, 149–51. Grand Rapids: Eerdmans, 1992.
Bulliet, Richard W. *Hunters, Herders, and Hamburgers: The Past and Future of Human-Animal Relationships*. New York: Columbia University Press, 2005.
Byrne, Brendan. "An Ecological Reading of Rom. 8.19–22: Possibilities and Hesitations." In *Ecological Hermeneutics: Biblical, Historical and Theological Perspectives*, edited by David G. Horrell et al., 83–93. London: T. & T. Clark, 2010.
Canadian Broadcasting Corporation. "Animal Abuse Alleged at Manitoba Hog Farm." http://www.cbc.ca/news/canada/manitoba/story/2012/12/10/mb-animal-abuse-hog-farm-puratone-manitoba.html/.
Cashin, Edward J. "The Real World of Bartram's *Travels*." In *Fields of Vision: Essays on the Travels of William Bartram*, edited by Kathryn E. Holland Braund and Charlotte M. Porter, 3–14. Tuscaloosa: University of Alabama Press, 2010.
Chitham, Edward. *A Life of Anne Brontë*. Oxford: Blackwell, 1991.
Clark, Stephen R. L. "Animals in Classical and Late Antique Philosophy." In *The Oxford Handbook of Animal Ethics*, edited by Tom L. Beauchamp and R. G. Frey, 35–60. Oxford Handbooks. Oxford: Oxford University Press, 2011.
Cohen, Noah J. *Tsa'ar Ba'alei Hayim: The Prevention of Cruelty to Animals—Its Bases, Development, and Legislation in Hebrew Literature*. 2nd ed. Nanuet, NY: Feldheim, 1976.
Cohn-Sherbok, Dan. "Hope for the Animal Kingdom: A Jewish Vision." In *A Communion of Subjects: Animals in Religion, Science, and Ethics*, edited by Paul Waldau and Kimberley Patton, 81–90. New York: Columbia University Press, 2006.
Conradie, Ernst M. "The Road towards an Ecological, Biblical and Theological Hermeneutics." *Scriptura* 85 (2004) 123–35.
Cook, Albert, trans. and ed. *The Odyssey: A New Verse Translation*. New York: Norton, 1974.
Crossan, John Dominic. *The Greatest Prayer: Rediscovering the Revolutionary Message of the Lord's Prayer*. New York: HarperCollins, 2010.
———. *Jesus: A Revolutionary Biography*. San Francisco: HarperCollins, 1994.
———. "The Power of the Dog." In *Postmodern Interpretations of the Bible: A Reader*, edited by A. K. M. Adam, 187–93. St. Louis: Chalice, 2001.
Davids, Peter H. *The Letters of 2 Peter and Jude*. Pillar New Testament Commentary. Grand Rapids: Eerdmans, 2006.
Davies, Philip R., et al. *The Complete World of the Dead Sea Scrolls*. New York: Thames & Hudson, 2002.

Bibliography

Davies, Stevie. "'Three Distinct and Unconnected Tales': *The Professor, Agnes Grey*, and *Wuthering Heights*." In *The Cambridge Companion to the Brontës*, edited by Heather Glen, 72–98. Cambridge Companions to Literature. Cambridge: Cambridge University Press, 2002.

Deane-Drummond, Celia E. *Eco-Theology*. Winona, MN: Anselm Academic, 2008.

———. *The Ethics of Nature*. New Dimensions to Religious Ethics. Malden, MA: Blackwell, 2004.

Derrida, Jacques. *The Animal That Therefore I Am*. Edited by Marie-Louise Mallet. Translated by David Wills. Perspectives in Continental Philosophy. New York: Fordham University Press, 2008.

DeSilva, David A. *Seeing Things John's Way: The Rhetoric of the Book of Revelation*. Louisville: Westminster John Knox, 2009.

Doniger, Wendy. "Zoomorphism in Ancient India: Humans More Bestial than Beasts." In *Thinking with Animals: New Perspectives on Anthropomorphism*, edited by Lorraine Daston and Gregg Mitman, 17–36. New York: Columbia University Press, 2005.

Douglas, Mary. "The Forbidden Animals in Leviticus." *JSOT* 59 (1993) 3–23.

Durham, John I. *The Biblical Rembrandt: Human Painter in a Landscape of Faith*. Macon, GA: Mercer University Press, 2004.

Eco, Umberto. *Inventing the Enemy, and Other Occasional Writings*. Translated by Richard Dixon. Boston: Houghton Mifflin Harcourt, 2012.

Eisenman, Robert. *James, the Brother of Jesus: The Key to Unlocking the Secrets of Early Christianity and the Dead Sea Scrolls*. New York: Penguin, 1997.

Fabre-Vassas, Claudine. *The Singular Beast: Jews, Christians & the Pig*. Translated by Carol Volk. European Perspectives. New York: Columbia University Press, 1997.

Farrell, Robert, and Catherine Karkov. "Serpent." In *A Dictionary of Biblical Tradition in English Literature*, edited by David Lyle Jeffrey, 693–95. Grand Rapids: Eerdmans, 1992.

Fee, Gordon D. *The First Epistle to the Corinthians*. NICNT. Grand Rapids: Eerdmans, 1987.

Ferguson, Everett. *Backgrounds of Early Christianity*. 2nd ed. Grand Rapids: Eerdmans, 1993.

Findley, Timothy. *From Stone Orchard: A Collection of Memories*. Toronto: HarperCollins, 1998.

———. *Inside Memory: Pages from a Writer's Perspective*. Toronto: HarperCollins, 1990.

———. *Not Wanted on the Voyage*. Toronto: Penguin, 1984, 1996.

———. *The Wars*. Toronto: Penguin, 1978, 1996.

Fitzmyer, Joseph A. *First Corinthians*. Anchor Yale Bible. New Haven: Yale University Press, 2008.

Fleming, Alison C. "Animals, Symbolism of." In *Dictionary of the Bible and Western Culture*, edited by Mary Ann Beavis and Michael J. Gilmour, 20–21. Sheffield: Sheffield Phoenix, 2012.

———. "Birds, Symbolism of." In *Dictionary of the Bible and Western Culture*, edited by Mary Ann Beavis and Michael J. Gilmour, 58–59. Sheffield: Sheffield Phoenix, 2012.

Foltz, Richard C. *Animals in Islamic Tradition and Muslim Cultures*. Oxford: Oneworld, 2005.

———. "'This she-camel of God is a sign to you': Dimensions of Animals in Islamic Tradition and Muslim Culture." In *A Communion of Subjects: Animals in Religion,*

Science, and Ethics, edited by Paul Waldau and Kimberley Patton, 149–59. New York: Columbia University Press, 2006.

Fradkin, Arlene, and Mallory McCane O'Connor. "Before Bartram: Artist-Naturalist Mark Catesby." In *Fields of Vision: Essays on the Travels of William Bartram*, edited by Kathryn E. Holland Braund and Charlotte M. Porter, 91–114. Tuscaloosa: University of Alabama Press, 2010.

Fredriksen, Paula, and Adele Reinhartz, eds. *Jesus, Judaism, and Christian Anti-Judaism: Reading the New Testament after the Holocaust*. Louisville: Westminster John Knox, 2002.

Gaffney, James. "Can Catholic Morality Make Room for Animals?" In *Animals on the Agenda: Questions about Animals for Theology and Ethics*, edited by Andrew Linzey and Dorothy Yamamoto, 100–112. Urbana: University of Illinois Press, 1998.

———. "The Relevance of Animal Experimentation to Roman Catholic Ethical Methodology." In *Animal Sacrifices: Religious Perspectives on the Use of Animals in Science*, edited by Tom Regan, 149–70. Ethics and Action. Philadelphia: Temple University Press, 1986.

Gaventa, Beverly Roberts. *Our Mother Saint Paul*. Louisville: Westminster John Knox, 2007.

Gilmour, Michael J. "The Far Side of Religion: Notes on the Prophet Gary Larson." *Direction* 39/2 (2010) 220–33.

———. "Goats and Gods, Demons and Dogs: Zoomorphism in Salman Rushdie's Novels." MA thesis, University of Manitoba, 2007.

———. *Gods and Guitars: Seeking the Sacred in Post-1960s Popular Music*. Waco, TX: Baylor University Press, 2009.

———. *The Significance of Parallels between 2 Peter and Other Early Christian Literature*. Academia Biblica 10. Atlanta: Society of Biblical Literature, 2002.

———. "Timothy Findley's Postmodern Flood: Rewriting Genesis in *Not Wanted on the Voyage*." *Didaskalia* 17/2 (2006) 51–63.

Goldingay, John E. *Daniel*. WBC 30. Dallas: Word, 1989.

Goldstein, Jonathan A. *I Maccabees*. AB 41. Garden City, NY: Doubleday, 1976.

Goodall, Jane. "The Dance of Awe." In *A Communion of Subjects: Animals in Religion, Science, and Ethics*, edited by Paul Waldau and Kimberley Patton, 651–56. New York: Columbia University Press, 2006.

———, with Phillip Berman. *Reason for Hope: A Spiritual Journey*. New York: Warner, 1999.

Gruen, Lori. "Empathy and Vegetarian Commitments." In *The Feminist Care Tradition in Animal Ethics: A Reader*, edited by Josephine Donovan and Carol J. Adams, 333–43. New York: Columbia University Press, 2007.

Guthrie, Woody. *Bound for Glory*. New York: Penguin, 1943, 1983.

Habel, Norman. *The Birth, the Curse and the Greening of Earth: An Ecological Reading of Genesis 1–11*. Earth Bible Commentary 1. Sheffield: Sheffield Phoenix, 2011.

———. "Earth." In *Dictionary of the Bible and Western Culture*, edited by Mary Ann Beavis and Michael J. Gilmour, 124–25. Sheffield: Sheffield Phoenix, 2012.

———. "'Is the Wild Ox Willing to Serve You?': Challenging the Mandate to Dominate." In *The Earth Story in Wisdom Traditions*, edited by Norman Habel and Shirley Wurst, 179–89. Earth Bible 3. Sheffield: Sheffield Academic, 2001.

———. *Rainbow of Mysteries: Meeting the Sacred in Nature*. Kelowna, BC: CopperHouse, 2012.

Bibliography

Harrington, Daniel J. *Invitation to the Apocrypha*. Grand Rapids: Eerdmans, 1999.
Harrington, Wilfrid J. *Revelation*. SP 16. Collegeville, MN: Liturgical, 1993.
Haught, John F. *Making Sense of Evolution: Darwin, God, and the Drama of Life*. Louisville: Westminster John Knox, 2010.
Hays, Richard B. *Echoes of Scripture in the Letters of Paul*. New Haven: Yale University Press, 1989.
———. *First Corinthians*. Interpretation. Louisville: John Knox, 1997.
Helyer, L. R. "Tobit." In *Dictionary of New Testament Backgrounds*, edited by Craig A. Evans and Stanley E. Porter, 1238–41. Downers Grove, IL: InterVarsity, 2000.
Henderson, Ian H., and Meredith Warren. "Mark, Gospel of." In *Dictionary of the Bible and Western Culture*, edited by Mary Ann Beavis and Michael J. Gilmour, 323–24. Sheffield: Sheffield Phoenix, 2012.
Hennecke, Edgar, and Wilhelm Schneemelcher, eds. *New Testament Apocrypha*. Vol. 2, *Writings Relating to the Apostles, Apocalypses and Related Subjects*. Translated by R. McL. Wilson. Louisville: Westminster John Knox, 1992.
Hobgood-Oster, Laura. "Does Christian Hospitality Require That We Eat Meat?" In *A Faith Embracing All Creatures: Addressing Commonly Asked Questions about Christian Care for Animals*, edited by Tripp York and Andy Alexis-Baker, 75–89. Peaceable Kingdom Series 2. Eugene, OR: Cascade Books, 2012.
———. *The Friends We Keep: Unleashing Christianity's Compassion for Animals*. Waco, TX: Baylor University Press, 2010.
———. *Holy Dogs and Asses: Animals in the Christian Tradition*. Urbana: University of Illinois Press, 2008.
Hopkins, Gerard Manley. *The Major Works: Including All the Poems and Selected Prose*. Edited by Catherine Phillips. Oxford: Oxford University Press, 2002.
Horrell, David G. *The Bible and the Environment: Towards a Critical Ecological Biblical Theology*. Biblical Challenges in the Contemporary World. London: Equinox, 2010.
———. "The Green Bible: A Timely Idea Deeply Flawed." *Expository Times* 121 (2010) 180–86.
Horrell, David G., Cheryl Hunt, and Christopher Southgate. *Greening Paul: Rereading the Apostle in a Time of Ecological Crisis*. Waco: Baylor University Press, 2010.
Horrell, David G., et al., eds. *Ecological Hermeneutics: Biblical, Historical and Theological Perspectives*. London: T. & T. Clark, 2010.
Houston, Walter. "What Was the Meaning of Classifying Animals as Clean or Unclean?" In *Animals on the Agenda: Questions about Animals for Theology and Ethics*, edited by Andrew Linzey and Dorothy Yamamoto, 18–24. Urbana: University of Illinois Press, 1998.
Hughes, Philip Edgcumbe. *The Book of Revelation: A Commentary*. Grand Rapids: Eerdmans, 1990.
Hurtado, Larry W. *At the Origins of Christian Worship: The Context and Character of Earliest Christian Devotion*. Grand Rapids: Eerdmans, 1999.
Hutcheon, Linda. *A Theory of Adaptation*. New York: Routledge, 2006.
Hyland, J. R. *God's Covenant with Animals: A Biblical Basis for the Humane Treatment of All Creatures*. New York: Lantern, 2004.
The Illuminator and a Bible for the Twenty-First Century. DVD. Produced by 3BM Television for BBC Wales and Saint John's University, 2005.
Jeffers, James S. *The Greco-Roman World of the New Testament Era: Exploring the Background of Early Christianity*. Downers Grove, IL: InterVarsity, 1999.

Bibliography

Johnson, Luke Timothy. *The Writings of the New Testament: An Interpretation*. Rev. ed. Minneapolis: Fortress, 1999.

Kalechofsky, Roberta. "Hierarchy, Kinship, and Responsibility: The Jewish Relationship to the Animal World." In *A Communion of Subjects: Animals in Religion, Science, and Ethics*, edited by Paul Waldau and Kimberley Patton, 91–99. New York: Columbia University Press, 2006.

Kalof, Linda, and Amy Fitzgerald, eds. *The Animal Reader: The Essential Classic and Contemporary Writings*. Oxford: Berg, 2007.

Kazez, Jean. *Animalkind: What We Owe to Animals*. Public Philosophy. Malden, MA: Wiley-Blackwell, 2010.

Kemmerer, Lisa. *Animals and World Religions*. New York: Oxford University Press, 2012.

Klawans, Jonathan. *Purity, Sacrifice, and the Temple: Symbolism and Supersessionism in the Study of Ancient Judaism*. Oxford: Oxford University Press, 2006.

———. "Sacrifice in Ancient Israel: Pure Bodies, Domesticated Animals, and the Divine Shepherd." In *A Communion of Subjects: Animals in Religion, Science, and Ethics*, edited by Paul Waldau and Kimberley Patton, 65–80. New York: Columbia University Press, 2006.

Knight, Douglas A., and Amy-Jill Levine. *The Meaning of the Bible: What the Jewish Scriptures and Christian Old Testament Can Teach Us*. New York: HarperCollins, 2011.

Koester, Helmut. *Introduction to the New Testament*. Vol. 1, *History, Culture, and Religion of the Hellenistic Age*. New York: de Gruyter, 1982.

Kornegay, Burt. "Nature, Man, and God: The Introduction to Bartram's *Travels*." In *Fields of Vision: Essays on the* Travels *of William Bartram*, edited by Kathryn E. Holland Braund and Charlotte M. Porter, 81–90. Tuscaloosa: University of Alabama Press, 2010.

Kowalski, Gary. *The Bible according to Noah: Theology as if Animals Mattered*. New York: Lantern, 2001.

Kreilkamp, Ivan. "Petted Things: *Wuthering Heights* and the Animal." *Yale Journal of Criticism* 18/1 (2005) 87–110.

Kuhn, Thomas. *The Structure of Scientific Revolutions*. 2nd ed. Chicago: University of Chicago Press, 1970.

Kurian, George Thomas, ed. *Nelson's New Christian Dictionary: The Authoritative Resource on the Christian World*. Nashville: Thomas Nelson, 2001.

Lamp, Jeffrey S. *The Greening of Hebrews? Ecological Readings in the Letter to the Hebrews*. Eugene, OR: Pickwick, 2012.

Lane, William L. *The Gospel according to Mark*. NICNT. Grand Rapids: Eerdmans, 1974.

Lane Fox, Robin. *Pagans and Christians*. New York: Knopf, 1987.

Lanham, J. Drew. "Bartram on Blacktop." In *Bartram's Living Legacy: The* Travels *and the Nature of the South*, edited by Dorinda G. Dallmeyer, 403–15. Macon, GA: Mercer University Press, 2010.

Larson, Gary. *There's a Hair In My Dirt! A Worm's Story*. New York: Harper, 1998.

Leonard, R. Maynard, ed. *The Dog in British Poetry*. San Francisco: Chronicle, 2005.

Lewis, C. S. *The Complete C. S. Lewis Signature Classics*. New York: HarperOne, 2002.

———. *The Magicians's Nephew*. New York: HarperCollins, 1955.

Li, Chien-Hui. "Mobilizing Christianity in the Antivivisection Movement in Victorian Britain." *Journal of Animal Ethics* 2/2 (2012) 141–61.

Linzey, Andrew. *Animal Theology*. Urbana: University of Illinois Press, 1994.

Bibliography

———. "C. S. Lewis's Theology of Animals." *Anglican Theological Review* 80 (1998) 60–81.
———. *Creatures of the Same God: Explorations in Animal Theology*. New York: Lantern, 2009.
———. "Introduction: Is Christianity Irredeemably Speciesist?" In *Animals on the Agenda: Questions about Animals for Theology and Ethics*, edited by Andrew Linzey and Dorothy Yamamoto, xi–xx. Urbana: University of Illinois Press, 1998.
Linzey, Andrew, and Dorothy Yamamoto, eds. *Animals on the Agenda: Questions about Animals for Theology and Ethics*. Urbana: University of Illinois Press, 1998.
Lohse, Eduard. *Colossians and Philemon*. Hermeneia. Translated by William R. Poehlmann and Robert J. Karris. Philadelphia: Fortress, 1971.
MacDonald, Nathan. *What Did the Ancient Israelites Eat? Diet in Biblical Times*. Grand Rapids: Eerdmans, 2008.
Maier, Harry O. "Green Millennialism: American Evangelicals, Environmentalism and the Book of Revelation." In *Ecological Hermeneutics: Biblical, Historical and Theological Perspectives*, edited by David G. Horrell et al., 246–65. London: T. & T. Clark, 2010.
Manitoba Government. "Pork." http://www.gov.mb.ca/trade/globaltrade/agrifood/po_livestock/pork.html.
Mason, Jim, and Mary Finelli. "Brave New Farm?" In *The Animals Reader: The Essential Classic and Contemporary Writings*, edited by Linda Kalof and Amy Fitzgerald, 158–70. Oxford: Berg, 2007.
Masure, Eugene. *The Christian Sacrifice*. New York: Kennedy, 1943.
Maudlin, Michael G., et al., eds. *The Green Bible*. New York: HarperCollins, 2008.
May, Herbert G., and Bruce M. Metzger, eds. *The New Oxford Annotated Bible with the Apocrypha*. Revised Standard Version. New York: Oxford University Press, 1977.
Mayer, Jed. "The Expression of the Emotions in Man and Laboratory Animals." *Victorian Studies* 50 (2008) 399–417.
McColley, Diane. "Raphael." In *A Dictionary of Biblical Tradition in English Literature*, edited by David Lyle Jeffrey, 768–69. Grand Rapids: Eerdmans, 1992.
———. "Tobit and Tobias." In *A Dictionary of Biblical Tradition in English Literature*, edited by David Lyle Jeffrey, 655–56. Grand Rapids: Eerdmans, 1992.
McCracken, David. "Narration and Comedy in the Book of Tobit." *JBL* 114 (1995) 401–18.
McDaniel, Jay. "Practicing the Presence of God: A Christian Approach to Animals." In *A Communion of Subjects: Animals in Religion, Science, and Ethics*, edited by Paul Waldau and Kimberley Patton, 132–45. New York: Columbia University Press, 2006.
McGinn, Bernard, ed. *The Essential Writings of Christian Mysticism*. New York: Modern Library, 2006.
Metzger, Bruce M. *The Text of the New Testament: Its Transmission, Corruption, and Restoration*. 3rd enlarged ed. Oxford: Oxford University Press, 1992.
———. *A Textual Commentary on the Greek New Testament*. Corrected ed. London: United Bible Societies, 1975.
Morgan, Jonathan. "Sacrifice in Leviticus: Eco-Friendly Ritual or Unholy Waste?" In *Ecological Hermeneutics: Biblical, Historical and Theological Perspectives*, edited by David G. Horrell et al., 32–45. London: T. & T. Clark, 2010.
Moritz, Joshua M. "Animals and the Image of God in the Bible and Beyond." *Dialog: A Journal of Theology* 48 (2009) 134–46.
Mounce, Robert H. *The Book of Revelation*. NICNT. Rev. ed. Grand Rapids: Eerdmans, 1998.

Bibliography

Muddiman, John. "A New Testament Doctrine of Creation?" In *Animals on the Agenda: Questions about Animals for Theology and Ethics*, edited by Andrew Linzey and Dorothy Yamamoto, 25–32. Urbana: University of Illinois Press, 1998.

Murti, Vasu. *They Shall not Hurt or Destroy: Animal Rights and Vegetarianism in the Western Religious Traditions*. Cleveland: Vegetarian Advocates, 2003.

Neusner, Jacob, trans. *The Mishnah: A New Translation*. New Haven: Yale University Press, 1988.

Neyrey, Jerome H. "Clean/Unclean, Pure/Polluted, and Holy/Profane: The Idea and the System of Purity." In *The Social Sciences and New Testament Interpretation*, edited by Richard L. Rohrbaugh, 80–104. Peabody, MA: Hendrickson, 1996.

———. "Meals, Food, and Table Fellowship." In *The Social Sciences and New Testament Interpretation*, edited by Richard L. Rohrbaugh, 159–82. Peabody, MA: Hendrickson, 1996.

Oleson, Brian, and Janet Honey. "Agricultural Review and Outlook, 2011–2012." Feb. 23, 2012, Online: http://www.umanitoba.ca/afs/agric_economics/staff/CUC_Outlook_November_2011_rev_Feb2012.pdf.

Osborne, Catherine. *Dumb Beasts and Dead Philosophers: Humanity and the Humane in Ancient Philosophy and Literature*. Oxford: Clarendon, 2007.

Oswalt, John N. *The Book of Isaiah: Chapters 1–39*. NICOT. Grand Rapids: Eerdmans, 1986.

Painter, John, and David A. DeSilva. *James and Jude*. Paideia. Grand Rapids: Baker, 2012.

Parsons, Mikeal C. *Body and Character in Luke and Acts: The Subversion of Physiognomy in Early Christianity*. Grand Rapids: Baker, 2006.

Penner, Jeremy. "Cock." In *Dictionary of the Bible and Western Culture*, edited by Mary Ann Beavis and Michael J. Gilmour, 93–94. Sheffield: Sheffield Phoenix, 2012.

Peterson, Dale. *The Moral Lives of Animals*. New York: Bloomsbury, 2011.

Phelps, Norm. *The Dominion of Love: Animal Rights according to the Bible*. New York: Lantern, 2002.

Preece, Rod. "Darwinism, Christianity, and the Great Vivisection Debate." *Journal of the History of Ideas* 64/3 (2003) 399–419.

Quammen, David. *Monster of God: The Man-Eating Predator in the Jungles of History and the Mind*. New York: Norton, 2003.

Rachels, Stuart. "Vegetarianism." In *The Oxford Handbook of Animal Ethics*, edited by Tom L. Beauchamp and R. G. Frey, 877–905. Oxford Handbooks. Oxford: Oxford University Press, 2011.

Reed, Stephen A. "Meat Eating and the Hebrew Bible." In *Problems in Biblical Theology: Essays in Honor of Rolf Knierim*, edited by Henry T. C. Sun and Keith L. Eades, with James M. Robinson and Garth I. Moller, 281–94. Grand Rapids: Eerdmans, 1997.

Regan, Tom. *Defending Animal Rights*. Urbana: University of Illinois Press, 2001.

Regan, Tom, and Andrew Linzey, eds. *Other Nations: Animals in Modern Literature*. Waco: Baylor University Press, 2010.

Resseguie, James L. *Spiritual Landscape: Images of the Spiritual Life in the Gospel of Luke*. Peabody, MA: Hendrickson, 2004.

Ritvo, Harriet. "Our Animal Cousins." *differences: A Journal of Feminist Cultural Studies* 15/1 (2004) 48–68.

Rogerson, John W. "The Creation Stories: Their Ecological Potential and Problems." In *Ecological Hermeneutics: Biblical, Historical and Theological Perspectives*, edited by David G. Horrell et al., 21–31. London: T. & T. Clark, 2010.

Bibliography

———. "What Was the Meaning of Animal Sacrifice?" In *Animals on the Agenda: Questions about Animals for Theology and Ethics*, edited by Andrew Linzey and Dorothy Yamamoto, 8–17. Urbana: University of Illinois Press, 1998.

Rubio, Julie Hanlon. "Toward a Just Way of Eating." In *Green Discipleship: Catholic Theological Ethics and the Environment*, edited by Tobias Winright, 360–78. Winona, MN: Anselm Academic, 2011.

Sacks, Jonathan. *The Great Partnership: Science, Religion, and the Search for Meaning.* New York: Schocken, 2011.

Said, Edward W. *Culture and Imperialism.* New York: Vintage, 1993.

———. *Freud and the Non-European.* London: Verso, 2003.

Santmire, H. Paul. *Nature Reborn: The Ecological and Cosmic Promise of Christian Theology.* Minneapolis: Fortress, 2000.

Sarna, Nahum M. *Understanding Genesis.* New York: Schocken, 1970.

Scheid, Daniel P. "Saint Thomas Aquinas, the Thomistic Tradition, and the Cosmic Common Good." In *Green Discipleship: Catholic Theological Ethics and the Environment*, edited by Tobias Winright, 129–47. Winona, MN: Anselm Academic, 2011.

Schmidt, T. E. "Taxes." In *Dictionary of Jesus and the Gospels*, edited by Joel B. Green and Scot McKnight, 804–7. Downers Grove, IL: InterVarsity, 1992.

Schwartz, Richard H. *Judaism and Vegetarianism.* New rev. ed. New York: Lantern, 2001.

Schweitzer, Albert. *Albert Schweitzer: Reverence for Life.* Selected by Peter Seymour. Kansas City: Hallmark, 1971.

———. *The Mysticism of Paul the Apostle.* Translated by William Montgomery. New York: Seabury, 1968.

Schweizer, Eduard. *The Good News according to Mark.* Translated by Donald H. Madvig. Richmond: John Knox, 1970.

Serpell, James A. "People in Disguise: Anthropomorphism and the Human-Pet Relationship." In *Thinking with Animals: New Perspectives on Anthropomorphism*, edited by Lorraine Daston and Gregg Mitman, 121–36. New York: Columbia University Press, 2005.

Shedinger, Robert F. "Kuhnian Paradigms and Biblical Scholarship: Is Biblical Studies a Science?" *JBL* 119/3 (2000) 453–71.

Silva, Moisés. *Philippians.* Wycliffe Exegetical Commentary. Chicago: Moody, 1988.

Singer, Peter. *Animal Liberation.* New York: Harper Perennial, 2009.

Slaughter, Thomas P. *The Natures of John and William Bartram.* Philadelphia: University of Pennsylvania Press, 1996.

Smith, Matthew C. "Stone Blind." In *Bartram's Living Legacy: The Travels and the Nature of the South*, edited by Dorinda G. Dallmeyer, 491–511. Macon, GA: Mercer University Press, 2010.

Soggin, J. Alberto. *Judges.* Translated by John Bowden. OTL. Philadelphia: Westminster, 1981.

Soulen, Richard N., and R. Kendall Soulen. *Handbook of Biblical Criticism.* 3rd ed. Louisville: Westminster John Knox, 2001.

Southgate, Christopher. *The Groaning of Creation: God, Evolution, and the Problem of Evil.* Louisville: Westminster John Knox, 2008.

Steiner, Gary. "Descartes, Christianity, and Contemporary Speciesism." In *A Communion of Subjects: Animals in Religion, Science, and Ethics*, edited by Paul Waldau and Kimberley Patton, 117–31. New York: Columbia University Press, 2006.

Bibliography

Thomas Aquinas, Saint. *Summa Theologica*. Translated by Fathers of the English Dominican Province. Westminster, MD: Christian Classics, 1981.

Thompson, Geoff. "'Remaining Loyal to the Earth': Humanity, God's Other Creatures and the Bible in Karl Barth." In *Ecological Hermeneutics: Biblical, Historical and Theological Perspectives*, edited by David G. Horrell et al., 181–95. London: T. & T. Clark, 2010.

Tirosh-Samuelson, Hava. "Judaism and the Care for God's Creation." In *Green Discipleship: Catholic Theological Ethics and the Environment*, edited by Tobias Winright, 286–319. Winona, MN: Anselm Academic, 2011.

Tuan, Yi-Fu. "Animal Pets: Cruelty and Affection." In *The Animals Reader: The Essential Classic and Contemporary Writings*, edited by Linda Kalof and Amy Fitzgerald, 141–53. Oxford: Berg, 2007.

VanderKam, James C. *The Dead Sea Scrolls Today*. Grand Rapids: Eerdmans, 1994.

Vauchez, André. *Francis of Assisi: The Life and Afterlife of a Medieval Saint*. Translated by Michael F. Cusato. New Haven: Yale University Press, 2012.

Waal, Frans de. *The Bonobo and the Atheist: In Search of Humanism among the Primates*. New York: Norton, 2013.

Walker-Jones, Arthur. "Serpent/Snake." In *Dictionary of the Bible and Western Culture*, edited by Mary Ann Beavis and Michael J. Gilmour, 478–79. Sheffield: Sheffield Phoenix, 2012.

Walters, Kerry. *Vegetarianism: A Guide for the Perplexed*. London: Continuum, 2012.

Warner, Keith Douglas. "Retrieving Saint Francis: Tradition and Innovation for Our Ecological Vision." In *Green Discipleship: Catholic Theological Ethics and the Environment*, edited by Tobias Winright, 114–28. Winona, MN: Anselm Academic, 2011.

Way, Kenneth C. *Donkeys in the Biblical World: Ceremony and Symbol*. History, Archaeology, and Culture of the Levant 2. Winona Lake, IN: Eisenbrauns, 2011.

Webb, Stephen H. "Didn't Jesus Eat Lamb? The Last Supper and the Case of the Missing Meat." In *A Faith Embracing All Creatures: Addressing Commonly Asked Questions about Christian Care for Animals*, edited by Tripp York and Andy Alexis-Baker, 53–63. Peaceable Kingdom Series 2. Eugene, OR: Cascade Books, 2012.

———. *On God and Dogs: A Christian Theology of Compassion for Animals*. New York: Oxford University Press, 1998.

Wenham, Gordon J. *Genesis 1–15*. WBC 1. Dallas: Word, 1987.

Whiston, William, trans. *The Works of Josephus: Complete and Unabridged*. New updated ed. Peabody, MA: Hendrickson, 1987.

White, Lynn, Jr. "The Historical Roots of Our Ecologic Crisis." *Science* 155 (1967) 1203–7.

White, Paul S. "The Experimental Animal in Victorian Britain." In *Thinking with Animals: New Perspectives on Anthropomorphism*, edited by Lorraine Daston and Gregg Mitman, 59–81. New York: Columbia University Press, 2005.

Williams, Guy. "An Apocalyptic and Magical Interpretation of Paul's 'Beast Fight' in Ephesus (1 Corinthians 15:32)." *Journal of Theological Studies* 57/1 (2006) 42–56.

Williams, Rowan. *The Lion's World: A Journey into the Heart of Narnia*. Oxford: Oxford University Press, 2012.

Wirzba, Norman. *Food and Faith: A Theology of Eating*. Cambridge: Cambridge University Press, 2001.

Wise, Michael, et al., trans. *The Dead Sea Scrolls: A New Translation*. New York: HarperCollins, 1996.

Bibliography

Witherington, Ben III. *The Gospel of Mark: A Socio-Rhetorical Commentary*. Grand Rapids: Eerdmans, 2001.

Wright, N. T. *Jesus and the Victory of God*. Christian Origins and the Question of God 2. Minneapolis: Fortress, 1996.

———. "Jesus Is Coming—Plant a Tree!" In *The Green Bible*, edited by Michael G. Maudlin et al., I-72–85. New York: HarperCollins, 2008.

———. *The New Testament and the People of God*. Christian Origins and the Question of God 1. Minneapolis: Fortress, 1992.

———. *Paul: In Fresh Perspective*. Minneapolis: Fortress, 2005.

———. *The Resurrection of the Son of God*. Christian Origins and the Question of God 3. Minneapolis: Fortress, 2003.

———. *Surprised by Hope: Rethinking Heaven, the Resurrection, and the Mission of the Church*. New York: HarperCollins, 2008.

Wynn, Mark. "Thomas Aquinas: Reading the Idea of Dominion in the Light of the Doctrine of Creation." In *Ecological Hermeneutics: Biblical, Historical and Theological Perspectives*, edited by David G. Horrell et al., 154–65. London: T. & T. Clark, 2010.

Yamamoto, Dorothy. "Aquinas and Animals: Patrolling the Boundary?" In *Animals on the Agenda: Questions about Animals for Theology and Ethics*, edited by Andrew Linzey and Dorothy Yamamoto, 80–89. Urbana: University of Illinois Press, 1998.

York, Tripp, and Andy Alexis-Baker, eds. *A Faith Embracing All Creatures: Addressing Commonly Asked Questions about Christian Care for Animals*. Peaceable Kingdom Series 2. Eugene, OR: Cascade Books, 2012.

Zamir, Tzachi. "Literary Works and Animal Ethics." In *The Oxford Handbook of Animal Ethics*, edited by Tom L. Beauchamp and R. G. Frey, 932–55. Oxford: Oxford University Press, 2011.

Subject Index

Acts of Thomas, xi–xii
advocacy, animal, 99n7, 100–101, 139, 145–46, 147, 153
Adam, Adam and Eve, 5, 41, 49, 61, 63, 64, 64n19, 65, 65n20, 68, 69, 71, 73, 103, 114, 114n4, 122, 140, 142, 145, 146, 147, 147n21, 149, 150
angel(s), 38–39, 45, 61, 68, 70, 71–75, 82, 83, 86, 88, 116–18, 120, 121
animal-based technologies, *see* animal bodies, use of
animal bodies, use of, 58–61
animal imagery, symbolism, 40n26, 41–42, 44, 68, 70n30, 116, 145, 153
anthropocentrism, 28, 33, 52, 74, 77, 142, 145, 153
Argus, *see* Odysseus
ark, *see* Noah
Assisi, St. Francis of, xiii, 56
Austen, Jane, ix, 29–36, 38, 69

Balaam, xi–xii, 38–39, 74, 86
Bartram, William, 14, 63, 140–53
bears, 7, 41, 42n31, 88, 89, 129, 135, 143–44, 148
bestial imagery, 41–44, 53n56, 116, 145, 153
blood, 89n63, 90, 92–112, 133, 136
Brontë, Anne, 14, 18–25, 46, 123

cat(s), 7n11, 57, 126–28
clean/unclean, *see* dietary laws
cock('s crow), 39–40
community, 3, 4, 10, 14, 26–28, 34, 45, 48, 49, 61, 94–97, 105, 108–10, 119, 120, 124–25, 133, 139
companion animals, *see* pets
concessions, divine, 66–68, 97–99, 108
coyote, 15–17
creation stories, 5, 51, 61–69, 132, 149–50
cruelty to animals, 5, 15, 19, 23–24, 29, 32n12, 45–48, 56n1, 119, 126–28, 134–35, 138, 148–49

David, 39–40, 41, 46, 89, 106, 120–21, 135
Dead Sea Scrolls, 58, 71n32, 102, 108n21, 135n31
deer, 59–60, 78, 80, 106, 125, 143, 146, 148
dietary laws, 46, 54, 73n34, 129–34
dog(s), ix–x, 7–8, 15, 22–23, 42, 55, 56–57, 70–83, 86, 88, 113–15, 129, 148
dominion (*radah*), 5, 14, 17n33, 48–49, 57n4, 63–67, 78n39, 79, 101n12, 116, 118, 136, 146, 150
domestic animals, 7n11, 10, 12, 46n39, 65, 116, 117, 119, 146

167

Subject Index

donkey(s), x, xi–xii, 9, 38–39, 74, 77, 86, 90–91, 119

Eden, *see* garden, gardener
environmental concern, 6, 31, 46–47, 50, 53n57, 54, 57, 64, 136, 141
eschatology, 15, 37, 41, 47n43, 49, 56–58, 62–63, 86, 114, 122, 125
Eve, *see* Adam, Adam and Eve
evolution, 50n49, 62, 63

factory farms, 11–12, 99n7, 105, 115, 134, 136–37, 139
Findley, Timothy, 15–17
fish, 40, 51, 65, 70, 74–76, 86, 88, 90, 99, 106, 131, 136n33, 137, 147, 150
four living creatures (Revelation), 86, 115–19

garden, gardener, 65–69, 71, 114n4, 128, 140–53
generosity, 1–4, 17, 34–35, 43n35, 55, 63, 119, 125, 135, 138, 148
Goodall, Jane, 87–88, 134
greyhounds, *see* dog(s)
groaning creation, 37, 49, 86, 113–15
Guthrie, Woody, x, 126–28

hermeneutics, 12, 30–31, 33, 37–41, 42, 46–47, 51–55, 89n62
hesed, 1–2
Hobgood-Oster, Laura, ix–x, 7n10, 44n36, 55, 70n30
Hopkins, Gerard Manley, 26–28, 77–78, 79, 81
hospitality, 1–4, 16, 17, 34–35, 54–55, 73, 125, 135, 139
hunting, 27, 43n34, 99n7, 101, 105, 136, 143, 148, 152

inclusivity (all-encompassing language), 13, 35, 40–41, 48, 55, 114, 119
interconnectedness, xv, 2n3, 6n8, 128–29

Jesus, x, xi, 1–4, 35n20, 39–40, 43–44, 49, 55, 57, 68–69, 81–87, 90–91, 98, 107, 118, 119–25, 135
Jonah, 5–6, 7, 74, 76, 86, 90, 129–32

kingdom of God, 37, 49, 55, 57, 71, 87, 118, 121, 122, 123, 125, 139

labor animals, *see* domestic animals
Lazarus (in Jesus's parable), 81–83, 88
Leviathan, 62, 73n34, 80
Lewis, C. S., 61, 114n2
Linzey, Andrew, 10, 15–16, 24n53, 43n35, 56, 101n12, 112
lion(s), 14n25, 42n31, 43, 44, 53n56, 61, 62, 80, 86, 88, 89, 115, 116, 124, 135

manger, 107, 119–21
manna, 67–68
meat eating, 12, 27, 65–68, 76, 88, 97, 109, 111, 132n28, 133–39, 146n17
Moses, 33, 52, 58, 67–68, 95–99, 105, 129, 138

Nathan's parable, 39, 44, 73n34
neighbor(s), 2, 4, 35, 36, 83, 93, 96, 99, 132
new creation, 49, 57, 69, 69n28, 139
Noah, 9n13, 17n33, 41, 53, 65, 66, 97, 98, 103, 124

Odysseus, 81–83
ox, oxen, 4, 5, 9, 18, 28–36, 37, 46, 48, 64, 77, 79, 80, 102, 105, 106, 110, 116, 119

palimpsest, 142–53
paradigm shift, 48–51
Paul, ix, 28–36, 37, 41–42, 48, 49, 69, 81, 94, 114, 122, 128, 130, 133–34, 135
pets, 7–9, 56–57, 73–74, 78–81, 115
pigs, *see* swine
Pope Francis, xii–xiii

Qumran, *see* Dead Sea Scrolls

Subject Index

rapture, the, 56–57
Ruth, 1–4

Sabbath, 6n8, 10, 35n20, 43, 108, 116n5, 119, 138, 149
sacrifice, animal, x, 41, 53n56, 54, 58, 76, 83, 86, 92–112, 135, 137
Said, Edward W., ix, 29–31, 35, 38, 41, 47, 52, 69
Saint John's Bible, The, 58–59
Sampson, 45–46, 52, 135
Schweitzer, Albert, 13, 32, 78, 153
science, 14, 16n29, 49–50, 62n14, 63, 142
snake(s), 42n31, 121–23, 129, 148
snake handling, 121–23
Sowa, Michael, 123–25
sparrow(s), 23–24, 43, 74–77, 85, 112, 115
steward, stewardship, 48, 54, 55, 57, 64n19
subdue (*kabash*), 63–67
swine, 11–12, 81n44, 83–87, 88, 91, 137

tabernacle, temple, 58, 60, 76, 93n2, 100–108, 112, 116
tsa'ar ba'alei chayim, 9, 119
Tobit, book of, 70–77, 78, 82–83
Torah, mandates concerning animals, x, 3–4, 9–10, 28–36, 40n27, 46, 48, 51–52, 67, 83, 92–112, 119, 132, 134, 137–38
triads (divine, animal, human), x, 7, 38–40, 41, 58–59, 71, 74, 76, 87, 90, 91, 97, 98, 101, 110, 111, 129, 131, 139

unclean/clean, *see* dietary laws

veganism, vegetarianism, 49, 65, 67–68, 98, 134–39, 149

wild animals, 9, 10, 41, 42n31, 64, 65, 79, 80, 81, 84, 86, 88, 89, 106, 116, 117, 121, 123, 129, 146, 150
worship, vi, 10, 42, 58, 62, 87, 92–112, 117–19

Zacchaeus, 1–4, 138

www.ingramcontent.com/pod-product-compliance
Lightning Source LLC
Chambersburg PA
CBHW020851160426
43192CB00007B/871